CW00819518

BAZI STRUCTURES

&

Structural Useful Gods

WATER 水 | 壬 Ren / 癸 Gui

BaZi Structures & Structural Useful Gods
Water Structure

The author can be reached at:

Mastery Academy of Chinese Metaphysics Sdn. Bhd. (611143-A)
19-3, The Boulevard, Mid Valley City,
59200 Kuala Lumpur, Malaysia.
Tel   : +603-2284 8080
Fax   : +603-2284 1218
Email   : info@masteryacademy.com
Website: www.masteryacademy.com

Published by JY Books Sdn. Bhd. (659134-T)

Table of Contents

Table of Contents

About The Chinese Metaphysics Reference Series

Reference Series

The Chinese Metaphysics Reference Series of books are designed primarily to be used as complimentary textbooks for scholars, students, researchers, teachers and practitioners of Chinese Metaphysics.

The goal is to provide quick easy reference tables, diagrams and charts, facilitating the study and practice of various Chinese Metaphysics subjects including Feng Shui, BaZi, Yi Jing, Zi Wei, Liu Ren, Ze Ri, Ta Yi, Qi Men and Mian Xiang.

This series of books are intended as reference text and educational materials principally for the academic syllabuses of the **Mastery Academy of Chinese Metaphysics**. The contents have also been formatted so that Feng Shui Masters and other teachers of Chinese Metaphysics will always have a definitive source of reference at hand, when teaching or applying their art.

Because each school of Chinese Metaphysics is different, the Reference Series of books usually do not contain any specific commentaries, application methods or explanations on the theory behind the formulas presented in its contents. This is to ensure that the contents can be used freely and independently by all Feng Shui Masters and teachers of Chinese Metaphysics without conflict.

If you would like to study or learn the applications of any of the formulas presented in the Reference Series of books, we recommend that you undertake the courses offered by Joey Yap and his team of Instructors at the Mastery Academy of Chinese Metaphysics.

Titles offers in the Reference Series:

1. The Chinese Metaphysics Compendium
2. Dong Gong Date Selection
3. Earth Study Discern Truth
4. Xuan Kong Da Gua Structure Reference Book
5. San Yuan Dragon Gate Eight Formations Water Method
6. Xuan Kong Da Gua Ten Thousand Year Calendar
7. Plum Blossom Divination Reference Book
8. The Date Selection Compendium (Book 1) - The 60 Jia Zi Attributes
9. BaZi Structures & Structural Useful Gods Reference Series

Preface

The study and practice of BaZi is an infinitely rewarding and intriguing one, with literally an inexhaustible depth and range from which we can mine our information on a person's character, temperament, life outlook and personal destiny. The simplest data – your birth date and time – can yield a rich treasure trove of knowledge, most of which can help shed new light on old perceptions.

The idea for this BaZi Structures and Structural Useful God Reference Series came out of a common need among my BaZi students, many of whom wanted to learn more about how the various structures in BaZi are derived. This series was therefore created to help students learn and absorb the methods and techniques in which a structure is created and developed mainly from a classical standpoint.

While initially it was my idea to create one BaZi Structures book to accommodate all 10 Heavenly Stems (Day Masters), I soon found out that it would not be a book that could reasonably be used by anyone – because it would be too heavy to lift! So I decided to break it apart into five different books, with each one corresponding to each Element. The book you're holding in your hands is on Water Structures, for both Ren 壬 and Gui 癸 Water Day Masters.

There are many traditional sources available on the BaZi structures, and the derivation of those structures. One of the more well-known texts is the *Qiong Tong Bao Jian* 窮通寶鑑, written by a famous master, *Xu Le Wu* 徐樂吾. Another popular BaZi scholar of recent past who contributed a lot to mainstream BaZi theories, especially those relating to structures, is *Wei Qian Li* 韋千里.

It's difficult for most students to have access to this information because it's scattered about in various texts and documents, and also – all of it is available only in Chinese. It was my intention, therefore, to compile this information into one convenient source, and to present the transliterated version of these traditional texts for the modern, English-speaking practitioner and student without losing the essence of the original.

To derive a structure and structural Useful God in BaZi, one must know and understand the Day Master and the month of birth, and its variations in a BaZi chart. There are traditional methods on how this is derived, and there are newer interpretations on these methods.

As such, different practitioners and teachers have different methods and formats to derive these structures, and it is recommended that you use the techniques outlined in this book with care and thought. As always, there is much merit in using traditional practices, but students who are learning BaZi should use this under the supervision of a teacher in order to better understand the subject. A good teacher will help you understand the different ways of interpreting these traditional texts.

Do note that these texts should not be taken literally. Different masters may agree or disagree with the classical commentaries included here, and as a student, it's important for you to know the reasons why. Better yet, it's important for you to know those reasons and then go on to form your own conclusions, based on your understanding of the various interpretations.

For that reason, this book was designed to be a reference accompaniment for the students of my BaZi Mastery Series, where you'll be able to get the guidance you need in interpreting these traditional methods. I encourage you to take a class because it will help to place this material in context and give you the added knowledge you need to help you make the most of the information contained within this book. Each and every structure in this book could be its own chapter, because it can literally explain a person and his or her modus operandi!

I hope you enjoy your research on this subject, and here's to many pleasurable hours of BaZi Structural study!

Warm regards,

Joey Yap
June 2009

Author's personal websites :
www.joeyyap.com | www.fengshuilogy.com (Personal blog)

Academy websites :
www.masteryacademy.com | www.masteryjournal.com | www.maelearning.com

Follow Joey's current updates on Twitter :
www.twitter.com/joeyyap

MASTERY ACADEMY
OF CHINESE METAPHYSICS™

At **www.masteryacademy.com**, you will find some useful tools to ascertain key information about the Feng Shui of a property or for the study of Astrology.

The Joey Yap Flying Stars Calculator can be utilised to plot your home or office Flying Stars chart. To find out your personal best directions, use the 8 Mansions Calculator. To learn more about your personal Destiny, you can use the Joey Yap BaZi Ming Pan Calculator to plot your Four Pillars of Destiny – you just need to have your date of birth (day, month, year) and time of birth.

For more information about BaZi, Xuan Kong or Flying Star Feng Shui, or if you wish to learn more about these subjects with Joey Yap, logon to the Mastery Academy of Chinese Metaphysics website at **www.masteryacademy.com.**

MASTERY ACADEMY
E-LEARNING CENTER
w w w . m a e l e a r n i n g . c o m

www.maelearning.com

Bookmark this address on your computer, and visit this newly-launched website today. With the E-Learning Center, knowledge of Chinese Metaphysics is a mere 'click' away!

Our E-Learning Center consists of 3 distinct components.

1. Online Courses
These shall comprise of 3 Programs: our Online Feng Shui Program, Online BaZi Program, and Online Mian Xiang Program. Each lesson contains a video lecture, slide presentation and downloadable course notes.

2. MA Live!
With MA Live!, Joey Yap's workshops, tutorials, courses and seminars on various Chinese Metaphysics subjects broadcasted right to your computer screen. Better still, participants will not only get to see and hear Joey talk 'live', but also get to engage themselves directly in the event and more importantly, TALK to Joey via the MA Live! interface. All the benefits of a live class, minus the hassle of actually having to attend one!

3. Video-On-Demand (VOD)
Get immediate streaming-downloads of the Mastery Academy's wide range of educational DVDs, right on your computer screen. No more shipping costs and waiting time to be incurred!

Study at your own pace, and interact with your Instructor and fellow students worldwide… at your own convenience and privacy. With our E-Learning Center, knowledge of Chinese Metaphysics is brought DIRECTLY to you in all its clarity, with illustrated presentations and comprehensive notes expediting your learning curve!

Welcome to the Mastery Academy's E-LEARNING CENTER…YOUR virtual gateway to Chinese Metaphysics mastery!

Introduction - Water Day Masters

In the study of Chinese Metaphysics, the Water element usually pertains to intelligence, wisdom and IQ. Water of course is also known for its ability to move, flow and change forms. And Water is capable of harboring a thousand and one secrets.

There are 2 types of Water Day Masters: Ren 壬 Water and Gui 癸 Water.

Of the two, Ren Water Day Masters are usually robust and on the move. Due to their inherently restless nature, however, they tend to become distracted easily. Intelligent and adaptive, they are virtually unstoppable when they put their mind to a task. Ren Water Day Masters can, however, be rather rebellious and non-conformist.

Gui Water Day Masters tend to be imaginative and creative, and make good teachers and educationists. They are also not the type to remain still, although they are usually introverted by nature.

Since a certain amount of visualization or the ability to picture the Five Elements – or Wu Xing 五行 - is required in order to truly master BaZi, think of large, massive bodies of water whenever Ren Water is mentioned. Think of the world's great oceans or roaring rapids, such as Niagara Falls. And imagine the power they generate to the extent that we are even able to harness these massive bodies of water for useful intents such as hydroelectric energy. Unsurprisingly, Ren Water Day Masters are usually intelligent, adaptive, extroverted and rebellious.

Likewise, where Gui Water is concerned, think of the mists, dew and rain; which are examples of Yin and hence softer, gentler bodies of water. Gui Water Day Masters are hence imaginative, creative and introverted characters by nature, who also make good teachers and mentors.

Ren (壬) Water Day Master

Overview:

Ren 壬 Water is Yang Water. One can therefore think or picture Ren Water as massive, converging bodies of water, such as the world's great oceans, lakes and waterfalls.

As such, Ren Water people – just like the water of the river and sea – are always on the move. Adaptive, intelligent and usually unable to remain still, Ren Water people are often extroverts by nature. They always tend to be on the move, but also run the risk of becoming easily distracted and lacking focus.

Being adventurous people, Ren Water types usually enjoy robust, even physical, activities to keep them occupied. Indeed, whenever they put their mind to it, Ren Water people can be unstoppable in their quest to complete or perfect something. Nevertheless, they are also often rebellious by nature and dislike being made to conform.

Ren 壬 Water Day Master, Born in First Month 正月

Yin 寅 (Tiger) Month
February 4th – March 5th

Do note that the dates provided above are subject to slight yearly variations. Please refer to the Ten Thousand Year Calendar for the accurate transition dates for each year.

Day Master	Ren 壬 Water		Month	Yin 寅 (Tiger)

日元 **Day Master**	月 **Month**
壬 *Ren* **Yang Water**	寅 *Yin* **Tiger** **Yang Wood**

A Ren Water Day Master born in a Yin (Tiger) Month, an Eating God Structure is formed where Jia Wood is revealed as one of the Heavenly Stems.

Where Bing Fire is revealed as one of the Heavenly Stems, an Indirect Wealth Structure is formed.

Where Wu Earth is revealed as one of the Heavenly Stems, a Seven Killings Structure is formed.

Should, however, neither Jia Wood nor Bing Fire nor Wu Earth happen to be revealed within the Heavenly Stems, one should select the BaZi Chart's most prominent Qi attribute at one's discretion.

| Day Master | Ren 壬 Water | Month | Yin 寅 (Tiger) |

喜用神提要 **Regulating Useful God Reference Guide**

月 Month	用神 Useful God
1st Month 正月 Yin 寅 **(Tiger) Month**	庚 *Geng* **Yang Metal** 丙 *Bing* **Yang Fire** 戊 *Wu* **Yang Earth**

For a Ren Water Day Master born in the Yin (Tiger) Month, Geng Metal, Bing Fire and Wu Earth are its Regulating Useful Gods.

Where there are no Friends Stars in the BaZi Chart, there would be no need or use for Wu Earth as a Useful God. Under such circumstances, one should concentrate on utilizing Geng Metal and Bing Fire as Useful Gods.

Where Friends Stars are present in abundance throughout the BaZi Chart, as long as there is at least a Wu Earth penetrating through the Heavenly Stems, it should be fairly easy to maintain control and balance throughout the entire BaZi Chart.

BaZi Structures & Structural Useful Gods 格局與格局用神

| Day Master | Ren 壬 Water | | Month | Yin 寅 (Tiger) |

4th day of February – 5th day of March, Gregorian Calendar

A Yin (Tiger) Month contains the elements of Wood, Fire and Earth as its Hidden Stems.

Ren Water Day Master born in a Yin (Month), the presence of Fire and Earth will make Wealth and Officer Structures. Consequently, Metal and Water stars would be weak.

Where the Wood Qi is prosperous, Metal Qi is weak. And where Metal Qi is weak, Ren Water shall also, by extension, be weakened, resulting in a weak Ren Water Self Element Day Master. Since Metal, however, produces Ren Water, the former serves as the latter's Useful God.

Fire and Earth should preferably not be prominently present or seen throughout the BaZi Chart, for strong Fire Qi will directly weaken Metal Qi. Likewise, strong Earth Qi will only serve to 'cripple' or prevent Water Qi from thriving.

A Ren Water Day Master born in a Chen (Dragon) Hour where Fire and Earth are strong can easily encourage a Fire Formation with the Earthly Branches of Yin (Tiger) and Wu (Horse). Under such circumstances, strong Metal Qi is needed to help bring balance to the BaZi Chart.

Tiger

Day Master	Ren 壬 Water		Month	Yin 寅 (Tiger)

Commentary

In addition to the preceding narratives on the potential Structures and scenarios resulting from a Ren Water Day Master born in a Yin (Tiger) Month, the following circumstances also play their respective roles in determining the overall strength of this Day Master's BaZi Chart.

Note:

Tiger

- Bing Fire and Wu Earth are this Ren Water Day Master's most important Useful Gods.

- Jia Wood should be prevented from penetrating through to the Heavenly Stems.

- Since a Yin (Tiger) Month falls in early spring, Ren Water would have thawed and hence freed itself of 'cold' Qi by then. As such, Ren Water should be 'flowing' in a Yin (Tiger) Month. Jia Wood is strong in a Yin (Tiger) Month. It would hence be preferable for Jia Wood not to be revealed or featured prominently, as it would invariably control Wu Earth, which is one of this Ren Water Day Master's primary choice of Useful Gods.

- Where Jia Wood, Bing Fire and Wu Earth are revealed amongst the Heavenly Stems, and in a Yin (Month), this Ren Water Day Master's BaZi Chart would be fairly ideal and well-balanced. This chart therefore would belong to a highly successful individual who would enjoy a noble life.

- Where Wu Earth is revealed in the Heavenly Stems, this Ren Water Day Master shall be famous in life.

- Where Wu Earth is appearing amongst the Earthly Branches, this Ren Water Day Master shall be blessed with abundant skills in life. Skills enough to generate great wealth.

- Bing Fire should not be absent from this BaZi Chart. Since Bing Fire is the Indirect Wealth Star of this Ren Water Day Master, without it, the person may experience difficulty in accumulating or saving wealth, no matter how much he or she may generate it.

- Where the Earthly Branches in the BaZi Chart forms a Fire Structure, this Day Master may suffer from a lack of status or authority in life. In fact, life would be hindered by incessant obstacles and mishaps.

- Where there are four 壬寅 Ren Yin (Water Tiger) Pillars forming the BaZi Chart, this Ren Water Day Master may enjoy extraordinary prosperity in life, although he or she shall still lack real status or authority.

正月 First Month

寅
Tiger

| Day Master | Ren 壬 Water | | Month | Yin 寅 (Tiger) |

Additional Attributes

格局 Structural Star	偏印 Indirect Resource	偏財 Indirect Wealth	七殺 Seven Killings
用神 Useful God	Geng 庚 Metal	Bing 丙 Fire	Wu 戊 Earth
Conditions	Where Geng Metal, Bing Fire and Wu Earth are revealed in the BaZi Chart, this Ren Water Day Master shall enjoy immense prosperity in life. Even if only one Geng Metal element were to be revealed, this Day Master would still not lack either fame or fortune in life.		
Positive Circumstances	Geng Metal, Bing Fire and Wu Earth appearing the Heavenly Stems.		
Negative Circumstances	Ding Fire weakens Geng Metal (Resource Star)		

格局 Structural Star	七殺 Seven Killings
用神 Useful God	Wu 戊 Earth
Conditions	A Seven Killings Star should only be used where a Zi (Rat) Earthly Branch forms a Goat Blade Structure with this Ren Water Day Master. Otherwise, all things remain status quo.
Positive Circumstances	Wu Earth rooted in the Branches.
Negative Circumstances	Ji Earth also appearing on the Heavenly Stems.

| Day Master | Ren 壬 Water | Month | Yin 寅 (Tiger) |

Additional Attributes

格局 Structural Star	偏財 Indirect Wealth	正財 Direct Wealth
用神 Useful God	Bing 丙 Fire	Ding 丁 Fire
Conditions	Where the Earthly Branches forms a Fire Structure, a Direct Wealth Structure would ensue. Although Water and Fire counter each other in maintaining the balance of this BaZi Chart, this Ren Water Day Master would still lack fame and fortune in life.	
Positive Circumstances	Ren Water should be rooted.	
Negative Circumstances	Too much Water in the Branches.	

* *Geng Metal and Bing Fire are the preferred Useful Gods.*

** *Wu Earth is the second-choice Useful God.*

Tiger

Day Master	Ren 壬 Water	Month	Yin 寅 (Tiger)

Summary

- Where there are four Ren Yin 壬寅 (Tiger) Pillars forming the BaZi Chart of a Ren Water Day Master born in a Yin (Tiger) Month, this Day Master shall enjoy a high official status or even a king's fortune in life. This is a special structure.

- Where a *Follow the Wealth Structure* is formed, it would still be considered a substandard structure. A Ren Water Day Master with such a structure in his or her BaZi Chart would be prone to making empty promises. The person would be looking good, but often going nowhere.

- A Seven Killings Structure may be used in the presence of a Goat Blade Star. Where a Seven Killings Structure is seen, a strong Direct Resource would be needed. Where an Eating God Star is present to control a Seven Killings Structure, this Ren Water Day Master would amass power, authority and recognition. This chart would belong to an exceptional individual with great achievements.

- An Indirect Resource Star would serve as this Ren Water Day Master's preferred Useful God.

Ren 壬 Water Day Master, Born in Second Month 二月

Mao 卯 (Rabbit) Month
March 6th – April 4th

Do note that the dates provided above are subject to slight yearly variations. Please refer to the Ten Thousand Year Calendar for the accurate transition dates for each year.

| Day Master | Ren 壬 Water | Month | Mao 卯 (Rabbit) |

日元 Day Master	月 Month
壬 *Ren* **Yang Water**	卯 *Mao* **Rabbit** **Yin Wood**

For a Ren Water Day Master born in a Mao (Rabbit) Month, a Hurting Officer Structure is formed where Yi Wood is revealed in the Heavenly Stem. Even if Yi Wood does not penetrate through the Heavenly Stem, a Hurting Officer Structure is still considered to have been formed.

二月 Second Month

| Day Master | Ren 壬 Water | Month | Mao 卯 (Rabbit) |

喜用神提要 **Regulating Useful God Reference Guide**

月 Month	用神 Useful God
2nd Month 二月 Mao 卯 **(Rabbit) Month**	戊 辛 庚 *Wu* *Xin* *Geng* **Yang Earth** **Yin Metal** **Yang Metal**

Rabbit

For a Mao (Rabbit) Month, Wu Earth, Xin Metal and Geng Metal are its Regulating Useful Gods.

Ren Water, in spring, should use Geng Metal and Xin Metal as its source, since Metal produces Water.

Where Water is present in abundance, Wu Earth should be used to control it.

BaZi Structures & Structural Useful Gods 格局與格局用神

| Day Master | Ren 壬 Water | Month | Mao 卯 (Rabbit) |

6th day of March – 4th day of April, Gregorian Calendar

Mao (Rabbit) Month denotes the mid point in the spring season months. Wood Qi is at its peak in spring. As such, in the case of a Ren Water Day Master born in a Mao (Rabbit) Month, Ren Water is weakened by such strong Wood Qi. Since wood is the strongest, Metal Qi would be very weak.

Given that Wood Qi is prosperous in spring, there would be a 'leakage' or weakening of Water Qi. Furthermore, an abundance of Fire Qi would also control Metal Qi. Earth Qi should equally be avoided, since Ren Water must be free to 'flow'.

A Ren Water Day Master born in a Mao (Rabbit) Month would be averse toward Fire, Earth and Wood Qi together, as these elements will 'hurt' or weaken Ren Water. It would hence be best to use Metal and Water, both of which shall strengthen and hence turn a weak Ren Water Day Master into a stronger one.

Day Master	Ren 壬 Water		Month	Mao 卯 (Rabbit)

Commentary

In addition to the preceding narratives on the potential Structures and scenarios resulting from a Ren Water Day Master born in a Mao (Rabbit) Month, the following circumstances also play their respective roles in determining the overall strength of this Day Master's BaZi Chart.

Note:

- Wu Earth and Xin Metal can be directly employed as Useful Gods.

- Bing Fire and Ding Fire should be avoided, where possible.

- A Ren Water Day Master born in either a Yin (Tiger) or Mao (Rabbit) Month may be subject to varying circumstances, in selecting a Useful God to suit the varying chart conditions of early and mid-spring months. For instance, Wood Qi is particularly strong in a Mao (Rabbit) Month, with Xin Metal a must-have.

- Where Jia Wood and Ding Fire are not revealed in the Heavenly Stems, this Ren Water Day Master will lead only an average life.

- Where the Earthly Branches form a Wood Structure and Geng Metal is revealed in the Heavenly Stems, this Ren Water Day Master may enjoy unexpected results, good coincidences and sudden successes in life.

- Where the Earthly Branches forms a Water Structure and Water Qi is revealed in the Heavenly Stems, Wu Earth is needed to penetrate through to the Heavenly Stems. Otherwise, this Ren Water Day Master may lead a life of uncertainty and hardship.

- Wu Earth brings stability, calmness and direction in the life of a Ren Water.

二月 Second Month

Rabbit

BaZi Structures & Structural Useful Gods 格局與格局用神

Day Master	Ren 壬 Water	Month	Mao 卯 (Rabbit)

Additional Attributes

格局 Structural Star	七殺 Seven Killings	正印 Direct Resource
用神 Useful God	Wu 戊 Earth	Xin 辛 Metal
Conditions	Where Wu Earth and Xin Metal are revealed in the BaZi Chart, this Ren Water Day Master shall enjoy a successful professional life.	
Positive Circumstances	Presence of both Wu Earth and Xin Metal in the Heavenly Stems.	
Negative Circumstances	Ding Fire penetrates through to the Heavenly Stems and controls Xin Metal as well as combines with the Ren Water Day Master.	

格局 Structural Star	食神 Eating God	傷官 Hurting Officer
用神 Useful God	Jia 甲 Wood	Yi 乙 Wood
Conditions	Where the Earthly Branches form a Wood Structure, along with a Geng Metal Resource Star – this would allow this Ren Water Day Master to enjoy a fairly successful life.	
Positive Circumstances	Geng Metal as a Resource Star penetrates through to the Heavenly Stems.	
Negative Circumstances	The absence of Wu Earth to penetrate through to the Heavenly Stems.	

Day Master	Ren 壬 Water		Month	Mao 卯 (Rabbit)

Additional Attributes

格局 **Structural Star**	比肩 Friend
用神 **Useful God**	Ren 壬 Water
Conditions	Where the relevant Earthly Branches form a Water Structure, much would still depend on the presence of Wu Earth as a Seven Killings Star to control and hence bring balance to this Ren Water Day Master's BaZi Chart.
Positive Circumstances	Rooted Wu Earth on the Heavenly Stems.
Negative Circumstances	Absence of Wu Earth.

*   *Wu Earth and Xin Metal are the most-preferred Useful Gods.*

** *Ding Fire, if present, should not penetrate through the Heavenly Stems as well.*

17

二月
Second Month

卯
Rabbit

| Day Master | Ren 壬 Water | Month | Mao 卯 (Rabbit) |

Summary

- Even where Water Qi features prominently in this chart, it is still insufficient due to the strong presence of Wood in this season. Water needs the Wu Earth to keep it in flow. Hence, much will depend on Wu Earth's capability – as a Seven Killings Star - to penetrate through to the Heavenly Stems, as a Useful God.

- In a Mao (Rabbit) Month, even if Jia Wood and Ding Fire do not penetrate through to the Heavenly Stems, this Ren Water Day Master would still be able to lead a fairly average, well-balanced life.

- In a Mao (Rabbit) Month, even if Ding Fire (Direct Wealth Star) is not used, a Seven Killings or Direct Resource Star may still be used to allow this Ren Water Day Master to prosper in life.

Ren 壬 Water Day Master, Born in Third Month 三月

Chen 辰 (Dragon) Month
April 5th - May 5th

Do note that the dates provided above are subject to slight yearly variations. Please refer to the Ten Thousand Year Calendar for the accurate transition dates for each year.

三月 Third Month

Dragon

Day Master Ren 壬 Water   **Month** Chen 辰 (Dragon)

日元 Day Master	月 Month
壬 Ren **Yang Water**	辰 Chen **Dragon** **Yang Earth**

For a Ren Water Day Master born in a Chen (Dragon) Month, a Seven Killings Structure is formed where Wu Earth is revealed as one of the Heavenly Stems.

Where Yi Wood is revealed as one of the Heavenly Stems, a Hurting Officer Structure is formed.

Where the Gui Water is revealed as one of the Heavenly Stems, a Goat Blade Structure is formed when the support is derived from the Earthly Branches.

Should, however neither Wu Earth, Yi Wood nor Gui Water happen to be revealed within the Heavenly Stems, one should select a Structure according to the BaZi Chart's most prominent Qi attribute at one's discretion.

| Day Master | Ren 壬 Water | Month | Chen 辰 (Dragon) |

喜用神提要 Regulating Useful God Reference Guide

月 Month	用神 Useful God
3rd Month 三月 Chen 辰 (Dragon) Month	甲 *Jia* **Yang Wood** 庚 *Geng* **Yang Metal**

Dragon

For a Chen (Dragon) Month, Jia Wood and Geng Metal are its Regulating Useful Gods.

Where Jia Wood is lacking during the earlier part of a Chen (Dragon) Month, one should use Geng Metal as an alternative Resource Star and hence Useful God.

Where Metal is present in abundance, it would be preferable to have Bing Fire to exert at least a certain amount of control over Metal.

BaZi Structures & Structural Useful Gods 格局與格局用神

| Day Master | Ren 壬 Water | Month | Chen 辰 (Dragon) |

5th day of April – 5th day of May, Gregorian Calendar

Chen (Dragon), being one of the Four Graveyard Earthly Branches, serves as 'storage' for excess Water Qi. In addition, Earth Qi also features strongly or prominently in a Chen (Dragon) Month.

In a Chen (Dragon) Month, however, Ren Water is limited by Earth.

With the presence of Wood Qi to control Earth Qi, however, Metal Qi and Water Qi can hence flourish simultaneously in bringing balance to this Ren Water Day Master's BaZi Chart.

Dragon

Nevertheless, a Ren Water Day Master born in a Chen (Dragon) Month should avoid encountering Excessive Fire Qi. This is because even though Fire is this Ren Water Day Master's Wealth Star, it also has the capacity to produce Earth Qi and also weaken or 'hurt' Metal Qi, which is a Useful God.

As long as there is sufficient Wood Qi to keep the excessive Earth Qi brought about by a Chen (Dragon) Month under control, the Ren Water Day Master shall enjoy a well-balanced life.

Day Master	Ren 壬 Water	Month	Chen 辰 (Dragon)

三
月
Third Month

Commentary

In addition to the preceding narratives on the potential Structures and scenarios resulting from a Ren Water Day Master born in a Chen (Dragon) Month, the following circumstances also play their respective roles in determining the overall strength of this Day Master's BaZi Chart.

Note:

Dragon

- Jia Wood is the primary or preferred Useful God, while Geng Metal can be used where Jia Wood is absent or weak.

- Where Jia Wood and Geng Metal are both revealed in the BaZi Chart, this Ren Water Day Master shall enjoy fame, fortune and all the best that life has to offer. Where either Jia Wood or Geng Metal happens to be missing, however, the outcomes would be vastly different, and definitely nowhere as excellent as under the preceding circumstances.

- Should all Four Graveyard or Storages Earthly Branches of Chen (Dragon), Xu (Dog), Chou (Ox) and Wei (Goat) happen to be present, this Ren Water Day Master shall enjoy fame in life when Jia Wood is revealed in the Heavenly Stems; even though Geng Metal may be missing from the BaZi Chart.

- Ding Fire combines with a Ren Water Day Master to form Wood. Under such circumstances, this Ren Water Day Master shall still lead an average life, at least, unless a successful transformation to Wood Qi takes place.

- Where the Earthly Branches form a Wood Structure, Geng Metal must be revealed amongst the Heavenly Stems.

三月 Third Month

Dragon

| Day Master | Ren 壬 Water | | Month | Chen 辰 (Dragon) |

Additional Attributes

格局 Structural Star	食神 Eating God	偏印 Indirect Resource
用神 Useful God	Jia 甲 Wood	Geng 庚 Metal
Conditions	Geng Metal is the preferred useful Resource Star for this Ren Water Day Master. Without the presence of Jia Wood, however, this Ren Water Day Master may possess overly strong reliance and emotional nature. Without the presence of Geng Metal, this Ren Water Day Master may even possess an extremely stubborn or obstinate personality.	
Positive Circumstances	Even though Jia Wood and Geng Metal may be present in the BaZi Chart, both should preferably be separated or at least, not present side-by-side in the Heavenly Stems.	
Negative Circumstances	Absence of Geng Metal in the chart.	

格局 Structural Star	正財 Direct Wealth
用神 Useful God	Ding 丁 Fire
Conditions	Ding Fire combines with the Ren Water Day Master to form Wood. A Ren Water Day Master born in a Chen (Dragon) Month may transform or be combined away, should it encounter Ding Fire.
Positive Circumstances	Earthly Branches that are of the Water element are also present.
Negative Circumstances	Without Water in the BaZi Chart, this Ren Water Day Master may only lead an average life, at best.

Day Master Ren 壬 Water	**Month** Chen 辰 (Dragon)

Additional Attributes

格局 **Structural Star**	七殺 Seven Killings
用神 **Useful God**	Wu 戊 Earth
Conditions	Where the Four Graveyard Earthly Branches of Chen (Dragon), Xu (Dog), Chou (Ox) and Wei (Goat) happen to be present, there must be at least one Jia Wood in the Heavenly Stems, in order for this Ren Water Day Master to prosper in life.
Positive Circumstances	Presense of two or more Jia Wood.
Negative Circumstances	Ji Earth, as a Direct Officer Star, penetrates through to the Heavenly Stems and combines with Jia Wood to produce Earth.

*   *Jia Wood and Geng Metal are the preferred Useful Gods, but both should be separated and must not be present side-by-side in the BaZi Chart.*

Dragon

三月 Third Month

三
月

Third Month

| **Day Master** | Ren 壬 Water | **Month** | Chen 辰 (Dragon) |

Summary

Dragon

- Do note that Ren Water and Ding Fire shall combine and may be transformed into Wood in this month. Successful transformation would denote a immensely noble life.

- Wu Earth (Seven Killings Star) should not penetrate through to the Heavenly Stems. As long as there are plenty of the Chen (Dragon), Xu (Dog), Chou (Ox) and Wei (Goat) Earthly Branches present, this Ren Water Day Master's BaZi Chart should be fairly well-balanced in itself. But for this chart to enjoy superiority, Jia Wood needs to be revealed in the Heavenly Stems. Where Jia Wood is revealed in the BaZi Chart, this person shall enjoy an extraordinary life. Jia Wood keeps the balance of the chart.

- Where there are four Chen (Dragon) Earthly Branches in the BaZi Chart, a structure known as 'Ren Water riding atop the Dragon's back' (壬騎龍背) is formed, where the Jia Wood also appears on the stem, this chart's quality is similar to a highest class of Seven Killings Structure. Such special formations like these denote an extraordinary life of power, fame and fortune.

Ren 壬 Water Day Master, Born in Fourth Month 四月

Si 巳 (Snake) Month
May 6th - June 5th

Do note that the dates provided above are subject to slight yearly variations. Please refer to the Ten Thousand Year Calendar for the accurate transition dates for each year.

| Day Master | Ren 壬 Water | Month | Si 巳 (Snake) |

日元 Day Master	月 Month
壬	巳
Ren	Si
Yang Water	Snake
	Yin Fire

For a Ren Water Day Master born in a Si (Snake) Month, an Indirect Wealth Structure is formed where Bing Fire is revealed as one of the Heavenly Stems.

Where Geng Metal is revealed as one of the Heavenly Stems, an Indirect Resource Structure is formed.

Where Wu Earth is revealed as one of the Heavenly Stems, a Seven Killings Structure is formed.

Should, however, neither Bing Fire, Geng Metal nor Wu Earth happen to be revealed within the Heavenly Stems, one should select a Structure according to the BaZi Chart's most prominent Qi attribute at one's discretion.

Day Master Ren 壬 Water   **Month** Si 巳 (Snake)

喜用神提要 **Regulating Useful God Reference Guide**

月 Month	用神 Useful God

4th Month 四月
Si 巳 (Snake) Month

壬
Ren
Yang Water

辛
Xin
Yin Metal

Snake

四月 Fourth Month

For a Si (Snake) Month, Ren Water, Xin Metal, Geng Metal and Gui Water are the Regulating Useful Gods.

Since Ren Water is weak in a Si (Snake) Month, Geng Metal and Xin Metal should be chosen as Useful Resource Stars to this Ren Water Day Master. With the support of Geng Metal and Xin Metal, both Ren Water and Gui Water may also assist as favourable Companion Stars for this Ren Water Day Master.

BaZi Structures & Structural Useful Gods 格局與格局用神

Day Master	Ren 壬 Water	Month	Si 巳 (Snake)

6th day of May – 5th day of June, Gregorian Calendar

Snake

Geng Metal is hidden within Si (Snake). Fire Qi is extremely vibrant in summer. Being strong, Fire Qi shall hence control Metal Qi. Consequently, a Ren Water Day Master born in a Si (Snake) Month shall be weak or at least considered weakened.

Since Metal and Water are inclined towards being in the weak state, the Metal element serves as the primary Useful Resource Star for Ren Water. Thus, in a Si (Snake) Month, Geng Metal needs to be referenced as Useful God to strengthen Ren Water.

Where Ren Water is able to flow the proverbial 'thousand miles', this Ren Water Day Master would be able to tap into the Qi of Wealth Stars. However, it is advidable for this chart not encounter additional Fire, Earth and Wood Qi. This is because Wood Qi produces Fire Qi which, in turn, would weaken or exert an overly strong control over Metal Qi.

| Day Master | Ren 壬 Water | Month | Si 巳 (Snake) |

Commentary

In addition to the preceding narratives on the potential Structures and scenarios resulting from a Ren Water Day Master born in a Si (Snake) Month, the following circumstances also play their respective roles in determining the overall strength of this Day Master's BaZi Chart.

Note:

Snake

- Ren Water and Xin Metal are the preferred Useful Gods.

- Bing Fire should be prevented from combining with Xin Metal to form Water, if both are to serve as Useful Gods.

- Geng Metal and Xin Metal (Resource Stars) are the preferred choices for this chart as they are needed to produce and strengthen a Water Day Master born in summer.

- Ren Water and Gui Water (Companion Stars) are also favoured to support and strengthen the Water Day Master.

- Where Jia Wood and Yi Wood are present in the BaZi Chart, Geng Metal is needed to penetrate to the Heavenly Stems and rooted in the branches. With this, the chart may hold infinite potential for its bearer.

- Where Ding Fire is absent from the chart, but Ren Water and Gui Water are present in abundance, this Ren Water Day Master shall enjoy fame, wealth and happiness in life.

- Where the Earthly Branches of Si (Snake), You (Rooster) and Chou (Ox) combine to form a Metal Structure, it would be preferable to have Wu Earth in the Heavenly Stems.

- Earth and Wood should not be present in abundance throughout the chart, since they may suppress the Ren Water's performance in this month. Where excessive Wood and Earth is found, this Ren Water Day Master may not be privileged enough to enjoy sustainable fame and fortune throughout his or her entire life. Life would be an empty promise.

- Where only Geng Metal is revealed amongst the Heavenly Stems, while Ren Water and Gui Water are unable to penetrate through to the Heavenly Stems, this Ren Water Day Master will probably lead an average life, at best.

- Where Fire Qi is present in abundance, but only Gui Water is present while an additional Ren Water is missing, this Ren Water Day Master may be blessed with wealth, but also suffer from poor health.

Snake

| Day Master | Ren 壬 Water | Month | Si 巳 (Snake) |

Additional Attributes

格局 Structural Star	食神 Eating God	比肩 Friend
用神 Useful God	Jia 甲 Wood	Ren 壬 Water
Conditions	Where this Eating God Structure is accompanied by Friends and Direct Resource Stars, this Ren Water Day Master shall enjoy enviable fame in life.	
Positive Circumstances	Jia Wood appearing on the Stem and Ren Water in the Branches.	
Negative Circumstances	Where Jia Wood does not penetrate through to the Heavenly Stems, this Ren Water Day Master shall only enjoy short term fame.	

格局 Structural Star	正財 Direct Wealth
用神 Useful God	Ding 丁 Fire
Conditions	Where Ding Fire (Direct Wealth Star), penetrates through to the Heavenly Stems and combines with this Ren Water Day Master, Gui Water would be needed as a Rob Wealth Star in penetrating through to the Heavenly Stems. Otherwise, this Ren Water Day Master may not achieve the level of fame he or she desires in life.
Positive Circumstances	Yi Wood penetrate through to the Heavenly Stem.
Negative Circumstances	Gui Water penetrates through to the Heavenly Stems.

Day Master Ren 壬 Water	**Month** Si 巳 (Snake)

四月

Fourth Month

Additional Attributes

格局 **Structural Star**	偏印 Indirect Resource	正印 Direct Resource
用神 **Useful God**	Geng 庚 Metal	Xin 辛 Metal
Conditions	Where the Earthly Branches encounter a Metal Structure, Jia Wood should not be seen at the same time. Otherwise, this Ren Water Day Master may be susceptible to poor health and illness in life.	
Positive Circumstances	Bing Fire and Wu Earth, as Direct Wealth and Seven Killings Stars, serve as Useful Gods.	
Negative Circumstances	Where Jia Wood sits atop a Yin (Tiger) Earthly Branch but its Qi penetrates through the Heavenly Stems, this Ren Water Day Master may suffer from a lack of fame and fortune in life.	

Snake

* *Ren Water and Xin Metal are the preferred Useful Gods.*

四月 **Fourth Month**

Snake

| Day Master | Ren 壬 Water | | Month | Si 巳 (Snake) |

Summary

- Where the Earthly Branches are more inclined towards forming a Water Structure, this Ren Water Day Master shall enjoy great prosperity in life.

- Where Gui Water is present but additional Ren Water missing, this Day Master may encounter a potentially life-threatening disease or ailment.

- Where Geng Metal forms an Indirect Resource Structure, the absence of Friends and Rob Wealth Stars coupled with the interference of any other threatening elements, will produce only a substandard BaZi Chart.

- Where the Earthly Branches form a Metal Structure, the Bing Fire and Wu Earth Hidden Stems of the Si (Snake) Earthly Branch should be used, if this Ren Water Day Master is to prosper in life.

Ren 壬 Water Day Master, Born in Fifth Month 五月

Wu 午 (Horse) Month
June 6th - July 6th

Do note that the dates provided above are subject to slight yearly variations. Please refer to the Ten Thousand Year Calendar for the accurate transition dates for each year.

| Day Master | Ren 壬 Water | | Month | Wu 午 (Horse) |

五月
Fifth Month

Horse

日元 Day Master	月 Month
壬 *Ren* **Yang Water**	午 *Wu* **Horse** **Yang Fire**

For a Ren Water Day Master born in a Wu (Horse) Month, a Direct Wealth Structure is formed where Ding Fire is revealed as one of the Heavenly Stems.

Where Ji Earth is revealed as one of the Heavenly Stems, a Direct Officer Structure is formed.

Should, however, neither Ding Fire nor Ji Earth happen to be revealed within the Heavenly Stems, one should select a Structure according to the BaZi Chart's most prominent Qi attribute at one's discretion.

| Day Master | Ren 壬 Water | | Month | Wu 午 (Horse) |

喜用神提要 **Regulating Useful God Reference Guide**

月 **Month**	用神 **Useful God**

5th Month 五月
Wu 午 **(Horse) Month**

Gui
Yin Water

Geng
Yang Metal

Xin
Yin Metal

Horse

For a Wu (Horse) Month, Gui Water, Geng Metal and Xin Metal are the Regulating Useful Gods.

Where possible, Geng Metal (Resource Star) should be chosen as the preferred Useful God, with Gui Water as the second-choice Useful God.

In the absence of Geng Metal, Xin Metal may be used as a suitable alternative Useful God in its stead.

BaZi Structures & Structural Useful Gods 格局與格局用神

五月 Fifth Month

Day Master	Ren 壬 Water		Month	Wu 午 (Horse)

6th day of June – 6th day of July, Gregorian Calendar

A Ren Water Day Master born in a Wu (Horse) Month will invariably be weak. This is because Earth is inevitably dry in mid-summer, and hence weakening Water Qi.

Metal and Water that are rooted in Earth Branches serve as supporting Stars for a Ren Water Day Master born in a Wu (Horse) Month. Wood Qi should, however, be avoided, as it would only strengthen the already excessive Fire Qi in a Wu (Horse) Month.

As such, additional Fire and Earth Qi should be avoided, as both serve as the proverbial 'Achilles' Heel' of this Ren Water Day Master.

Horse

| Day Master | Ren 壬 Water | Month | Wu 午 (Horse) |

Commentary

In addition to the preceding narratives on the potential Structures and scenarios resulting from a Ren Water Day Master born in a Wu (Horse) Month, the following circumstances also play their respective roles in determining the overall strength of this Day Master's BaZi Chart.

Horse

Note:

- Geng Metal and Ren Water are the preferred Useful Gods.

- Gui Water may be used to control and hence prevent Ding Fire from becoming overly strong.

- Ding Fire should be prevented from combining with Ren Water to form Wood. Wu Earth should also be avoided or at least, not be present in abundance in the BaZi Chart.

- Where Geng Metal and Gui Water are revealed in the Heavenly Stems, this Ren Water Day Master shall enjoy immense success in life.

- Where Geng Metal is but Gui Water is not revealed in the Heavenly Stems, this Ren Water Day Master will not lack the requisite skills to succeed in life; although he or she will probably only lead an average life, at best.

- Where Ding Fire and Wu Earth are revealed in the Heavenly Stems and their Qi also seen throughout the entire BaZi Chart, this Ren Water Day Master may struggle to achieve success in life. The person would encounter many self created obstructions in life.

- Where additional Jia Wood and Yi Wood happen to form a Wood Structure, this Ren Water Day Master shall tend to be learned and knowledgeable; although he or she may also suffer from loneliness in life.

五
月

Fifth Month

Horse

Day Master	Ren 壬 Water		Month	Wu 午 (Horse)

Additional Attributes

格局 Structural Star	劫財 Rob Wealth	偏印 Indirect Resource
用神 Useful God	Gui 癸 Water	Geng 庚 Metal
Conditions	Where Geng Metal and Gui Water are revealed in the BaZi Chart, this Ren Water Day Master shall enjoy immense fame and good fortune in life.	
Positive Circumstances	Geng Metal penetrate through the Heavenly Stems.	
Negative Circumstances	Ding Fire penetrate through the Heavenly Stems.	

| Day Master | Ren 壬 Water | Month | Wu 午 (Horse) |

五月

Additional Attributes

Horse

格局 Structural Star	偏財 Indirect Wealth	正財 Direct Wealth
用神 Useful God	Bing 丙 Fire	Ding 丁 Fire
Conditions	Where the Earthly Branches encounter Fire Qi forming a Direct Wealth Structure with Ren Water – coupled with the total absence of Geng Metal and Gui Water, it would be possible for a Follow the Wealth Structure to be formed.	
Positive Circumstances	Geng Metal and Gui Water penetrate through the Heavenly Stems.	
Negative Circumstances	In the absence of Metal and Water, this Ren Water Day Master may still suffer from poverty; regardless of how affluent his or her household may be.	

* *Geng Metal and Gui Water are the best or most-preferred Useful Gods.*

BaZi Structures & Structural Useful Gods 格局與格局用神

Day Master	Ren 壬 Water	Month	Wu 午 (Horse)

Summary

- A Ren Water Day Master born in a Wu (Horse) Month is subject to the same circumstances governing a Ren Water Day Master born in a Si (Snake) Month. The only difference is that a Gui Water Day Master born in either a Wu (Horse) or Si (Snake) Month would fare better than a Ren Water Day Master born in either month.

- Wu Earth and Gui Water must be 'protected' or 'defended' at all costs. As such, one should first use Ren Water, where available, as the primary Useful God.

- Ding Fire and Ren Water should be prevented from being combined away with one another to form Wood. As such, one should first use Gui Water, where available, as the Useful God – while reserving Ren Water as the last option.

- In the absence of Ding Fire penetrating through the Heavenly, Xin Metal may be used to replace Geng Metal as a Useful God.

Ren 壬 Water Day Master, Born in Sixth Month 六月

Wei 未 (Goat) Month
July 7th - August 7th

Do note that the dates provided above are subject to slight yearly variations. Please refer to the Ten Thousand Year Calendar for the accurate transition dates for each year.

六
月

Sixth Month

Goat

| Day Master | Ren 壬 Water | Month | Wei 未 (Goat) |

日元 **Day Master**	月 **Month**
壬 *Ren* **Yang Water**	未 *Wei* **Goat** **Yin Earth**

For a Ren Water Day Master born in a Wei (Goat) Month, a Direct Officer Structure is formed where Ji Earth is revealed as one of the Heavenly Stems.

Where Ding Fire is revealed as one of the Heavenly Stems, a Direct Wealth Structure is formed.

Where Yi Wood is revealed as one of the Heavenly Stems, a Hurting Officer Structure is formed.

Should, however, neither Ji Earth nor Ding Fire nor Yi Wood happen to be revealed within the Heavenly Stems, one should select a Structure according to the BaZi Chart's most prominent Qi attribute at one's discretion.

| Day Master | Ren 壬 Water | Month | Wei 未 (Goat) |

喜用神提要 **Regulating Useful God Reference Guide**

| 月 **Month** | 用神 **Useful God** |

6th Month 六月
Wei 未 (Goat) Month

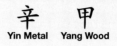

辛   甲
Yin Metal   Yang Wood

Goat

For a Wei (Goat) Month, Xin Metal and Jia Wood are the Regulating Useful Gods.

As a Useful God, Xin Metal produces and strengthens Water Qi. Meanwhile, Jia Wood may be used to 'plough' and hence make Earth Qi softer and useable.

45

BaZi Structures & Structural Useful Gods 格局與格局用神

Day Master	Ren 壬 Water	Month	Wei 未 (Goat)

7th day of July – 7th day of August, Gregorian Calendar

Fire and Earth are very strong in a Wei (Goat) Month. Consequently, the Wood Qi hidden inside the Wei (Goat) Earthly Branch would bring about a leakage of Water Qi, while simultaneously produce and cause Fire Qi to become stronger.

Ren Water would therefore need the assistance or support of Metal elements, in order for it to grow and thrive. It is only with the assistance of Metal and Water that Ren Water will be able to prosper.

Goat

Even though Earth Qi is strong in a Wei (Goat) Month, Wood is still deemed unsuitable to be used to counter or control Earth. This is because Wood produces Fire, and this will invariably lead to a leakage and weakening of Water.

| Day Master | Ren 壬 Water | Month | Wei 未 (Goat) |

Commentary

In addition to the preceding narratives on the potential Structures and scenarios resulting from a Ren Water Day Master born in a Wei (Goat) Month, the following circumstances also play their respective roles in determining the overall strength of this Day Master's BaZi Chart.

Note:

- Xin Metal and Jia Wood are the Useful Gods for a Ren Water Day Master born in a Wei (Goat) Month.

- Earth Qi is strong in a Wei (Goat) Month. As such, Jia Wood should be used to 'plough' and hence make Earth Qi softer and useable.

- Presence of Bing Fire in the chart where there are Direct Officer Stars present in abundance, as well as Eating God and Hurting Officer Stars, this Ren Water Day Master will tend to possess an honest, straightforward personality – although he or she may only lead an average life.

- Where Geng Metal and an additional Ren Water are both revealed in the BaZi Chart, this Ren Water Day Master shall possess power, authority and wealth in life.

- Where Geng Metal is but an additional Ren Water is not revealed, this Day Master shall be learned and knowledgeable; although he or she may only lead an average life.

- Where Xin Metal and Jia Wood are both revealed, this Ren Water Day Master may possess status and authority in life; although his or her wealth may not equal his or her level of status.

- Where Wood and Earth both dominant in the chart, this person may struggle to achieve the outcomes he or she desires in life.

六月 Sixth Month

Goat

47

Day Master	Ren 壬 Water		Month	Wei 未 (Goat)

Goat

Additional Attributes

格局 **Structural Star**	正印 Direct Resource	食神 Eating God
用神 **Useful God**	Xin 辛 Metal	Jia 甲 Wood
Conditions	Where Jia Wood and Xin Metal are both revealed in the BaZi Chart, this Ren Water Day Master shall prosper and indeed, advance significantly in life.	
Positive Circumstances	There is at least a couple of Friend and Rob Wealth Stars contained within the Hidden Stems of the Earthly Branches.	
Negative Circumstances	Ding Fire penetrate through to the Heavenly Stems.	

格局 **Structural Star**	正官 Direct Officer
用神 **Useful God**	Ji 己 Earth
Conditions	In the absence of Jia Wood and Yi Wood (Eating God and Hurting Officer Stars) respectively, there may be certain 'hidden' characteristics of this Ren Water Day Master's BaZi Chart that may be difficult to be understood by others. This person may appear enigmatic. Consequently, this Ren Water Day Master may struggle throughout his or her life, even if only to make basic ends meet.
Positive Circumstances	Absence of Jia Wood next to Ji Earth.
Negative Circumstances	Jia Wood and Yi Wood do not penetrate through the Heavenly Stems.

Day Master	Ren 壬 Water		Month	Wei 未 (Goat)

Additional Attributes

Goat

格局 **Structural Star**	偏印 Indirect Resource
用神 **Useful God**	Geng 庚 Metal
Conditions	Only an Indirect Resource Star or a Friend Star, penetrating through the Heavenly Stems. Under such circumstances, this Ren Water Day Master shall be able to wield significant skills and authority that will help him or her to progress in life.
Positive Circumstances	Geng Metal and Ren Water appearing the Heavenly Stems.
Negative Circumstances	The presence of Bing Fire as an Indirect Wealth Star will weaken Geng Metal. Under such circumstances, this Ren Water Day Master may not possess the drive to generate wealth according to the best of his or her capabilities in life.

* *Before the advent of 'Greater Heat' (大暑) roughly from July 23rd to August 7th, a Ren Water Day Master born in a Wei (Goat) Month would be subject to the same circumstances governing a Ren Water Day Master born in a Wu (Horse) Month.*

** *After the advent of 'Greater Heat' (大暑) roughly from July 23rd to August 7th, Xin Metal and Jia Wood are the preferred Useful Gods for a Ren Water Day Master born in a Wei (Goat) Month.*

六月
Sixth Month

Goat

| Day Master | Ren 壬 Water | Month | Wei 未 (Goat) |

Summary

- A Ren Water Day Master born in a Wei (Goat) Month would find it unsuitable to encounter a dominant Direct Officer or Seven Killings Structure. Even though Jia Wood and Yi Wood may be revealed and penetrate through to the Heavenly Stems, both will control Ji Earth. Consequently, this Ren Water Day Master may struggle throughout his or her entire life, and perhaps barely even able to make ends meet.

- A Direct Resource Structure stars are the preferred Useful God as the Qi it produces would be strengthen, protect and nurture the Ren Day Master.

Ren 壬 Water Day Master, Born in Seventh Month 七月

Shen 申 (Monkey) Month
August 8th - September 7th

Do note that the dates provided above are subject to slight yearly variations. Please refer to the Ten Thousand Year Calendar for the accurate transition dates for each year.

| Day Master | Ren 壬 Water | Month | Shen 申 (Monkey) |

日元 Day Master	月 Month
壬 Ren Yang Water	申 Shen Monkey Yang Metal

For a Ren Water Day Master born in a Shen (Monkey) Month, an Indirect Resource Structure is formed where Geng Metal is revealed as one of the Heavenly Stems.

Where Wu Earth is revealed as one of the Heavenly Stems, a Seven Killings Structure is formed.

Where another Ren Water appears in the Heavenly Stems, a Thriving Structure may be formed depending on circumstances.

Should, however, neither Wu Earth, Ren Water, nor Geng Metal happen to be revealed amongst the Heavenly Stems, one should select a Structure according to the BaZi Chart's most prominent Qi attribute at one's discretion.

| Day Master | Ren 壬 Water | Month | Shen 申 (Monkey) |

喜用神提要 Regulating Useful God Reference Guide

月 Month	用神 Useful God

7th Month 七月
Shen 申 (Monkey) Month

戊 丁
Yang Earth | Yin Fire

Monkey

In a Shen (Monkey) Month, Wu Earth and Ding Fire are the Regulating Useful Gods for this Ren Water Day Master.

Ding Fire should be taken or used to assist Wu Earth, in producing Geng Metal.

In any case, Wu Earth must be rooted in either a Chen (Dragon) or Xu (Dog) Earthly Branch, with Ding Fire rooted in either a Wu (Horse) or Xu (Dog) Earthly Branch, if both are to be effectives as Useful Gods.

Day Master	Ren 壬 Water	Month	Shen 申 (Monkey)

8th day of August – 7th day of September, Gregorian Calendar

In a Shen (Monkey) Month, Metal Qi is vibrant while Water Qi is becoming prominent. As one of the Four Growths Earthly Branches, Shen (Monkey) also contains Ren Water in its Hidden Stem, which would also lends support and strengthen the Ren Water Day Master.

Where the Day Master or Self Element is strong, Fire will best be selected as this Ren Water Day Master's Useful Wealth Star.

Where Fire Qi and Earth Qi are prominent in the BaZi Chart, this Ren Water Day Master shall enjoy authority and power in life.

Where Wood Qi and Fire Qi are prominent in the BaZi Chart, this Ren Water Day Master shall prosper and become extremely wealthy in life.

However, this day master should not encounter additional Metal and Water Qi. This is because strong Metal Qi and Water Qi would weaken this Day Master's Wealth and Officer Stars.

Day Master	Ren 壬 Water	Month	Shen 申 (Monkey)

Commentary

In addition to the preceding narratives on the potential Structures and scenarios resulting from a Ren Water Day Master born in a Shen (Monkey) Month, the following circumstances also play their respective roles in determining the overall strength of this Day Master's BaZi Chart.

Monkey

Note:

- The Wu Earth Hidden Stem found inside the Shen (Monkey) Earthly Branch is regarded as hallowed Earth. As such, it would be of little, if any, use to this Ren Water Day Master.

- Where the Earthly Branches of Shen (Monkey), Zi (Rat) and Chen (Dragon) forms a Water Structure, Wu Earth would be needed to control Water, in order for this Ren Water Day Master to prosper in life.

- If, at the same time, Gui Water also happens to meet Wu Earth, this Ren Water Day Master may be prone towards harboring ill or malicious thoughts, or even possess subversive tendencies.

- Where this Ren Water Day Master encounters additional Water stars as well as an abundance of Wu Earth (Seven Killings Star), the ability of Wu Earth would be limited to only keeping Water under control but not serve it's Seven Killing prowess. Consequently, this Ren Water Day Master may possess a relaxed attitude towards life, which may even border on being lackadaisal.

- Where Water and Wood Qi are dominant in this chart, the person shall prosper to the extent of being able to accumulate large holdings of property and real estate globally.

- Where Geng Metal is revealed, this Ren Water Day Master would find it difficult to form any powerful or significant BaZi structures. Consequently, this Ren Water Day Master may only lead an average life, at best.

七
月

Seventh Month

Monkey

| Day Master | Ren 壬 Water | | Month | Shen 申 (Monkey) |

Additional Attributes

格局 Structural Star	七殺 Seven Killings	正財 Direct Wealth
用神 Useful God	Wu 戊 Earth	Ding 丁 Fire
Conditions	This Ren Water shall enjoy tremendous success, particularly in a Wu Earth Month of a Ding Fire Year.	
Positive Circumstances	Both Wu Earth and Ding Fire appearing on the Heavenly Stems.	
Negative Circumstances	The presence of Gui Water, as a Rob Wealth Star. Also, where a Direct Wealth Star penetrates through to the Heavenly Stems and combines the Wu Earth away.	

格局 Structural Star	七殺 Seven Killings
用神 Useful God	Wu 戊 Earth
Conditions	Only Wu Earth (Seven Killings Star), should be used, where there is an abundance of Ren Water in the Four Pillars.
Positive Circumstances	Absence of Gui Water in the Heavenly Stems.
Negative Circumstances	There are too many Jia Wood Eating God Stars present throughout the BaZi Chart.

Day Master	Ren 壬 Water	Month	Shen 申 (Monkey)

Additional Attributes

格局 **Structural Star**	食神 Eating God
用神 **Useful God**	Jia 甲 Wood
Conditions	Where the Earthly Branches forms a Wood structure, coupled with the absence of Geng Metal (Indirect Resource Star), this Ren Water Day Master will be outspoken but lack substance.
Positive Circumstances	Geng Metal (Indirect Resource Star), penetrates through to the Heavenly Stems right next to the Jia Wood (Eating God).
Negative Circumstances	Absence of roots for the Eating God.

Monkey

*   *Wu Earth and Ding Fire are the best or most-preferred Useful Gods.*

** *Where Wu Earth is absent on the Stems, the Wu Earth contained within the Shen (Monkey) Earthly Branch may be used instead. Nevertheless, it would be better or preferable to use the Wu Earth Hidden Stem contained within the Chen (Dragon) or Xu (Dog) Earthly Branches.*

Day Master	Ren 壬 Water	Month	Shen 申 (Monkey)

Summary

- A Ren Water Day Master born in a Shen (Monkey) Month should use Wu Earth as a Seven Killings Star where there is excessive Water stars.

- The Wu Earth Heavenly Stem contained within the Shen (Monkey) Earthly Branch is considered hallowed earth Earth. Best to select the Wu Earth in the Dragon or Dog branches.

Monkey

Ren 壬 Water Day Master, Born in Eighth Month 八月

You 酉 (Rooster) Month
September 8th - October 7th

Do note that the dates provided above are subject to slight yearly variations. Please refer to the Ten Thousand Year Calendar for the accurate transition dates for each year.

| Day Master | Ren 壬 Water | Month | You 酉 (Rooster) |

日元 Day Master	月 Month
壬 Ren Yang Water	酉 You Rooster Yin Metal

For a Ren Water Day Master born in a You (Rooster) Month, a Direct Resource Structure is formed where Xin Metal as a Heavenly Stem.

Even if Xin Metal is not revealed as a Heavenly Stem, the resultant structure formed is also known as a Direct Resource Structure.

Day Master Ren 壬 Water ·   **Month** You 酉 (Rooster)

喜用神提要 **Regulating Useful God Reference Guide**

月 Month	用神 Useful God
8th Month 八月 You 酉 **(Rooster) Month**	 甲 庚 Yang Wood Yang Metal

Rooster

For a You (Rooster) Month, Jia Wood and Geng Metal are the Regulating Useful Gods.

In the absence of Jia Wood, Metal should be used as a source or resource to purify the Water. Then use of Geng is merely to keep the water flowing.

八月 Eighth Month

酉 Rooster

| Day Master | Ren 壬 Water | Month | You 酉 (Rooster) |

8th day of August – 7th day of September, Gregorian Calendar

A Ren Water Day Master born in a You (Rooster) Month, both Metal Qi is prosperous while Water Qi is strong.

It would beneficial for this Day Master to have rooted Direct Wealth and Direct Officer Stars as Useful Gods.

Where Metal Qi are in abundance, Wood Qi would be automatically weakened. In this month, the Ren Water Day Master shall enjoy a good life where it encounters prominent Fire Qi, which is duly supported by Wood. A life of bliss and happiness is expected. A good condition is when additional Metal and Water Qi are not be present in the chart.

Where this Ren Water Day Master is to rooted, it would require the assistance of 'warm' or 'warmed' Wood star to serve as either a Direct or Indirect Wealth Star to bring life to the chart.

Day Master	Ren 壬 Water		Month	You 酉 (Rooster)

Commentary

In addition to the preceding narratives on the potential Structures and scenarios resulting from a Ren Water Day Master born in a You (Rooster) Month, the following circumstances also play their respective roles in determining the overall strength of this Day Master's BaZi Chart.

Note:

- Only Xin Metal should be used, where appropriate, to help keep strong Jia Wood under control.

- Wu Earth and Ji Earth should be prevented from penetrating through the Heavenly Stems.

- Where there are three rooted Geng Metal or Xin Metal revealed in the Heavenly Stems, this person shall be blessed with a extraordinary life. Only the purest Water has the potential to 'aggravate' or 'antagonize' three Xin Metal Stems. This is a very special structure.

- Where Jia Wood is revealed in the Heavenly Stems, and supported by the presence of 'brilliant' Metal and 'clear' Water, this person shall be blessed with admirable fame and great fortune in life. Especially when Geng Metal and Wu Earth are not seen penetrating through the Heavenly Stems. For this chart to fulfill the special structure, significant and non threatening Fire Qi is needed for this condition to work.

八
月

Eighth Month

Rooster

| Day Master | Ren 壬 Water | Month | You 酉 (Rooster) |

八月
Eighth Month

酉
Rooster

Additional Attributes

格局 Structural Star	食神 Eating God
用神 Useful God	Jia 甲 Wood
Conditions	Jia Wood is revealed as the Heavenly Stem of the Hour Pillar. This person shall enjoy a fortunate, smooth-sailing life.
Positive Circumstances	Jia Wood appears on the Heavenly Stems.
Negative Circumstances	Geng Metal penetrates through the Heavenly Stems.

格局 Structural Star	偏印 Indirect Resource	正印 Direct Resource
用神 Useful God	Geng 庚 Metal	Xin 辛 Metal
Conditions	Only Water has the potential to purify Xin Metal Stems. Water Qi is considered weak when Metal Qi is overly abundant.	
Positive Circumstances	Ren Water and Gui Water as Friend and Rob Wealth Stars respectively, occupying their proper places or positions in the BaZi Chart. Alternatively, rooted Fire Stars are present to keep the Metal under control.	
Negative Circumstances	Excessive Metal Stars in the chart.	

| Day Master | Ren 壬 Water | Month | You 酉 (Rooster) |

Additional Attributes

格局 Structural Star	比肩 Friend	劫財 Rob Wealth
用神 Useful God	Wu 戊 Earth	Gui 癸 Water
Conditions	Where the Earthly Branches encounter a Zi (Rat) Earthly Branch, a Goat Blade Structure is formed.	
Positive Circumstances	Wu Earth (Seven Killings Star), should be used as a Useful God.	
Negative Circumstances	Jia Wood or Gui Water appears right next to Wu Earth.	

Rooster

* *Jia Wood is the preferred Useful God.*

** *Wu Earth and Ji Earth should be prevented from penetrating through to the Heavenly Stems.*

八月

Eighth Month

Rooster

| Day Master | Ren 壬 Water | Month | You 酉 (Rooster) |

Summary

- A Goat Blade formation may be formed when the Ren Water Day Master born in a You (Rooster) Month encounter a Zi (Rat) Earthly Branch. When this is seen, the Wu Earth would be the Useful God.

- Jia Wood (Eating God Star) as the primary Useful God would be good for this Ren Water Day Master. The absence of Jia Wood would, in effect, result in any structure formed being a substandard one.

- Where both Metal and Water Structures are formed, Earth would still be needed to control and maintain balance in the BaZi Chart.

Ren 壬 Water Day Master, Born in Ninth Month 九月

Xu 戌 (Dog) Month
October 8th - November 6th

Do note that the dates provided above are subject to slight yearly variations. Please refer to the Ten Thousand Year Calendar for the accurate transition dates for each year.

| Day Master | Ren 壬 Water | Month | Xu 戌 (Dog) |

戌
Dog

日元 Day Master	月 Month
壬 *Ren* **Yang Water**	戌 *Xu* **Dog** **Yang Earth**

For a Ren Water Day Master born in a Xu (Dog) Month, a Seven Killings Structure is formed where Wu Earth is revealed as one of the Heavenly Stems.

Where Ding Fire is revealed as one of the Heavenly Stems, a Direct Wealth Structure is formed.

Where Xin Metal is revealed as one of the Heavenly Stems, a Direct Resource Structure is formed.

Should, however, neither Wu Earth nor Ding Fire nor Xin Metal happen to be revealed within the Heavenly Stems, one should select a Structure according to the BaZi Chart's most prominent Qi attribute at one's discretion.

Day Master Ren 壬 Water   **Month** Xu 戌 (Dog)

喜用神提要 **Regulating Useful God Reference Guide**

月 **Month**	用神 **Useful God**

9th Month 九月
Xu 戌 (Dog) Month

甲 丙
Jia *Bing*
Yang Wood **Yang Fire**

Dog

For a Xu (Dog) Month, Jia Wood and Bing Fire are the Regulating Useful Gods.

Jia Wood should be used to keep the Wu Earth under control. Meanwhile, Bing Fire serves as an intermediary to maintain the overall balance between Jia Wood and Wu Earth in the BaZi Chart.

69

BaZi Structures & Structural Useful Gods 格局與格局用神

Day Master	Ren 壬 Water	Month	Xu 戌 (Dog)

8th day of October – 7th day of November, Gregorian Calendar

Earth is invariably leaden and thick in the autumn month of the Dog. Earth would be thick the moment Wu Earth is seen reaching the Heavenly Stems.

The strength of Ren Water depends greatly on the clarity of Metal Qi in the chart.

Wood, only in moderate or small amounts, may be used, since Wood Qi is particularly brittle and unstable this month.

Abundance of Metal and Water Qi in the chart may result in the person encountering constant legal obstacles and petty-minded or malicious people throughout his or her life.

戌
Dog

Day Master	Ren 壬 Water	Month	Xu 戌 (Dog)

Commentary

In addition to the preceding narratives on the potential Structures and scenarios resulting from a Ren Water Day Master born in a Xu (Dog) Month, the following circumstances also play their respective roles in determining the overall strength of this Day Master's BaZi Chart.

Dog

Note:

- Jia Wood is the preferred Useful God, although in its absence, Bing Fire and Ding Fire can also serve as Useful Gods.

- Ji Earth should be prevented from combining with Jia Wood, as this would result in Earth being produced.

- Earth Qi is also dominant in a Xu (Dog) Month. Although the presence of Water may support the flow of this Ren Water Day Master, its ability to 'contaminate' Earth makes Water's presence in a Xu (Dog) Month rather untimely.

- Jia Wood should be used to 'loosen' Earth, making this star more useable in a Xu (Dog) Month.

- Where any of the Four Graveyards Earthly Branches - Chen (Dragon), Xu (Dog), Chou (Ox) and Wei (Goat) are present, select Jia Wood, as the preferred Useful God. This star will keep the balance in the chart. However, Jia Wood needs to penetrate through the Heavenly Stems to be effective.

- Where Bing Fire is missing or absent from the chart, this Ren Water Day Master shall only lead an average life, at best.

Dog

Day Master	Ren 壬 Water	Month	Xu 戌 (Dog)

Additional Attributes

格局 **Structural Star**	偏印 Indirect Resource
用神 **Useful God**	Geng 庚 Metal
Conditions	Where an Indirect Resource Structure is formed, Ding Fire needs to be revealed in the BaZi Chart. The absence of Ding Fire, it would be difficult to maintain balance. This chart would be disastrous without Ding.
Positive Circumstances	Ding Fire (Direct Wealth Star), penetrates through the Heavenly Stems.
Negative Circumstances	Ding Fire, is absent from the BaZi Chart. Instead, Jia Wood penetrates through the Heavenly Stems.

Day Master	Ren 壬 Water		Month	Xu 戌 (Dog)

Additional Attributes

格局 **Structural Star**	食神 Eating God
用神 **Useful God**	Jia 甲 Wood
Conditions	The best-case scenario would be where Jia Wood is revealed in the Hour Pillar of the BaZi Chart. The Hour Pillar prevents the useful Jia Wood from being harmed by external factors. A protected Eating God denotes heightened prowess of creativity and intelligence.
Positive Circumstances	Jia Wood in the Hour Pillars Heavenly Stem.
Negative Circumstances	Ji Earth combining with Jia Wood. Whole life loss of opportunities.

Dog

* *Jia Wood is the preferred Useful God.*

73

| Day Master | Ren 壬 Water | | Month | Xu 戌 (Dog) |

Summary

Dog

- Since Earth Qi is obstructing in a Xu (Dog) Month, Jia Wood is needed to keep the Earth under control; regardless of whether Wu Earth is revealed in the BaZi Chart or otherwise.

- Where Jia Wood is missing or absent from the BaZi Chart, this Ren Water Day Master may lack a sense of purpose in life.

- The best-case scenario would be where Ding Fire, revealed and rooted in the chart. Take note however that Ding Fire should not be on the Month or Hour Stems. This is to prevent an undesirable combination rendering the Ding Fire's function useless.

- Bing Fire can also be interspersed and used as a Useful God.

Ren 壬 Water Day Master, Born in Tenth Month 十月

Hai 亥 (Pig) Month
November 7th - December 6th

Do note that the dates provided above are subject to slight yearly variations. Please refer to the Ten Thousand Year Calendar for the accurate transition dates for each year.

| Day Master | Ren 壬 Water | | Month | Hai 亥 (Pig) |

日元 Day Master	月 Month
壬 *Ren* **Yang Water**	亥 *Hai* **Pig** **Yin Water**

For a Ren Water Day Master born in a Hai (Pig) Month, an Eating God Structure is formed where Jia Wood is revealed as a Heavenly Stem.

Where another Ren Water is revealed in the stem, a Thriving Structure may be formed.

Even if Jia Wood is not revealed as a Heavenly Stem, the resultant structure formed is also known as the Thriving Structure.

| Day Master | Ren 壬 Water | Month | Hai 亥 (Pig) |

喜用神提要 **Regulating Useful God Reference Guide**

月 **Month**	用神 **Useful God**

10th Month 十月
Hai 亥 (Pig) Month

戊   丙   庚
Wu   *Bing*   *Geng*
Yang Earth   **Yang Fire**   **Yang Metal**

Pig

Ren in a Hai (Pig) Month, Wu Earth, Bing Fire and Geng Metal are the Regulating Useful Gods.

Where Jia Wood penetrates through the Heavenly Stems, the assistance of Geng Metal would be needed to chop wood and produce Fire, in order to support the Earth and hence maintain balance in the BaZi Chart.

BaZi Structures & Structural Useful Gods 格局與格局用神

Day Master	Ren 壬 Water	Month	Hai 亥 (Pig)

7th day of November – 6th day of December, Gregorian Calendar

Pig

It would be preferable to have Fire and Earth present and be selected as Useful Wealth and Officer Stars.

The Qi of the BaZi Chart would invariably tend to be 'cold' or 'chilly' this month; resulting in Water being frozen and Earth being weak. As such, where there is at least enough Fire to 'warm' Earth, this Ren Water Day Master shall be blessed with wealth, power and status in life.

Wood Qi Earthly Branches, which contains or harbors Fire Qi, may also be used to serve the this purpose.

| Day Master | Ren 壬 Water | Month | Hai 亥 (Pig) |

Commentary

In addition to the preceding narratives on the potential Structures and scenarios resulting from a Ren Water Day Master born in a Hai (Pig) Month, the following circumstances also play their respective roles in determining the overall strength of this Day Master's BaZi Chart.

Pig

Note:

- Wu Earth is a preferred Useful God, while Bing Fire may be used as yet another Useful God to produce and support Wu Earth.

- Gui Water is undesirable to be seen from penetrating through to the Heavenly Stems.

- Where the Earthly Branches of Hai (Pig), Mao (Rabbit) and Wei (Goat) form a Wood Structure, there may be a Qi leakage from the Ren Water. Under such circumstances, Geng Metal, may act as a Useful God, used to keep Wood under control. Here, the role of a Useful God is to 'medicate' an unstable Day Master. As such, Jia Wood should be inseparable from Geng Metal, as Geng Metal should be inseparable from Ding Fire.

- A self punishment between two dragons while Wu Earth is absent from the Heavenly Stems may indicate that this person is prone to meeting accidents and mishaps his/her whole life.

- Where the Earthly Branches forms a complete Water Structure, and while Wu Earth and Ji Earth happen to be absent, this Ren Water Day Master shall prosper during Metal and Water Luck Periods, but fare poorly during Wood and Fire Luck Periods. This is because it will form a Follow Prosperous Structure.

- Where Bing Fire is missing or absent from the chart, this person would only lead an average life, at best.

- Ding Fire may not be enough to warm the chart.

Day Master	Ren 壬 Water		Month	Hai 亥 (Pig)

Additional Attributes

格局 Structural Star	七殺 Seven Killings	偏印 Indirect Resource
用神 Useful God	Wu 戊 Earth	Geng 庚 Metal
Conditions	Where Wu Earth and Geng Metal are both revealed in the BaZi Chart, but there is no sign of Jia Wood penetrating through the Heavenly Stems next to Geng, this Ren Water Day Master shall be blessed with fame, fortune and longevity in life.	
Positive Circumstances	Fire element is already present in the chart.	
Negative Circumstances	Jia Wood penetrates through the Heavenly Stems, right next to Geng.	

格局 Structural Star	食神 Eating God	傷官 Hurting Officer
用神 Useful God	Jia 甲 Wood	Yi 乙 Wood
Conditions	Where the Earthly Branches forms Wood stars, while Geng Metal (Resource Star) is missing from the Heavenly Stems, this Ren Water Day Master would only lead an average life, at best.	
Positive Circumstances	Geng Metal penetrates through the Heavenly Stems.	
Negative Circumstances	Absence of Fire element in the chart.	

Day Master	Ren 壬 Water		Month	Hai 亥 (Pig)

Additional Attributes

亥
Pig

格局 Structural Star	比肩 Friend	劫財 Rob Wealth
用神 Useful God	Ren 壬 Water	Gui 癸 Water
Conditions	Where the Earthly Branches form a Water Structure, Wu Earth would be needed to penetrate through the Heavenly Stems. The absence of Wu Earth would make this a substandard structure.	
Positive Circumstances	This Ren Water Day Master enters Metal and Water Luck. (Take note: this is only applicable when the Follow Prosperous structure is formed).	
Negative Circumstances	This Ren Water Day Master enters Earth Element. (Assuming it has entered the Follow Prosperous Structure).	

格局 Structural Star	七殺 Seven Killings
用神 Useful God	Wu 戊 Earth
Conditions	A Seven Killings Structure should only be used, when Bing is missing. Even so, this Ren Water Day Master may find it difficult to accumulate or generate wealth in life without Fire.
Positive Circumstances	This Ren Water Day Master enters a Fire or Earth Luck Period.
Negative Circumstances	Absence of fire element in the chart.

*   Wu Earth and Bing Fire are the preferred Useful Gods.

BaZi Structures & Structural Useful Gods 格局與格局用神

十
月

Tenth Month

Day Master	Ren 壬 Water		Month	Hai 亥 (Pig)

- Where Wu Earth and Bing Fire are absent from this chart, any structure formed will tend to be a substandard.

- Where the Earthly Branches form a Water Structure, the resultant Goat Blade Structure formed would definitely need Wu Earth (Seven Killings Star) - to counter and control Water, as a Useful God.

- Bing Fire is essential for the Well-being and prosperity of this chart.

亥
Pig

Ren 壬 Water Day Master, Born in Eleventh Month 十一月

Zi 子 (Rat) Month
December 7th - January 5th

Do note that the dates provided above are subject to slight yearly variations. Please refer to the Ten Thousand Year Calendar for the accurate transition dates for each year.

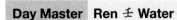

| Day Master | Ren 壬 Water | Month | Zi 子 (Rat) |

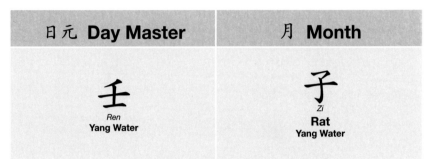

日元 Day Master	月 Month
壬 *Ren* **Yang Water**	子 *Zi* **Rat** **Yang Water**

For a Ren Water Day Master born in a Zi (Rat) Month, the Zi (Rat) Earthly Branch stores Gui Water as its sole Heavenly Stem and hence source of Qi.

In general circumstances, the Goat Blade Structure would be formed.

Day Master	Ren 壬 Water		Month	Zi 子 (Rat)

喜用神提要 Regulating Useful God Reference Guide

十一月

Eleventh Month

Rat

月 Month	用神 Useful God
11th Month 十一月 Zi 子 (Rat) Month	戊 丙 *Wu* *Bing* Yang Earth Yang Fire

For a Zi (Rat) Month, Wu Earth and Bing Fire are the Regulating Useful Gods.

Since Water Qi is very strong in a Zi (Rat) Month, Wu Earth is necessarily to keep the water in control. Meanwhile, Bing Fire is essential, for adjusting and varying the 'climate' or 'environment' to maintain the Qi balance in the BaZi Chart.

In any case, both Bing Fire and Wu Earth are needed to play their respective roles as Useful Gods for this Ren Water Day Master.

| Day Master | Ren 壬 Water | Month | Zi 子 (Rat) |

7th day of December – 5th day of January, Gregorian Calendar

In this month, both Metal and Water are extremely cold. As such, additional Friend and Rob Wealth Stars are capable of forming a special alliance with this Day Master. Indeed, the presence of the preceding Stars would allow the Self Element of this Ren Water Day Master to super thrive and become excessively strong. This will form a special structure.

In ordinary circumstances, where Fire is present and there is also Wood to continue to support and produce Fire, this Ren Water Day Master's BaZi Chart should be a fairly sentimental and well-balanced one. A life of happiness and prosperity is a certainty.

Wood, Fire and Earth should be rooted and properly positioned in this BaZi Chart. Then, and only then, would any structures be able to support the BaZi Chart. The person would be successful and happy.

In general circumstances, Metal and Water should also be avoided altogether, if possible, as they will invariably 'hurt' or weaken Wood, Fire and Earth.

| Day Master | Ren 壬 Water | Month | Zi 子 (Rat) |

Commentary

In addition to the preceding narratives on the potential Structures and scenarios resulting from a Ren Water Day Master born in a Zi (Rat) Month, the following circumstances also play their respective roles in determining the overall strength of this Day Master's BaZi Chart.

Note:

- Bing Fire is the preferred or first-choice Useful God, with Wu Earth as the second-choice Useful God.

- There are two basic rules of thumb to follow, in determining the Useful Gods for a winter month. Regulating Useful God comes before Medicating Useful God.

- Where the Earthly Branches form a Water Structure, Wu Earth should be revealed as the primary Useful God.

- Where two Ding Fire elements 'fight' with one another to combine with this Ren Water Day Master in the Heavenly Stems, this Ren Water Day Master would only lead an average life, at best. In most instance found between relationship matters

Rat

十一月 Eleventh Month

Day Master	Ren 壬 Water	Month	Zi 子 (Rat)

Additional Attributes

格局 Structural Star	偏財 Indirect Wealth	七殺 Seven Killings
用神 Useful God	Bing 丙 Fire	Wu 戊 Earth
Conditions	Where Bing Fire and Wu Earth are both revealed in the BaZi Chart, this Ren Water Day Master's skill and knowledge in life would be incomparable. Where Wu Earth is but Bing Fire is not revealed, this Ren Water Day Master shall possess excellent managerial skills, and hence be systematic in his or her approach towards matters. Where Bing Fire is but Wu Earth is not revealed, this Ren Water Day Master shall possess an abundance of ideas in life; although he or she may not achieve the level of success corresponding to his or her intellect.	
Positive Circumstances	Presence of Wu Earth to control excessive water.	
Negative Circumstances	Over flowing of Water elements.	

格局 Structural Star	比肩 Friend	劫財 Rob Wealth
用神 Useful God	Ren 壬 Water	Gui 癸 Water
Conditions	Where the Earthly Branches forms excessive Water turning this chart into a overly unstable Goat Blade Structure - Wu Earth as a Seven Killings Star would be useless. Instead, Bing Fire as a Wealth Star should be used.	
Positive Circumstances	Wu Earth and Bing Fire are both able to be used.	
Negative Circumstances	Where only Wu Earth as a Seven Killings Star is used, this Ren Water Day Master would probably only lead an average life, at best.	

| Day Master | Ren 壬 Water | | Month | Zi 子 (Rat) |

Additional Attributes

Rat

格局 Structural Star	偏財 Indirect Wealth	七殺 Seven Killings
用神 Useful God	Bing 丙 Fire	Ding 丁 Fire
Conditions	Where the Earthly Branches form a Fire Structure, a Wealth Structure would be formed this person hall prosper and become wealthy in life.	
Positive Circumstances	Presence of Wood to support the Fire.	
Negative Circumstances	Additional Metal element.	

* *Bing Fire and Wu Earth are the preferred Useful Gods.*

| Day Master | Ren 壬 Water | | Month | Zi 子 (Rat) |

Summary

- Where two Ding Fire elements 'fight' with one another to combine with this Ren Water Day Master in the Heavenly Stems, he or she may find it difficult to achieve fame and fortune in life. For ladies particularly, this scenario denotes problems in relationship matters.

- A chart without Bing Fire cannot find contentment.

Rat

十一月

Eleventh Month

Ren 壬 Water Day Master, Born in Twelfth Month 十二月

Chou 丑 (Ox) Month
January 6th - February 3th

Do note that the dates provided above are subject to slight yearly variations. Please refer to the Ten Thousand Year Calendar for the accurate transition dates for each year.

| Day Master | Ren 壬 Water | Month | Chou 丑 (Ox) |

日元 Day Master	月 Month
壬 *Ren* **Yang Water**	丑 *Chou* **Ox** **Yin Earth**

For a Ren Water Day Master born in a Chou (Ox) Month, a Direct Officer Structure is formed where Ji Earth is revealed as one of the Heavenly Stems.

Where Xin Metal is revealed as one of the Heavenly Stems, a Direct Resource Structure is formed.

Where Gui Water appears on the Heavenly Stems, and the conditions are right for Water, the Goat Blade Structure may be formed.

Should, however, neither Ji Earth, Gui Water, nor Xin Metal happen to be revealed within the Heavenly Stems, one should select the BaZi Chart's most prominent Qi attribute at one's discretion

Day Master Ren 壬 Water	Month Chou 丑 (Ox)

喜用神提要 Regulating Useful God Reference Guide

月 Month	用神 Useful God

12th Month 十二月
Chou 丑 (Ox) Month

丙
Bing
Yang Fire

丁
Ding
Yin Fire

甲
Jia
Yang Wood

Ox

In a Chou (Ox) Month, Bing Fire, Ding Fire and Jia Wood are the Regulating Useful Gods.

In the first-half of a Chou (Ox) Month, Bing Fire should be employed as the preferred Useful God. In the second-half of a Chou (Ox) Month, Bing Fire may be employed as the preferred Useful God, provided there is also Jia Wood to play the role of an 'intermediary' or 'mediator' to maintain the balance in the BaZi Chart.

BaZi Structures & Structural Useful Gods 格局與格局用神

Day Master	Ren 壬 Water		Month	Chou 丑 (Ox)

6th day of January – 3rd day of February, Gregorian Calendar

The Chou (Ox) Earthly Branch – being one of the Four Graveyards – also serves as storage for excess Metal Qi.

Since both Earth and Metal form a proverbial mud-pile, however, one can only imagine how chilly and freezing the scene may be. Since Water and Earth invariably form ice in winter, Fire is needed to bring warmth to the elements.

Where Ren Water is 'lively' or flowing smoothly, the Qi of this BaZi Chart is considered healthy and e well-balanced. The person would enjoy a blissful life. Health-wise, his or her blood vessels shall also function healthily.

Since Wood is the source needed to produce Fire, it should not be deficient or lacking in the BaZi Chart. Both Wood and Fire are the Useful Gods for a Ren Water Day Master born in a Chou (Ox) Month.

A Chou (Ox) Month contains Metal in its Hidden Stems. The roots of wood is therefore weak. Hence, Wood Qi is also, by extension, weak in this month. As such, only 'warm' Wood that harbors or contains Fire Qi within may support and strengthen the fire. Metal and Water should also be avoided, where possible, otherwise the chart will freeze.

Ox

| Day Master | Ren 壬 Water | | Month | Chou 丑 (Ox) |

Commentary

In addition to the preceding narratives on the potential Structures and scenarios resulting from a Ren Water Day Master born in a Chou (Ox) Month, the following circumstances also play their respective roles in determining the overall strength of this Day Master's BaZi Chart.

Note:

Ox

- The Qi will be invariably 'cold' this month. As such, Bing Fire should be used to 'adjust' or 'reacclimatize' the 'climate' or 'weather' which the elements in this Day Master's BaZi Chart are subject to. Without Bing Fire, this chart will not prosper.

- Where the Earthly Branches form a Metal Structure, and while Bing Fire and Ding Fire are completely absent from the Heavenly Stems, this Ren Water Day Master may find it difficult to succeed in his or her career-related pursuits. In fact, life would be a lack luster.

- Where the Four Storages Earthly Branches are all present, Jia Wood would still serve as a Useful God.

95

Day Master	Ren 壬 Water	Month	Chou 丑 (Ox)

Additional Attributes

格局 Structural Star	偏財 Indirect Wealth	正印 Direct Resource
用神 Useful God	Bing 丙 Fire	Xin 辛 Metal
Conditions	Where Bing Fire and Xin Metal are both separately revealed in the BaZi Chart, this Ren Water Day Master shall succeed in life.	
Positive Circumstances	Bing Fire and Xin Metal not located side-by-side.	
Negative Circumstances	Where Bing Fire is absent from the BaZi Chart, Ren Water may be 'chilled' or even 'frozen' prematurely.	

格局 Structural Star	偏印 Indirect Resource	正印 Direct Resource
用神 Useful God	Geng 庚 Metal	Xin 辛 Metal
Conditions	Where the Earthly Branches form Metal– but Bing Fire and Ding Fire are absent from the BaZi Chart, any pertinent structure formed would be a substandard.	
Positive Circumstances	Bing Fire and Ding Fire penetrate through the Heavenly Stems.	
Negative Circumstances	Additional Gui Water element.	

十二月 Twelfth Month

丑 Ox

| Day Master | Ren 壬 Water | Month | Chou 丑 (Ox) |

Additional Attributes

格局 **Structural Star**	正財 Direct Wealth
用神 **Useful God**	Ding 丁 Fire
Conditions	Even though Ding Fire and Ren Water may combine with one another, this Ren Water Day Master shall still prosper in life; provided there is no Gui Water to provoke or dampen the Ding Fire.
Positive Circumstances	Wood element is needed to keep the Ding Fire burning.
Negative Circumstances	Gui Water penetrates through the Heavenly Stems.

* *Bing Fire and Jia Wood are the preferred Useful Gods.*

Ox

97

| Day Master | Ren 壬 Water | | Month | Chou 丑 (Ox) |

Summary

- A Ren Water Day Master born in a Chou (Ox) Month forming a Resource Structure, while Bing Fire and Ding Fire are also absent from the BaZi Chart, the person may seriously struggle to achieve success in life.

- In the absence of Bing Fire in this chart, any structure formed would be inferior.

- When Ding Fire is used as Useful God, Gui Water should not be next to it.

Gui (癸) Water Day Master

Overview:

Gui (癸) Water is Yin Water. It represents the mist or dew, and has the capacity to consistently replenish and nourish, due to its seemingly infinite nature. As such, Gui Water is capable of nurturing and growing life. Gui Water Day Masters also tend to have good memory or mnemonic capabilities.

Where a Gui Water Day Master or Self Element is weak, however, Metal will be needed to further strengthen it. Where a Gui Water Day Master or Self Element is weakened by Fire or Earth, Gui Water becomes particularly susceptible to being combined with the latter, and transformed into Fire.

Gui 癸 Water Day Master, Born in First Month 正月

Yin 寅 (Tiger) Month
February 4th – March 5th

Do note that the dates provided above are subject to slight yearly variations. Please refer to the Ten Thousand Year Calendar for the accurate transition dates for each year.

| Day Master | Gui 癸 Water | Month | Yin 寅 (Tiger) |

Tiger

日元 Day Master	月 Month
癸	寅
Gui	Yin
Yin Water	Tiger
	Yang Wood

For a Gui Water Day Master born in a Yin (Tiger) Month, a Hurting Officer Structure is formed where Jia Wood is revealed as one of the Heavenly Stems.

Where Bing Fire is revealed as one of the Heavenly Stems, a Direct Wealth Structure is formed.

Where Wu Earth is revealed as one of the Heavenly Stems, a Direct Officer Structure is formed.

Should, however, neither Jia Wood nor Bing Fire nor Wu Earth happen to be revealed within the Heavenly Stems, one should select the BaZi Chart's most prominent Qi attribute at one's discretion.

| Day Master | Gui 癸 Water | Month | Yin 寅 (Tiger) |

喜用神提要 **Regulating Useful God Reference Guide**

月 **Month**	用神 **Useful God**

1st Month 正月
Yin 寅 (Tiger) Month

辛 　 丙
Xin 　 *Bing*
Yin Metal 　 **Yang Fire**

Tiger

Xin Metal is the preferred Regulating Useful God here, for it is used to further produce Gui Water. In this context, Xin Metal serves as the primary 'source' that will further strengthen this Gui Water Day Master.

In the absence of Xin Metal, however, Geng Metal may serve as the second-choice Regulating Useful God.

Bing Fire should, however, be present in the BaZi Chart, for either Xin Metal or Geng Metal to play the role of a Regulating Useful God.

BaZi Structures & Structural Useful Gods 格局與格局用神

| Day Master | Gui 癸 Water | Month | Yin 寅 (Tiger) |

4th day of February – 5th day of March, Gregorian Calendar

A Yin (Tiger) Month contains the elements of Wood, Fire and Earth in its Hidden Stems.

As such, where a Gui Water Day Master happens to be born in a Yin (Tiger) Month, the presence of Wood, Fire and Earth will possibly form Wealth and Officer Structures.

Tiger

Where Wood Qi is prosperous, Metal Qi is automatically weak. And where Metal Qi is weak, Gui Water would lack support, resulting in a weak Gui Water Self Element or Day Master. Since Metal, however, produces Gui Water, it may serve as the Useful God.

Fire and Earth Qi should preferably not be prominently seen throughout the BaZi Chart. This is because strong Fire Qi will weaken Metal Qi. Likewise, strong Earth Qi will only serve to 'cripple' or prevent Water Qi from thriving.

Day Master	Gui 癸 Water	Month	Yin 寅 (Tiger)

Commentary

In addition to the preceding narratives on the potential Structures and scenarios resulting from a Gui Water Day Master born in a Yin (Tiger) Month, the following circumstances also play their respective roles in determining the overall strength of this Day Master's BaZi Chart.

Note:

Tiger

- Where Xin Metal and Bing Fire are revealed amongst the Heavenly Stems, this Day Master shall be privileged enough to enjoy a prosperous and happy life.

- Should the Earthly Branches happen to form a Fire Structure, the resultant Fire Qi shall greatly weaken Xin Metal, which is this Gui Water Day Master's Regulating Useful God. Under such circumstances, a Ren Water Heavenly Stem should preferably be present in the BaZi Chart, in order to prevent this Gui Water Day Master from being weakened completely. If this condition is met, the person prospers financially through superior networks and connection with others.

- Where the Earthly Branches forms a Water Structure along with Bing Fire revealed amongst the Heavenly Stems, this Day Master may look forward to a fairly successful life. In the absence of Xin Metal in the BaZi Chart, the presence of Geng Metal may still serve to support Xin. But the structure is merely substandard.

- Where Fire and Earth Qi happen to be prominently featured amongst the Heavenly Stems, this Day Master will be troubled by poor health and poverty.

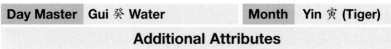

| Day Master | Gui 癸 Water | | Month | Yin 寅 (Tiger) |

Additional Attributes

Tiger

格局 Structural Star	偏印 Indirect Resource	正財 Direct Wealth
用神 Useful God	Xin 辛 Metal	Bing 丙 Fire
Conditions	Bing Fire and Xin Metal should not be found side-by-side in the BaZi Chart, for both would combine to form Water. If found separately in the BaZi Chart, the presence of both Xin Metal and Bing Fire shall support the Gui Water Day Master and enable success and good fortune for its entire life	
Positive Circumstances	Presence of Bing Fire and Xin Metal separately.	
Negative Circumstances	Bing Fire and Ding Fire appear side by side. Additional water formation in the Earthly branches.	

格局 Structural Star	正財 Direct Wealth
用神 Useful God	Bing 丙 Fire
Conditions	Where the Earthly Branches in the BaZi Chart form a Fire Structure, along with and additional Ren Water penetrating through the Heavenly Stems, this person may enjoy immense wealth and prosperity. He or she is exceptionally good in connecting with people.
Positive Circumstances	Presence of Ren Water to reflect the Bing Fire sunlight.
Negative Circumstances	Where Ren Water penetrates through the Heavenly Stems and beside it, a Ding Fire Heavenly Stem.

Day Master	Gui 癸 Water		Month	Yin 寅 (Tiger)

Additional Attributes

格局 Structural Star	劫財 Rob Wealth	比肩 Friend
用神 Useful God	Ren 壬 Water	Gui 癸 Water
Conditions	Where there are too many Earthly Branches that form a Water Structure, and Bing Fire is revealed amongst the Heavenly Stems, this Gui Water Day Master shall enjoy extraordinary fame and recognition in life.	
Positive Circumstances	Where the Rob Wealth and Friend Star does not appear in the Heavenly Stems.	
Negative Circumstances	Ji Earth appears to contaminate Water Qi.	

* *Xin Metal and Bing Fire are the best or most-preferred Useful Gods.*

正月 First Month

Tiger

107

First Month 正月

Day Master	Gui 癸 Water	Month	Yin 寅 (Tiger)

Summary

Tiger

- Should the Heavenly Stems of Wu Earth and Gui Water meet, both may combine to form Fire. This would only be possible with the Earthly Branches forming a Fire structure to facilitate this transformation.

- The absence of Xin Metal and Bing Fire in the BaZi Chart will result in this Gui Water Day Master lacking status or authority in life.

- The absence of Geng Metal and Xin Metal (Resource Stars), as well as the absence of Bing Fire and Ding Fire, will result in this Gui Water Day Master lacking initiative and direction in life.

Gui 癸 Water Day Master, Born in Second Month 二月

Mao 卯 (Rabbit) Month
March 6th – April 4th

Do note that the dates provided above are subject to slight yearly variations. Please refer to the Ten Thousand Year Calendar for the accurate transition dates for each year.

| Day Master | Gui 癸 Water | Month | Mao 卯 (Rabbit) |

日元 Day Master	月 Month
癸 *Gui* **Yin Water**	卯 *Mao* **Rabbit** **Yin Wood**

For a Gui Water Day Master born in a Mao (Rabbit) Month, an Eating God Structure is formed where Yi 乙 Wood is revealed in the Heavenly Stem. Even if Yi Wood does not penetrate through the Heavenly Stem, an Eating God Structure is still considered to have been formed.

| Day Master | Gui 癸 Water | Month | Mao 卯 (Rabbit) |

喜用神提要 Regulating Useful God Reference Guide

月 Month	用神 Useful God
2nd Month 二月 Mao 卯 (Rabbit) Month	庚 辛 *Geng* *Xin* **Yang Metal** **Yin Metal**

Rabbit

For a Mao (Rabbit) Month, Geng Metal and Xin Metal are its Regulating Useful Gods.

Yi Wood is the most prominent Qi in the Mao (Rabbit) Month. Geng Metal is the preferred Regulating Useful God with Xin Metal the second-choice Regulating Useful God.

二月 Second Month

Day Master Gui 癸 Water | **Month** Mao 卯 (Rabbit)

6th day of March – 4th day of April, Gregorian Calendar

Rabbit

Wood Qi is at its peak in spring. Gui Water is weakened by the strong Wood Qi, thereby causing it to become fragile.

Metal is therefore this weak Gui Water Day Master's Useful God. Given that Wood Qi is prosperous in spring, it would be easy for Wood to produce Fire. An abundance or strong presence of Fire Qi would in turn produce Earth Qi. And strong Fire Qi would weaken the Useful Metal Qi.

An abundance of Fire and Earth Qi in this BaZi Chart would only restrict or further weaken this Gui Water Day Master. As such, this chart would be most averse toward Fire, Earth and additional Wood Qi.

The best choice for Gui Water born this month is to use Metal and Water stars, both of which shall strengthen and hence turn a weak Gui Water Day Master into a stronger one.

| Day Master | Gui 癸 Water | Month | Mao 卯 (Rabbit) |

Commentary

In addition to the preceding narratives on the potential Structures and scenarios resulting from a Gui Water Day Master born in a Mao (Rabbit) Month, the following circumstances also play their respective roles in determining the overall strength of this Day Master's BaZi Chart.

Notes:

Rabbit

- Since Wood Qi is prosperous in a Mao (Rabbit) Month, Fire Qi would consequently be strong, since Wood produces Fire. There would hence be very little, if any, need at all for Bing Fire and Ding Fire to be present in the BaZi Chart.

- Where Geng Metal or Xin Metal are revealed amongst the Heavenly Stems, this Gui Water Day Master shall enjoy a successful career or professional life.

- Where the Earthly Branches in the chart form a strong Wood Structure, this Gui Water Day Master shall fare best when he or she is not entering a Metal Cycle. Entering Metal would present the possibility of encountering accidents and mishaps.

- Even if Geng Metal and Xin Metal this Gui Water Day Master will tend to be sentimental and artistic in nature. This is because the presence of strong Eating God Structure will allow this Gui Water Day Master to enjoy a relatively stable life, with at least average fortunes.

Day Master	Gui 癸 Water	Month	Mao 卯 (Rabbit)

Additional Attributes

Rabbit

格局 **Structural Star**	正印 Direct Resource	偏印 Indirect Resource
用神 **Useful God**	Geng 庚 Metal	Xin 辛 Metal
Conditions	Presence of Ding 丁 Fire along with a Geng Metal Hidden Stem that penetrates through to the Heavenly Stems. This person would be able to enjoy admirable success in life.	
Positive Circumstances	Rooted Geng Metal with suporting Ding Fire.	
Negative Circumstances	Yi Wood combining away the Geng Metal.	

| Day Master | Gui 癸 Water | | Month | Mao 卯 (Rabbit) |

Additional Attributes

格局 Structural Star	傷官 Hurting Officer	食神 Eating God
用神 Useful God	Jia 甲 Wood	Yi 乙 Wood
Conditions	Where excessive Wood is formed in the branches, and with the absence of Geng Metal and Xin Metal in the chart, a possible Follow the Son Structure may be formed. Where this formation is successful, the person would enjoy immense success and prosperity.	
Positive Circumstances	No Metal element exist in the chart, allowing the chart to Follow The Leader.	
Negative Circumstances	Encountering Metal Luck cycles.	

Rabbit

* *Geng Metal and Xin Metal are the best or most-preferred Useful Gods.*

** *Ding Fire, if present, should not penetrate through the Hidden Stems as well.*

| Day Master | Gui 癸 Water | Month | Mao 卯 (Rabbit) |

Summary

- A Gui Water Day Master born in a Mao (Rabbit) Month along with good support from Metal or Water Qi, may form a powerful Eating God Structure in this chart. With the presence of Wealth Stars, this chart may belong to an immensely wealthy and successful person.

- Any Wealth Stars present in the BaZi Chart must be compatible with Resource Stars present. In the absence of Resource Stars, however, the presence of any such Wealth Structure will still be useless.

Rabbit

Gui 癸 Water Day Master, Born in Third Month 三月

Chen 辰 (Dragon) Month
April 5th - May 5th

Do note that the dates provided above are subject to slight yearly variations. Please refer to the Ten Thousand Year Calendar for the accurate transition dates for each year.

| Day Master | Gui 癸 Water | Month | Chen 辰 (Dragon) |

Dragon

日元 Day Master	月 Month
癸 *Gui* **Yin Water**	辰 *Chen* **Dragon** **Yang Earth**

For a Gui Water Day Master born in a Chen (Dragon) Month, a Direct Officer Structure is formed where Wu Earth is revealed as one of the Heavenly Stems.

Where Yi Wood is revealed as one of the Heavenly Stems, an Eating God Structure is formed.

Where Gui Water is revealed as one of the Heavenly Stems, a Thriving Structure may be formed depending on circumstances.

Should, however, neither Wu Earth, Gui Water nor Yi Wood happen to be revealed within the Heavenly Stems, one should select a Structure according to the BaZi Chart's most prominent Qi attribute at one's discretion.

| Day Master | Gui 癸 Water | Month | Chen 辰 (Dragon) |

喜用神提要 Regulating Useful God Reference Guide

月 Month	用神 Useful God
3rd Month 三月 Chen 辰 (Dragon) Month	丙 辛 甲 *Bing* *Xin* *Jia* Yang Fire Yin Metal Yang Wood

Dragon

For a Chen (Dragon) Month, Bing Fire and Xin Metal are its most important Regulating Useful Gods.

Bing Fire should be used as the Regulating Useful God for the first half of a Chen (Dragon) Month. The support of Xin Metal and Jia Wood as Regulating Useful Gods are, however, more needed during the second half of a Chen (Dragon) Month.

Day Master	Gui 癸 Water	Month	Chen 辰 (Dragon)

5th day of April – 5th day of May, Gregorian Calendar

Chen (Dragon), being one of the Four Graveyard Earthly Branches, serves as 'storage' 庫 for excess Water Qi. In addition, Earth Qi also features prominently in a Chen (Dragon) Month. This depends on how much Earth is revealed.

With the presence of Wood Qi (of the Spring Season) to control Earth Qi (weaking the Water), Metal stars and Water stars are therefore needed to support this Gui Water Day Master.

This Day Master should avoid encountering additional Fire Qi. This is because even though Fire is this Gui Water Day Master's Wealth Star, it also has the capacity to produce Earth Qi and weaken or 'hurt' Metal Qi, which is a Useful God.

As long as there is sufficient Wood Qi to keep the excessive Earth Qi brought about by a Chen (Dragon) Month under control, a Gui Water Day Master is considered well-balanced.

Dragon

| Day Master | Gui 癸 Water | | Month | Chen 辰 (Dragon) |

Commentary

In addition to the preceding narratives on the potential Structures and scenarios resulting from a Gui Water Day Master born in a Chen (Dragon) Month, the following circumstances also play their respective roles in determining the overall strength of this Day Master's BaZi Chart.

Note:

- The Earthly Branches of Shen (Monkey), Zi (Rat) and Chen (Dragon) forms a Water Structure. Where Wu Earth is revealed in the BaZi Chart, this Gui Water Day Master shall prosper in life. Bing Fire must, however, be present in the BaZi Chart for this to be effective.

- Should all Four Graveyard be present, Jia Wood would be the only option available as Useful God.

- The Earthly Branches of Yin (Tiger), Mao (Rabbit) and Chen (Dragon) form the Wood Structure. Under such circumstances, the Eating God is turned into a Hurting Officer Structure. Bing Fire is needed to channel the excessive Qi. A special Hurting Officer Structure like this would, however, not be able to serves its purpose should Xin Metal be absent.

- Both Xin Metal and Bing Fire should also be separated from each other, in order to prevent them from combining to form Water.

三月 Third Month

Dragon

121

Day Master Gui 癸 Water		**Month** Chen 辰 (Dragon)

Additional Attributes

格局 **Structural Star**	正官 Direct Officer	七殺 Seven Killings
用神 **Useful God**	Wu 戊 Earth	Ji 己 Earth
Conditions	Should all Four Graveyard happen to be present, Jia Wood would be the only option available as Useful God.	
Positive Circumstances	Even if Jia Wood penetrates across the Heavenly Stems, Xin Metal must also be present.	
Negative Circumstances	Jia Wood and Ji Earth should not be side-by-side, since both will combine to produce Earth.	

格局 **Structural Star**	傷官 Hurting Officer	食神 Eating God
用神 **Useful God**	Jia 甲 Wood	Yi 乙 Wood
Conditions	Where the Earthly Branches forms Wood formation, Xin Metal would be needed in the Heavenly Stems and rooted in the branches.	
Positive Circumstances	The appearance of Jia Wood on the Monthly Branch denotes great fame and nobility.	
Negative Circumstances	Without Xin Metal (Resource Star), this Gui Water Day Master will probably be unable to accumulate wealth in life, although he or she may be knowledgeable and intelligent.	

| Day Master | Gui 癸 Water | Month | Chen 辰 (Dragon) |

Additional Attributes

格局 **Structural Star**	劫財 Rob Wealth	比肩 Friend
用神 **Useful God**	Ren 壬 Water	Gui 癸 Water
Conditions	Where the Earthly Branches form a Water Structure, the Wu Earth and Bing Fire should penetrate to the Heavenly Stems. When this criteria is fulfilled, the person would enjoy immense nobility.	
Positive Circumstances	Whenever this Gui Water Day Master goes through Metal Luck, he or she shall prosper.	
Negative Circumstances	Where the Jia Wood (Hurting Officer Star) combines with Ji Earth to produce Earth, this Gui Water Day Master Day Master will only lead a normal, average life.	

Dragon

123

Day Master	Gui 癸 Water		Month	Chen 辰 (Dragon)

Summary

- Where Wu Earth and Gui Water are revealed amongst the Heavenly Stems of a Gui Water Day Master born in a Chen (Rabbit) Month, Bing Fire is still needed if this Gui Water Day Master is to prosper and become wealthy in life.

- Where Wu Earth and Gui Water happen to be separated, Xin Metal is needed as a Resource Star to penetrate through to the Heavenly Stems, if this Gui Water Day Master is to prosper in life.

Dragon

Gui 癸 Water Day Master, Born in Fourth Month 四月

Si 巳 (Snake) Month
May 6th - June 5th

Do note that the dates provided above are subject to slight yearly variations. Please refer to the Ten Thousand Year Calendar for the accurate transition dates for each year.

| Day Master | Gui 癸 Water | Month | Si 巳 (Snake) |

四月
Fourth Month

Snake

日元 **Day Master**	月 **Month**
癸 *Gui* **Yin Water**	巳 *Si* **Snake** **Yin Fire**

For a Gui Water Day Master born in a Si (Snake) Month, a Direct Wealth Structure is formed where Bing Fire is revealed as one of the Heavenly Stems.

Where Wu Earth is revealed as one of the Heavenly Stems, a Direct Officer Structure is formed.

Where Geng Metal is revealed as one of the Heavenly Stems, a Direct Resource Structure is formed.

Should, however, neither Bing Fire nor Wu Earth nor Geng Metal happen to be revealed within the Heavenly Stems, one should select a Structure according to the BaZi Chart's most prominent Qi attribute at one's discretion.

126

| Day Master Gui 癸 Water | Month Si 巳 (Snake) |

喜用神提要 **Regulating Useful God Reference Guide**

月 **Month**	用神 **Useful God**
4th Month 四月 **Si 巳 (Snake) Month**	辛 *Xin* **Yin Metal**

Snake

For a Si (Snake) Month, Xin Metal is the Regulating Useful God.

In the absence of Xin Metal, however, Geng Metal may still be used as a second-choice Regulating Useful God.

BaZi Structures & Structural Useful Gods 格局與格局用神

| Day Master | Gui 癸 Water | Month | Si 巳 (Snake) |

6th day of May – 5th day of June, Gregorian Calendar

Fire Qi is extremely vibrant in summer, although Geng Metal is hidden within Si (Snake), it is considered considerably weak. In the snake month, both Metal and Water Qi are weak.

Metal serves as the main useful Resource Star for Gui Water. Geng Metal, revealed amongst the Heavenly Stems are the best choice for Useful God.

A Gui Water Day Master born in a Si (Snake) Month, should not encounter additional Fire and Earth Qi.

Day Master	Gui 癸 Water		Month	Si 巳 (Snake)

Commentary

In addition to the preceding narratives on the potential Structures and scenarios resulting from a Gui Water Day Master born in a Si (Snake) Month, the following circumstances also play their respective roles in determining the overall strength of this Day Master's BaZi Chart.

Snake

Note:

- Xin Metal and Geng Metal should be used as the preferred Useful Resource Stars.

- It is undesirable for Ding Fire and Ji Earth to be seen penetrating through to the Heavenly Stems.

- Where Ding Fire and Ji Earth penetrate through to the Heavenly Stems, this Gui Water Day Master may be afflicted by poverty and illness in life.

- Where Geng Metal and Ren Water are aligned in the rooted and revealed in the Heavenly Stems, this Gui Water Day Master shall enjoy fame and fortune in life.

- Where Geng Metal is revealed amongst the Heavenly Stems but Ren Water is not in the stems but rooted in the Branches, and while Ding Fire will is absent from sight this Gui Water Day Master shall be learned, knowledgeable and skillful.

- Where Ding Fire is revealed amongst the Heavenly Stems and also happens to be present in abundance amongst the Earthly Branches, this Gui Water Day Master may lack the drive and initiative to succeed in life.

- It is undesirable for Ding Fire should to be revealed in the Heavenly Stems for this a Gui Water Day Master unless there is support for Water.

Day Master	Gui 癸 Water		Month	Si 巳 (Snake)

Additional Attributes

Snake

格局 **Structural Star**	偏印 **Indirect Resource**	劫財 **Rob Wealth**
用神 **Useful God**	Xin 辛 Metal	Ren 壬 Water
Conditions	Where Xin Metal and Ren Water are revealed amongst the Heavenly Stems, the absence of Ding Fire will make for a prosperous Gui Water Day Master.	
Positive Circumstances	Where Ding Fire is present in the BaZi Chart, it will co-exist with Gui Water as a Friends Star, with each exerting equal control over the other.	
Negative Circumstances	Where Ding Fire as a Wealth Star penetrates through to the Heavenly Stems, this Gui Water Day Master may only enjoy an average life of mediocrity.	

| Day Master | Gui 癸 Water | Month | Si 巳 (Snake) |

Additional Attributes

格局 **Structural Star**	正財 Direct Wealth	偏財 Indirect Wealth
用神 **Useful God**	Bing 丙 Fire	Ding 丁 Fire
Conditions	In the absence of Ren Water or even Gui Water as a Friends Star, this Gui Water Day Master may be afflicted by illness throughout his or her entire life.	
Positive Circumstances	Ren Water and Gui Water are Companion Stars to this Gui Water Day Master, with Ren Water as Rob Wealth and Gui Water as Friend; both penetrating through to the Heavenly Stems.	
Negative Circumstances	It is undesirable to have Xin Metal right next to Bing Fire. The Person would have the mishap of losing all his wealth.	

*   *Xin Metal and Geng Metal are the preferred Useful Gods.*

**   *Ding Fire should be avoided or prevented from penetrating through to the Heavenly Stems.*

四月 Fourth Month

Snake

131

四月 Fourth Month

| Day Master | Gui 癸 Water | | Month | Si 巳 (Snake) |

Summary

Snake

- Where Ding Fire penetrates through to the Heavenly Stems, it will clash with Geng Metal and Xin Metal, but combine with Ren Water to form Wood. Under such circumstances, this Gui Water Day Master may suffer from the loss or demise of his or her mother, as well as lack the initiative and drive to succeed in life.

- Where Ding Fire penetrates through to the Heavenly Stems, Gui Water as this Gui Water Day Master's Friend will serve to control Ding Fire. Under such circumstances, this Gui Water Day Master may encounter a Punishment relationship in his or her BaZi Chart, and the spouses of male Gui Water Day Masters may be accident-prone in life.

- The absence of Xin Metal may still be replaced by Geng Metal as a second-choice Useful God. Should this be the case, however, this Gui Water Day Master may prosper in life, although probably only to a certain extent or limit.

Gui 癸 Water Day Master, Born in Fifth Month 五月

Wu 午 (Horse) Month
June 6th - July 6th

Do note that the dates provided above are subject to slight yearly variations. Please refer to the Ten Thousand Year Calendar for the accurate transition dates for each year.

Horse

| Day Master | Gui 癸 Water | Month | Wu 午 (Horse) |

| 日元 Day Master | 月 Month |

癸
Gui
Yin Water

午
Wu
Horse
Yang Fire

For a Gui Water Day Master born in a Wu (Horse) Month, an Indirect Wealth Structure is formed where Ding Fire is revealed as one of the Heavenly Stems.

Where Ji Earth is revealed as one of the Heavenly Stems, a Seven Killings Structure is formed.

Should, however, neither Ding Fire nor Ji Earth happen to be revealed within the Heavenly Stems, one should select a Structure according to the BaZi Chart's most prominent Qi attribute at one's discretion.

| Day Master | Gui 癸 Water | Month | Wu 午 (Horse) |

喜用神提要 **Regulating Useful God Reference Guide**

月 Month	用神 Useful God

5th Month 五月
Wu 午 (Horse) Month

庚	辛	壬	癸
Geng	*Xin*	*Ren*	*Gui*
Yang Metal	Yin Metal	Yang Water	Yin Water

Horse

For a Wu (Horse) Month, Geng Metal, Xin Metal, Ren Water and Gui Water are the Regulating Useful Gods.

Geng Metal and Xin Metal serve as the beneficial Resource Stars that strengthen this Gui Water Day Master's Self Element.

Unfortunately this in this month, the Ding Fire is the strongest Qi. Metal Qi cannot overcome or surmount Fire Qi under such circumstances, this Gui Water Day Master needs to be supported by Friends or Rob Wealth Stars, in order for both Geng Metal and Xin Metal to play their supporting or augmentative roles.

Day Master	Gui 癸 Water	Month	Wu 午 (Horse)

6th day of June – 6th day of July, Gregorian Calendar

A Gui Water Day Master born in a Wu (Horse) Month will invariably be weak. This is because Earth is dry and hot in mid-summer, and hence clash with Water.

Where Fire encounters Water in a Wu (Horse) Month, a clash between both elements would inevitably take place. Obviously, this would make for a weak Gui Water Day Master.

Metal and Water Qi that are rooted in Earthly Branches serve as supporting Stars for a Gui Water Day Master born in a Wu (Horse) Month.

Wood Qi should, however, be avoided, as it would only strengthen Fire Qi in a Wu (Horse) Month.

Additional Fire and Earth Qi should be avoided, as both serve as the proverbial 'Achilles' Heel' or undoing of this Gui Water Day Master.

| Day Master | Gui 癸 Water | Month | Wu 午 (Horse) |

Commentary

In addition to the preceding narratives on the potential Structures and scenarios resulting from a Gui Water Day Master born in a Wu (Horse) Month, the following circumstances also play their respective roles in determining the overall strength of this Day Master's BaZi Chart.

Horse

Note:

- Xin Metal and or Geng Metal should be used as the preferred Regulating Useful Gods.

- Where Ding Fire is seen in the Heavenly Stems. the Geng Metal and Xin Metal stars would be dampened.

- Ren Water may be used as the alternative choice where Geng Metal is absent.

- Gui Water may also be used as alternative Useful God where both Geng Metal and Ren Water are absent.

- Where the Earthly Branches of Si (Snake), Wu (Horse) and Wei (Goat) form a Southern Fire Structure, it would possible to form a Follow the Wealth Structure. But the absence of Ren Water in the chart is crucial for this structure to take shape. If the structure fails to form, this Gui Water Day Master may be afflicted by extreme loneliness and hardship in life.

- If a Follow Wealth Structure is to be formed, none of the Elements should strengthen the Day Master.

- Where Ji Earth is revealed in the Heavenly Stem, this person may encounter inherited illnesses.

- Where proper support for Gui Water is found, this chart is able to enjoy immense wealth, prosperity, fame and fortune.

五月
Fifth Month

Horse

Day Master	Gui 癸 Water	Month	Wu 午 (Horse)

Additional Attributes

格局 Structural Star	正印 Direct Resource	偏印 Indirect Resource
用神 Useful God	Geng 庚 Metal	Xin 辛 Metal
Conditions	Where Geng Metal and Xin Metal are revealed amongst the Heavenly Stems, this chart enjoys success, good health and happiness.	
Positive Circumstances	It is prefered to have Water Earthly Branches to support the Gui Day Master.	
Negative Circumstances	Excessive Fire Qi revealed in the Heavenly Stems.	

格局 Structural Star	正財 Direct Wealth	偏財 Indirect Wealth
用神 Useful God	Bing 丙 Fire	Ding 丁 Fire
Conditions	Where the Earthly Branches forms a Fire formation, and at the same time, Geng Metal and Ren Water are revealed amongst the Heavenly Stems, this Gui Water Day Master shall prosper or enjoy immense wealth, fame and fulfillment in life.	
Positive Circumstances	Geng Metal and Ren Metal appearing in the Heavenly Stems. Or at least, available in the Earthly Branches.	
Negative Circumstances	With the absence of Ren Water, this Day Master may be afflicted with loneliness in life, or may be inclined towards leading a hermit-like life of seclusion.	

Day Master	Gui 癸 Water		Month	Wu 午 (Horse)

Additional Attributes

五月 Fifth Month

格局 Structural Star	正官 Direct Officer	七殺 Seven Killings
用神 Useful God	Wu 戊 Earth	Ji 己 Earth
Conditions	Geng Metal and Xin Metal present in the chart as Useful Resource Stars; otherwise it may be difficult for this Gui Water Day Master to find help and support in life.	
Positive Circumstances	Where Geng Metal or Xin Metal are present in the chart.	
Negative Circumstances	Geng Metal and Xin Metal are absent or unavailable as Useful Resource Stars.	

Horse

* *Geng Metal and Xin Metal are the best or most-preferred Useful Gods.*

** *Ren Water and Gui Water are the second-choice Useful Gods.*

五月 Fifth Month

Horse

| Day Master | Gui 癸 Water | Month | Wu 午 (Horse) |

Summary

- A Gui Water Day Master born in a Wu (Horse) Month is considered very weak. Its chart should not see any Earthly Branches Clashes or Punishments. Should a Clash or Punishment occur, this Day Master's BaZi Chart would be considered to be of a substandard structure.

- A powerful Wealth Structure is formed where neither Ren Water nor Gui Water is revealed in the Heavenly Stems. Under such circumstances, however, this Gui Water Day Master may be afflicted with loneliness in life. With the presence of Rob Wealth or Friends Stars rooted in the Earthly Branches, this chart belong to a person of great nobility, wealth and fortune.

- Where Xin Metal is used as a Useful Resource Star, it would be best to avoid having it combined away with Bing Fire.

- Even when Geng Metal and Xin Metal are present as Useful Resource Stars for this Gui Water Day Master, the absence of Ren Water or Gui Water may still prevent this Day Master from attaining fame and fortune in life.

Gui 癸 Water Day Master, Born in Sixth Month 六月

Wei 未 (Goat) Month
July 7th - August 7th

Do note that the dates provided above are subject to slight yearly variations. Please refer to the Ten Thousand Year Calendar for the accurate transition dates for each year.

Day Master	Gui 癸 Water	Month	Wei 未 (Goat)

日元 **Day Master**	月 **Month**
癸 *Gui* **Yin Water**	未 *Wei* **Goat** **Yin Earth**

For a Gui Water Day Master born in a Wei (Goat) Month, a Seven Killings Structure is formed where Ji Earth is revealed as one of the Heavenly Stems.

Where Ding Fire is revealed as one of the Heavenly Stems, an Indirect Resource Structure is formed.

Where Yi Wood is revealed as one of the Heavenly Stems, an Eating God Structure is formed.

Should, however, neither Ji Earth nor Ding Fire nor Yi Wood happen to be revealed within the Heavenly Stems, one should select a Structure according to the BaZi Chart's most prominent Qi attribute at one's discretion.

Day Master	Gui 癸 Water		Month	Wei 未 (Goat)

喜用神提要 Regulating Useful God Reference Guide

月 Month	用神 Useful God

6th Month 六月
Wei 未 (Goat) Month

庚 *Geng* **Yang Metal**　辛 *Xin* **Yin Metal**　壬 *Ren* **Yang Water**　癸 *Gui* **Yin Water**

Goat

For a Wei (Goat) Month, Geng Metal, Xin Metal, Ren Water and Gui Water are the Regulating Useful Gods.

Since Metal Qi is in its weak stages and Fire Qi remains strong in most of the Wei (Goat) Month, this Gui Water Day Master needs the support of Friends or Rob Wealth Stars during this particular period in time. In this context, a Gui Water Day Master born in a Wei (Goat) Month would be encountering circumstances similar as those of a Gui Water Day Master born in a Wu (Horse) Month.

六
月
Sixth Month

Goat

| Day Master | Gui 癸 Water | | Month | Wei 未 (Goat) |

7th day of July – 7th day of August, Gregorian Calendar

Fire and Earth Qi are the strongest this month, and for a Gui Water Day Master, it is draining. The Wood Qi hidden inside the Wei (Goat) Earthly Branch would bring about a leakage of Water Qi in subtle way, while it also simultaneously produce and cause Fire Qi to become stronger.

Gui Water would therefore need the assistance or support of Metal and Water, in order for it to grow and thrive. It is only with the assistance of Metal and Water that Gui Water will be able to prosper.

Even though Earth Qi is very strong in a Wei (Goat) Month, Wood is still deemed unsuitable to be used to counter or control Earth. This is because Wood produces Fire, and this will invariably lead to a leakage and weakening of Water unless the Wood is wet.

| Day Master | Gui 癸 Water | Month | Wei 未 (Goat) |

Commentary

In addition to the preceding narratives on the potential Structures and scenarios resulting from a Gui Water Day Master born in a Wei (Goat) Month, the following circumstances also play their respective roles in determining the overall strength of this Day Master's BaZi Chart.

Note:

Goat

- There are both favorable and unfavorable circumstances that may affect a Gui Water Day Master born in a Wei (Goat) Month. It much depends on the hour of birth. If Wood is present at the born of birth, a life of great wealth and nobility is expected. This will only happens when wood is wet.

- Geng Metal and Xin Metal remain the generally preferred Useful Gods for a Gui Water Day Master born in the Wei (Goat) Month.

Day Master	Gui 癸 Water		Month	Wei 未 (Goat)

Additional Attributes

格局 **Structural Star**	正印 Direct Resource	偏印 Indirect Resource
用神 **Useful God**	Geng 庚 Metal	Xin 辛 Metal
Conditions	Where Geng Metal and Xin Metal are revealed amongst the Heavenly Stems, this Day Master shall enjoy fame and fortune.	
Positive Circumstances	Presence of Wood at the Hour Pillar can bring great wealth and nobility	
Negative Circumstances	Additional Fire element at the Hour Pillar denotes a tough old age.	

格局 **Structural Star**	正財 Direct Wealth	偏財 Indirect Wealth
用神 **Useful God**	Bing 丙 Fire	Ding 丁 Fire
Conditions	Where the Earthly Branches form a Fire structure, and with the presence of Geng Metal and Ren Water revealed amongst the Heavenly Stems, this Gui Water Day Master shall prosper or enjoy immense wealth in life.	
Positive Circumstances	Friends or Rob Wealth Stars at the Hour Pillar denotes a life of great abundance.	
Negative Circumstances	With the absence of Ren Water this person may be afflicted with loneliness in life, or may be inclined towards leading a hermit-like life of seclusion	

Day Master	Gui 癸 Water		Month	Wei 未 (Goat)

Additional Attributes

格局 **Structural Star**	正官 Direct Officer	七殺 Seven Killings
用神 **Useful God**	Wu 戊 Earth	Ji 己 Earth
Conditions	Geng Metal and Xin Metal should be supportive as Useful Resource Stars; otherwise it may be difficult for this Gui Water Day Master to find help and support in life.	
Positive Circumstances	Presence of Water in the Earthly Branches.	
Negative Circumstances	Geng Metal and Xin Metal are absent or unavailable as Resource Stars.	

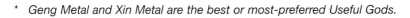

Goat

* *Geng Metal and Xin Metal are the best or most-preferred Useful Gods.*

** *Ren Water and Gui Water are the second-choice Useful Gods.*

| Day Master | Gui 癸 Water | | Month | Wei 未 (Goat) |

Summary

- The primary choice for Useful God would be Geng Metal or Xin Metal.

- Where wet wood is found in the Hour Pillar, the person may enjoy immense success and prosperity. Especially through the academic fields.

- Gui Water born this month may have a possibility of forming the Follow The Leader (Follow Officer) structure when abundance of Earth Qi is found in the chart. However, should this structure be formed, there must be no Clash or Punishment in the Branches. Where Clashes and/ or Punishments are present, this chart would be disastrous.

- A powerful Wealth Structure is formed where neither Ren Water nor Gui Water is revealed in the Heavenly Stems. Under such circumstances, however, this Gui Water Day Master may be afflicted with loneliness in life. Unless it is rooted in the Earthly Branches.

- Where Xin Metal is used as a Useful Resource Star, it would be best to avoid having it combined away with Bing Fire. This indicates massive loss of wealth.

- Where Ji Earth appears in the Heavenly Stems, wood Qi is necessary to keep the Water clean from contamination.

- Although Geng Metal and Xin Metal are present as Resource Stars for this Gui Water Day Master, the absence of Ren Water or Gui Water may still prevent this Day Master from attaining fame and fortune in life.

Goat

Gui 癸 Water Day Master, Born in Seventh Month 七月

Shen 申 (Monkey) Month
August 8th - September 7th

Do note that the dates provided above are subject to slight yearly variations. Please refer to the Ten Thousand Year Calendar for the accurate transition dates for each year.

| Day Master | Gui 癸 Water | | Month | Shen 申 (Monkey) |

日元 Day Master	月 Month
癸 *Gui* **Yin Water**	申 *Shen* **Monkey** **Yang Metal**

For a Gui Water Day Master born in a Shen (Monkey) Month, a Direct Resource Structure is formed where Geng Metal is revealed as one of the Heavenly Stems.

Where Wu Earth is revealed as one of the Heavenly Stems, a Direct Officer Structure is formed.

Where Ren Water is revealed as one of the Heavenly Stems, a Goat Blade Structure may be formed depending on supportive circumstances.

Should, however, neither Geng Metal nor Wu Earth happen to be revealed amongst the Heavenly Stems, one should select a Structure according to the BaZi Chart's most prominent Qi attribute at one's discretion.

| Day Master | Gui 癸 Water | Month | Shen 申 (Monkey) |

喜用神提要 Regulating Useful God Reference Guide

月 Month	用神 Useful God
7th Month 七月 Shen 申 (Monkey) Month	丁 *Ding* **Yin Fire**

Monkey

For a Shen (Monkey) Month, Ding Fire is the Regulating Useful God.

Since Geng Metal is at its peak or most prosperous stage in a Shen (Monkey) Month, Ding Fire would hence be needed to control, forge and make Metal more malleable, in order for Metal for the chart to be balanced.

In order for Ding Fire to serve this particular purpose effectively, it has to be rooted in either a Wu (Horse), Xu (Dog) or Wei (Goat) Earthly Branch.

BaZi Structures & Structural Useful Gods 格局與格局用神

Day Master	Gui 癸 Water	Month	Shen 申 (Monkey)

8th day of August – 7th day of September, Gregorian Calendar

A Gui Water Day Master born in a Shen (Monkey) Month shall form a Direct Resource Structure. As one of the Four Growths Earthly Branches, Shen (Monkey) contains Ren Water in its Hidden Stem, which would also support and strengthen Gui Water. Fire is this Gui Water Day Master's Wealth Star.

Rooted in Water Qi, this Gui Water Day Master shall enjoy fortune in life, when both Wood and Fire stars are revealed amongst the Heavenly Stems of the chart.

A Gui Water Day Master born in a Shen (Monkey) Month should, however, not encounter additional Metal and Water Qi. This is because strong Metal Qi and Water Qi would weaken this Day Master's Wealth and Officer Stars. It is important that this Day Master be further strengthened.

| Day Master | Gui 癸 Water | Month | Shen 申 (Monkey) |

Monkey

Commentary

In addition to the preceding narratives on the potential Structures and scenarios resulting from a Gui Water Day Master born in a Shen (Monkey) Month, the following circumstances also play their respective roles in determining the overall strength of this Day Master's BaZi Chart.

Note:

- Ding Fire is the prefered Useful God for a Gui Water Day Master born in a Shen (Monkey) Month, although Jia Wood may also serve as a Useful God.

- It is undesirable for Ren Water and additional Gui Water stems be seen penetrating through to the Heavenly Stems.

- Where Ding Fire and Jia Wood are revealed amongst the Heavenly Stems, this Gui Water Day Master shall enjoy a solid reputation and great fame in life.

- Where Ding Fire is revealed amongst the Heavenly Stems but Jia Wood is missing or absent from the chart this Gui Water Day Master will probably lead an average life.

- Where the Earthly Branches forms a Metal Structure, and Ding Fire is missing and or absent from the Heavenly Stems, this Gui Water Day Master may not be privileged enough to enjoy the fame he or she desires in life. Life would be a lot of missed opportunities.

- Where Ding Fire is revealed as one of the Heavenly Stems, this Gui Water Day Master shall prosper and may even become immensely wealthy in life.

Monkey

| Day Master | Gui 癸 Water | Month | Shen 申 (Monkey) |

Additional Attributes

格局 Structural Star	偏財 Indirect Wealth	傷官 Hurting Officer
用神 Useful God	Ding 丁 Fire	Jia 甲 Wood
Conditions	Where there is neither Ren Water nor Gui Water to penetrate through the Heavenly Stems, and there is Ding Fire in the Heavenly Stems, firmly rooted - this Gui Water Day Master will enjoy prosperity in many facets of life.	
Positive Circumstances	Ding Fire rooted in the Earthly Branches.	
Negative Circumstances	Ren Water and Gui Water should be prevented from penetrating through the Hidden Stems.	

| **Day Master** Gui 癸 Water | | **Month** Shen 申 (Monkey) |

Additional Attributes

格局 **Structural Star**	正印 Direct Resource	偏印 Indirect Resource
用神 **Useful God**	Geng 庚 Metal	Xin 辛 Metal
Conditions	A Direct Resource Structure's role in this Gui Water Day Master's BaZi Chart is actually minimal. Too strong in fact renders this person emotional and feeble.	
Positive Circumstances	Presence of powerful Ding Fire to forge the Metal Qi.	
Negative Circumstances	The absence of Ding Fire will make for a substandard structure.	

*   Jia Wood and Ding Fire are the preferred Useful Gods.

** Ren Water and Gui Water should be avoided.

Monkey

七月
Seventh Month

155

BaZi Structures & Structural Useful Gods 格局與格局用神

Day Master	Gui 癸 Water		Month	Shen 申 (Monkey)

Summary

- A Gui Water Day Master born in a Shen (Monkey) Month should not have additional Geng Metal or Xin Metal appearing in the Heavenly Stems.

- If Ding Fire can successfully penetrate from the Earthly Branches of a Wu (Horse) Earthly Branch, this would be the most-preferred choice of Useful God.

- Even if Ding Fire is revealed from the Earthly Branches, a Wei (Goat) or Xu (Dog) Earthly Branch may still prove to be good choice.

- Regardless of whatever structure formed, it would still be best to avoid having a Friends or Rob Wealth Stars in the Heavenly Stems. Such a formation denotes a life of misery and intense competition.

- The absence of Ding Fire will still result in the formation of substandard structures, regardless of whatever structure that may be formed.

- Wu Earth and Ji Earth (Direct Officer and Seven Killings Stars), may be beneficial to this Day Master despite a leakage or weakening of Ding Fire. These stars are particularly favourable when there is presence of Friends and Rob Wealth Stars in the Heavenly Stems. Without Earth Qi, this chart belongs to an average or mediocre person. The Fire or Earth elements need to be rooted in order to be of service to the Gui Day Master.

Gui 癸 Water Day Master, Born in Eighth Month 八月

You 酉 (Rooster) Month
September 8th - October 7th

Do note that the dates provided above are subject to slight yearly variations. Please refer to the Ten Thousand Year Calendar for the accurate transition dates for each year.

Day Master	Gui 癸 Water		Month	You 酉 (Rooster)

日元 Day Master	月 Month
癸 *Gui* **Yin Water**	酉 *You* **Rooster** **Yin Metal**

For a Gui Water Day Master born in a You (Rooster) Month, an Indirect Resource Structure is formed where Xin Metal is revealed as a Heavenly Stem.

Even if Xin Metal is not revealed as a Heavenly Stem, the resultant structure formed is also known as an Indirect Resource Structure.

| Day Master | Gui 癸 Water | | Month | You 酉 (Rooster) |

八
月

Eighth Month

喜用神提要 Regulating Useful God Reference Guide

月 Month	用神 Useful God
8th Month 八月 You 酉 (Rooster) Month	 *Xin*　　*Bing* **Yin Metal**　**Yang Fire**

Rooster

For a You (Rooster) Month, Xin Metal and Bing Fire are the Regulating Useful Gods.

For Xin Metal to serve its purpose as a Useful God, however, it would need the support of Bing Fire. This is because the resultant scenario, also known as 'warm' or 'warmed' Metal and hence Water, is vital towards bringing balance to this Gui Water Day Master's BaZi Chart.

As such, both Xin Metal and Bing Fire must be able to penetrate through to the Heavenly Stems, for them to play their respective roles as Useful Gods.

159

BaZi Structures & Structural Useful Gods 格局與格局用神

Day Master Gui 癸 Water	Month You 酉 (Rooster)

8th day of August – 7th day of September, Gregorian Calendar

Metal Qi shall further produce and strengthen Water Qi, to the extent of making it very strong and prosperous. Thus, Wealth and Officer become Useful Gods.

Wu Earth, receiving the help of Fire would be a sentimental combination with this Day Master.

Wood plays the role of supporting the weak Fire Qi. Hence it is favoruable.

Metal and Water Qi should also not be present in abundance.

If this Gui Water Day Master is to be rooted, it would require the assistance of 'warm' or 'warmed' Wood to serve as either the support to a Direct or Indirect Wealth Star.

| Day Master | Gui 癸 Water | Month | You 酉 (Rooster) |

Commentary

In addition to the preceding narratives on the potential Structures and scenarios resulting from a Gui Water Day Master born in a You (Rooster) Month, the following circumstances also play their respective roles in determining the overall strength of this Day Master's BaZi Chart.

Note:

- It is important that the Useful Gods of Xin Metal and Bing Fire should be seen to be combining with one another. Such combination produces Water.

- Xin Metal keeps the water pure and flowing. But it cannot be used alone in this month.

八月

Eighth Month

Rooster

Day Master	Gui 癸 Water		Month	You 酉 (Rooster)

Additional Attributes

格局 **Structural Star**	偏印 Indirect Resource	正財 Direct Wealth
用神 **Useful God**	Xin 辛 Metal	Bing 丙 Fire
Conditions	Where Xin Metal and Bing Fire are not found side-by-side and yet revealed amongst the Heavenly Stems, this Gui Water Day Master shall enjoy status and authority in life.	
Positive Circumstances	Jia Wood (Hurting Officer Star), would further support Bing Fire and Xin Metal as a Useful God. The person would enjoy immense wealth and nobility.	
Negative Circumstances	Bing Fire and Xin Metal, appearing together, shall combine to produce Water. The renders the chart useless. Loss opportunities and emotional trauma may plague this person's life.	

| Day Master | Gui 癸 Water | Month | You 酉 (Rooster) |

Additional Attributes

Rooster

格局 Structural Star	正官 Direct Officer	七殺 Seven Killings
用神 Useful God	Wu 戊 Earth	Ji 己 Earth
Conditions	Ren Water and Gui Water are needed as Friends and Rob Wealth Stars respectively, and must be revealed simultaneously in the Heavenly Stems. Otherwise, even the positive qualities of the Direct Officer and Seven Killings Stars would not be felt.	
Positive Circumstances	It is preferred that the Bing Fire be rooted in the branches. Fire element present, serves to magnify the success of this person's life.	
Negative Circumstances	Excessive Water element creates chaos and confusion. The person would suffer emotional and financial setbacks his/her whole life.	

* Xin Fire and Bing Fire are the preferred Useful Gods.

八月
Eighth Month

酉
Rooster

Day Master	Gui 癸 Water	Month	You 酉 (Rooster)

Summary

- Only the Wealth and Resource Structures brought about by Xin Metal and Bing Fire are deemed suitable for a Gui Water Day Master born in a You (Rooster) Month. Successful structures promises great wealth, nobility and fame.

- If both Friends and Rob Wealth Structures do not happen to be revealed in the Heavenly Stems, there would be no use for Direct Officer and Seven Killings Structures Star.

- Bing Fire and Xin Metal should be prevented from being present side-by-side with one another, as both shall combine to form Water.

- Jia Wood and Yi Wood (Eating God and Hurting Officer Stars) help support the Fire element, generating never ending source of income.

Gui 癸 Water Day Master, Born in Ninth Month 九月

Xu 戌 (Dog) Month
October 8th - November 6th

Do note that the dates provided above are subject to slight yearly variations. Please refer to the Ten Thousand Year Calendar for the accurate transition dates for each year.

| Day Master | Gui 癸 Water | Month | Xu 戌 (Dog) |

日元 Day Master	月 Month
癸 Gui Yin Water	戌 Xu Dog Yang Earth

For a Gui Water Day Master born in a Xu (Dog) Month, a Direct Officer Structure is formed where Wu Earth is revealed as one of the Heavenly Stems.

Where Ding Fire is revealed as one of the Heavenly Stems, an Indirect Wealth Structure is formed.

Where Xin Metal is revealed as one of the Heavenly Stems, an Indirect Resource Structure is formed.

Should, however, neither Wu Earth nor Ding Fire nor Xin Metal happen to be revealed within the Heavenly Stems, one should select a Structure according to the BaZi Chart's most prominent Qi attribute at one's discretion.

| Day Master | Gui 癸 Water | Month | Xu 戌 (Dog) |

喜用神提要 **Regulating Useful God Reference Guide**

月 **Month**	用神 **Useful God**
9th Month 九月 **Xu** 戌 **(Dog) Month**	辛 甲 壬 癸 *Xin* *Jia* *Ren* *Gui* **Yin Metal** **Yang Wood** **Yang Water** **Yin Water**

Dog

The preferred Useful God is Xin Metal. It is advisable to avoid Wu Earth.

It is desirable to have the Friends and Rob Wealth Stars serve to support Jia Wood, to control Wu Earth.

BaZi Structures & Structural Useful Gods 格局與格局用神

Day Master	Gui 癸 Water	Month	Xu 戌 (Dog)

8th day of October – 7th day of November, Gregorian Calendar

This month, the Earth is found in abundance. Fire is brewing internally. The Earth is invariably leaden and thick in the autumn, while Gui Water invariably lacks vitality.

The strength of Gui Water depends greatly on the capacity of Metal to produce Water. Visible Metal Qi would allow Water to flow and flourish.

Dog

Wood, in moderate or small amounts, may also be used, since Wood Qi may be particularly brittle and unstable this month. The purpose of Wood is to control the thick Earth.

Day Master	Gui 癸 Water		Month	Xu 戌 (Dog)

Commentary

In addition to the preceding narratives on the potential Structures and scenarios resulting from a Gui Water Day Master born in a Xu (Dog) Month, the following circumstances also play their respective roles in determining the overall strength of this Day Master's BaZi Chart.

Note:

- For a Gui Water Day Master born in Xu(Dog) Month, the preferred Useful Gods are Xin and Jia.

- The presence of Fire on the Stem for the helps bring warmth and contentment to the person's life. However, Fire should not be next to Xin Metal.

- Additional Rob Wealth and Friends may increase the person's popularity and fame, but not necessarily his/her personal status.

九
月
Ninth Month

Dog

Day Master	Gui 癸 Water	Month	Xu 戌 (Dog)

Additional Attributes

格局 Structural Star	偏印 Indirect Resource	傷官 Hurting Officer
用神 Useful God	Xin 辛 Metal	Jia 甲 Wood
Conditions	A Gui Water Day Master born in a Xu (Dog) Month that has both Xin Metal and Jia Wood in his or her BaZi Chart shall enjoy a successful professional life.	
Positive Circumstances	Absence of Friends and Rob Wealth stars.	
Negative Circumstances	Wu Earth and Ji Earth happen to penetrate through the Heavenly Stems.	

* Xin Metal and Jia Metal are the most-preferred Useful Gods.

** Gui Water is the second-choice Useful God.

Day Master	Gui 癸 Water		Month	Xu 戌 (Dog)

Summary

- A Gui Water Day Master born in a Xu (Dog) Month should not use a Direct Wealth or Direct Officer stars, but instead, seek to match a Hurting Officer to a Direct Resource Structure. The Hurting Officer matching with Resource is a noble structure.

- Where Wu Earth penetrates through to the Heavenly Stems, Ren Water and Gui Water would be needed as Friends and Rob Wealth Stars to assist Jia Wood, the Hurting Officer Star, to control Wu Earth.

- Even though both Xin Metal and Gui Water may be absent or unavailable in the BaZi Chart, they may still be substituted by Jia Wood (Hurting Officer Star), which would allow this Gui Water Day Master to enjoy a fairly prosperous life.

Dog

171

Gui 癸 Water Day Master, Born in Tenth Month 十月

Hai 亥 (Pig) Month
November 7th - December 6th

Do note that the dates provided above are subject to slight yearly variations. Please refer to the Ten Thousand Year Calendar for the accurate transition dates for each year.

| Day Master | Gui 癸 Water | Month | Hai 亥 (Pig) |

日元 Day Master	月 Month
癸 Gui Yin Water	亥 Hai Pig Yin Water

For a Gui Water Day Master born in a Hai (Pig) Month, a Hurting Officer Structure is formed where Jia Wood is revealed as a Heavenly Stem.

Where the Ren (Yang Water) is revealed on the Heavenly Stems, a Goat Blade Structure is formed.

If Jia Wood is not revealed as a Heavenly Stem, the resultant structure formed is also known as either Goat Blade or a Hurting Officer Structure, depending on the overall condition of the chart.

| Day Master | Gui 癸 Water | | Month | Hai 亥 (Pig) |

喜用神提要 **Regulating Useful God Reference Guide**

月 **Month**	用神 **Useful God**
10th Month 十月 **Hai 亥 (Pig) Month**	庚 辛 戊 丁 *Geng* *Xin* *Wu* *Ding* **Yang Metal** **Yin Metal** **Yang Earth** **Yin Fire**

Pig

For a Hai (Pig) Month, Geng Metal, Xin Metal, Wu Earth and Ding Fire are the Regulating Useful Gods.

As Hai (Pig) is one of the Four Growths Earthly Branches, Jia Wood is rapidly growing or peaking during a Hai (Pig) Month. Since Jia Wood weakens Gui Water, it would be preferable to restore balance to the Qi of Gui Water, using either Geng Metal or Xin Metal.

Where Water is present in abundance, however, Wu Earth may be used to control the former. Where Metal is present in abundance, Ding Fire may be used to control and hone the former.

BaZi Structures & Structural Useful Gods 格局與格局用神

Day Master	Gui 癸 Water	Month	Hai 亥 (Pig)

7th day of November – 6th day of December, Gregorian Calendar

Fire is essential for this chart. It is the useful Wealth Star that restores balance to this chart.

It would also be good for Fire Qi to be supported by Wood Qi. This is because the presence of Wood Qi allows strong Fire Qi to be produced. Under such circumstances, this Gui Water Day Master can enjoy long lasting prosperity and happiness.

Pig

Day Master	Gui 癸 Water		Month	Hai 亥 (Pig)

Commentary

In addition to the preceding narratives on the potential Structures and scenarios resulting from a Gui Water Day Master born in a Hai (Pig) Month, the following circumstances also play their respective roles in determining the overall strength of this Day Master's BaZi Chart.

Note:

- Xin Metal and Ding Fire should be the preferred choices of Useful Gods. Another alternative choice of Useful Gods would be Geng Metal and Wu Earth.

- It is undesirable for additional Gui Water and Ren Water to be seen penetrating through to the Heavenly Stems.

- Bing Fire may also be selected as Useful God if and when Ding Fire is unavailable.

- Presence of the Yin (Tiger), Wu (Horse) and Xu (Dog) Earthly Branches forms a Fire Frame. This is highly beneficial for this chart.

- Where a complete Water Structure is formed and there is absence of Earth in the chart, a Super Vibrant Structure is formed. These are special conditions that denote an extraordinary life.

- Where Geng Metal and Xin Metal are both revealed amongst the Heavenly Stems, but Ding Fire is completely missing from the Heavenly Stems, this Gui Water Day Master will not enjoy a happy life.

十
月

Tenth Month

Pig

177

Pig

Day Master	Gui 癸 Water		Month	Hai 亥 (Pig)

Additional Attributes

格局 Structural Star	正印 Direct Resource	偏印 Indirect Resource
用神 Useful God	Geng 庚 Metal	Xin 辛 Metal
Conditions	Metal can only be used when Fire is present.	
Positive Circumstances	Absence of Fire and Earth may allow the chart to be super-vibrant.	
Negative Circumstances	The absence of Bing Fire may result in this Gui Water Day Master being afflicted by loneliness in life, or be inclined towards leading a hermit-like life of seclusion	

格局 Structural Star	傷官 Hurting Officer	食神 Eating God
用神 Useful God	Jia 甲 Wood	Yi 乙 Wood
Conditions	Where the Earthly Branches forms Wood Qi, the resultant quality of the Eating God Structure or Hurting Officer Structure shall depend greatly on the presence of Geng Metal and Xin Metal amongst the Heavenly Stems.	
Positive Circumstances	Presence of Fire helps keep the Water warm and clear.	
Negative Circumstances	Geng Metal and Xin Metal should not penetrate through to the Heavenly Stems.	

| Day Master | Gui 癸 Water | | Month | Hai 亥 (Pig) |

Additional Attributes

格局 Structural Star	劫財 Rob Wealth	比肩 Friend
用神 Useful God	Ren 壬 Water	Gui 癸 Water
Conditions	Where the Earthly Branches forms a Water Structure, and with the Wu Earth penetrating through to the Heavenly Stems , this person shall enjoy a good and stable life.	
Positive Circumstances	Presence of Fire element to keep the Water warm and flowing.	
Negative Circumstances	Without the presence of Wu Earth to penetrate through to the Heavenly Stems, this Gui Water Day Master may have to slog for a living.	

Pig

* *Bing Fire is the preferred Useful God.*

** *The Earthly Branches should not encounter Wood Qi, as well as Eating God and Hurting Officer Structures.*

179

| Day Master | Gui 癸 Water | Month | Hai 亥 (Pig) |

Summary

- Gui Water Day Master born in a Hai (Pig) Month, whose Earthly Branches form a Water Structure, needs Wu Earth (Direct Officer) to control it. It would be pointless using a Seven Killings Structure, even if it happens to be present, because Seven Killings would only contaminate the Water.

- Any additional Water would make this a powerful Goat Blade Structure. A Goat Blade needs Seven Killings to be its Blade. A Seven Killings need to be wielded carefully in the presence of Wood.

- In order for a Wealth Structure to play its role, the Companion Stars of Ren Water and Gui Water must penetrate through to the Heavenly Stems. When this happens, Wu Earth and Fire Qi are necessary to complete the structure. Otherwise, this Gui Water Day Master may be susceptible to poor health and illness throughout his or her entire life.

- Water helps reflect light from the Sun. This is known as reverse growth. Hence Bing Fire meeting Hai (Pig) Month is a good setup.

- Geng Metal and Xin Metal (Resource Stars) of this Gui Water Day Master, are incompatible with Ding Fire. Hence Ding Fire should not be next to them. Bing Fire may be used in tandem with Geng Metal.

Gui 癸 Water Day Master, Born in Eleventh Month 十一月

Zi 子 (Rat) Month
December 7th - January 5th

Do note that the dates provided above are subject to slight yearly variations. Please refer to the Ten Thousand Year Calendar for the accurate transition dates for each year.

BaZi Structures & Structural Useful Gods 格局與格局用神

| Day Master | Gui 癸 Water | | Month | Zi 子 (Rat) |

日元 **Day Master**	月 **Month**
癸 *Gui* **Yin Water**	子 *Zi* **Rat** **Yang Water**

For a Gui Water Day Master born in a Zi (Rat) Month, the Zi (Rat) Earthly Branch stores Gui Water as its sole Heavenly Stem and hence source of Qi. This source of Qi, however, is not contained within any Direct Structures that may be formed in the BaZi Chart.

The Gui Water inside the Zi (Rat) makes this chart a Thriving Structure.

| Day Master | Gui 癸 Water | | Month | Zi 子 (Rat) |

喜用神提要 Regulating Useful God Reference Guide

Rat

月 Month	用神 Useful God
11th Month 十一月 **Zi** 子 **(Rat) Month**	丙 辛 *Bing* *Xin* **Yang Fire** **Yin Metal**

For a Zi (Rat) Month, Bing Fire and Xin Metal are the Regulating Useful Gods.

Bing Fire helps to 'warm' things out and hence thaw the chill brought about by the winter season. Xin Metal plays the source of water that keeps the Qi flowing in this cold winter month.

BaZi Structures & Structural Useful Gods 格局與格局用神

Day Master	Gui 癸 Water	Month	Zi 子 (Rat)

7th day of December – 5th day of January, Gregorian Calendar

A Gui Water Day Master born in a Zi (Rat) Month, the Zi (Rat) Earthly Branch's only Hidden Stem of Gui serves as the main source of Qi.

Since both Metal and Water are extremely cold in winter only the Friends and Rob Wealth Stars are capable of supporting this Gui Water Day Master. Frozen water is strong yet weak at the same time. With ice and frost reigning supreme at this time of the year, Fire should be used to thaw the elements.

The presence of 'thick' Earth and fierce Fire shall enable this water to flow and bring about a wealthy, prosperous and happ life. Only with the support of Wealth and Officer Stars will this person enjoy a great life.

Day Master	Gui 癸 Water		Month	Zi 子 (Rat)

Commentary

In addition to the preceding narratives on the potential Structures and scenarios resulting from a Gui Water Day Master born in a Zi (Rat) Month, the following circumstances also play their respective roles in determining the overall strength of this Day Master's BaZi Chart.

Note:

- Since both the Zi (Rat) is considered mid-winter, Bing Fire should be used to thaw and bring warmth to the Day Master. Without Fire, this Water is considered weak.

- Where Bing Fire is absent from the chart, this Gui Water Day Master shall neither prosper nor progress in life. The person may be afflicted with poverty and misery throughout his or her entire life.

- Where Ren Water and Gui Water both appear in the chart, and Bing Fire is absent amongst the Heavenly Stems, this Day Master will be bogged by jealousy and emotional drama his/her whole life.

- Where Wu Earth and Ji Earth penetrate through the Hidden Stems, this Gui Water Day Master may suffer from poor health and illness in life.

十一月 Eleventh Month

Rat

BaZi Structures & Structural Useful Gods 格局與格局用神

Day Master	Gui 癸 Water	Month	Zi 子 (Rat)

Additional Attributes

格局 Structural Star	正財 Direct Wealth	劫財 Rob Wealth
用神 Useful God	Bing 丙 Fire	Ren 壬 Water
Conditions	Where Bing Fire and Ren Water are revealed amongst the Heavenly Stems ,this person will enjoy a blissful and successful life.	
Positive Circumstances	It would be preferable to have two Bing Fire Useful Gods present. One in the Stem and one in the Branch. Life of abundance, fortune and fame can be expected.	
Negative Circumstances	Ding Fire penetrates through the Hidden Stems and combines with Ren Water, to form Wood -Another scenario to be avoided.	

格局 Structural Star	比肩 Friend	偏財 Indirect Wealth
用神 Useful God	Gui 癸 Water	Ding 丁 Fire
Conditions	Where Ding Fire is revealed in the Year Pillar's Heavenly Stem, a Gui Water Day Master born at night shall prosper.	
Positive Circumstances	Where the Earthly Branches form a Water Structure, Fire Qi shall be extinguished. Under such circumstances, Wu Earth and Ji Earth may be used as Useful Direct Officer and Seven Killings Stars, respectively.	
Negative Circumstances	The absence of Fire in the BaZi Chart shall result in this Gui Water Day Master suffering from loneliness and poverty in life.	

| Day Master | Gui 癸 Water | Month | Zi 子 (Rat) |

Additional Attributes

格局 Structural Star	正官 Direct Officer	七殺 Seven Killings
用神 Useful God	Wu 戊 Earth	Ji 己 Earth
Conditions	Where Earth Qi is present in abundance amongst the Earthly Branches, this Gui Water Day Master may be afflicted with poverty and illness in life.	
Positive Circumstances	Presence of Wood to filter Water.	
Negative Circumstances	Absence of Wood. Water is contaminated.	

Rat

* Bing Fire is the most-preferred Useful God.

** Ren Water is the second-choice Useful God, although Ding Fire should be prevented from penetrating through to the Heavenly Stems.

BaZi Structures & Structural Useful Gods 格局與格局用神

| Day Master | Gui 癸 Water | Month | Zi 子 (Rat) |

Summary

- Where no Wealth or Resource Stars penetrate through to the Heavenly Stems - a male Gui Water Day Master may find it difficult to find a suitable companion or spouse in life.

- Where Bing Fire is absent from the chart, any Structure formed within the BaZi Chart would still be considered a substandard one.

- Where Eating God and Hurting Officer Stars are found but there is no Metal to serve as a useful Resource Star, this Gui Water Day Master may be afflicted with a disability or handicap in life.

- Where Bing Fire comes into play as a Useful God, it should be rooted in the Earthly Branches of Yin (Tiger), Si (Snake) and Wu (Horse). Otherwise, Bing Fire would still be unable to play its role as a Useful God, effectively.

- Where the Qi of the Heavenly Stems penetrates through to Xin Metal, it may not be wise to use Bing Fire, since Xin Metal combines with Bing Fire to form Water. However, the Qi of Ding Fire must still be transferred or allocated accordingly; otherwise, Ding Fire would still be of no use to this Gui Water Day Master.

Gui 癸 Water Day Master, Born in Twelfth Month 十二月

Chou 丑 (Ox) Month
January 6th - February 3th

Do note that the dates provided above are subject to slight yearly variations. Please refer to the Ten Thousand Year Calendar for the accurate transition dates for each year.

十二月 Twelfth Month

Ox

| Day Master | Gui 癸 Water | Month | Chou 丑 (Ox) |

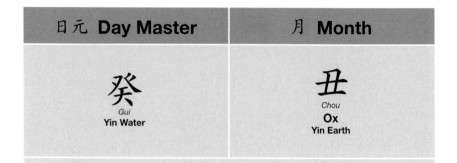

日元 Day Master	月 Month
癸 _Gui_ **Yin Water**	丑 _Chou_ **Ox** **Yin Earth**

For a Gui Water Day Master born in a Chou (Ox) Month, a Seven Killings Structure is formed where Ji Earth is revealed as one of the Heavenly Stems.

Where Xin Metal is revealed as one of the Heavenly Stems, an Indirect Resource Structure is formed.

Where Gui Water is revealed as one of the Heavenly Stems, a Thriving Structure may still be formed depending on supportive circumstances.

Should, however, neither Ji Earth, Gui Water nor Xin Metal happen to be revealed within the Heavenly Stems, one should select the BaZi Chart's most prominent Qi attribute at one's discretion.

| Day Master | Gui 癸 Water | Month | Chou 丑 (Ox) |

喜用神提要 **Regulating Useful God Reference Guide**

月 **Month**	用神 **Useful God**
12th Month 十二月 Chou 丑 (Ox) Month	丙　　丁 *Bing*　　*Ding* **Yang Fire**　**Yin Fire**

Ox

For a Chou (Ox) Month, Bing Fire and Ding Fire are the Regulating Useful Gods.

It would be ideal, should Fire also happen to be rooted in a Yin (Tiger), Si (Snake), Wu (Horse), Wei (Goat) or Xu (Dog) Earthly Branch. Under such circumstance, an ideal scenario also described in the classical texts as 'Light after the Snow' takes place.

Where the Earthly Branches form a Fire frame, it would be ideal to select Geng or Xin Metal as the Useful God.

BaZi Structures & Structural Useful Gods 格局與格局用神

Day Master	Gui 癸 Water	Month	Chou 丑 (Ox)

6th day of January – 3rd day of February, Gregorian Calendar

The Chou (Ox) Month also serves as storage for excess Metal Qi.

Since both 'cold' Earth and 'cold' Metal form a proverbial mud-pile, one can only imagine how chilly and freezing the scene may be. Water and Earth invariably form ice in winter, Fire is needed to bring warmth to the elements.

Where Gui Water is 'lively' or at least, flowing smoothly, the Qi of this Gui Water Day Master's BaZi Chart will be well-balanced and health-wise, his or her blood vessels shall also function healthily. Hence Fire Qi is of primary importance.

Since Wood is the source needed to produce Fire, it should not be deficient or lacking in the BaZi Chart.

A Gui Water Day Master born in a Chou (Ox) Month with a strong Metal Structure in his or her BaZi Chart will still need Ding Fire, in order to bring the prevalent Metal Qi under control. As such, where Wood and Fire are available to further support Ding Fire, this Gui Water person would enjoy long lasting happiness and good health.

Day Master	Gui 癸 Water	Month	Chou 丑 (Ox)

Commentary

In addition to the preceding narratives on the potential Structures and scenarios resulting from a Gui Water Day Master born in a Chou (Ox) Month, the following circumstances also play their respective roles in determining the overall strength of this Day Master's BaZi Chart.

Note:

- Bing Fire is of utmost importance for Gui Water born in the Ox Month. Without Fire, water is frozen and this denotes a life that is emotionally draining and tiresome.

- The presence of Si (Snake) in the chart helps bring peace and harmony.

- The presence of Ding Fire illuminates the snow, bringing beauty and elegance.

- Where Bing Fire is absent from the chart, this Gui Water Day Master shall neither prosper nor progress in life. The person may even be afflicted with poverty and misery throughout his or her entire life.

- Where Ji Earth penetrate through the Hidden Stems, this Gui Water Day Master may suffer from poor health and illness in life.

- Where Ji Earth is in the Heavenly Stems, Jia Wood is needed to filter the dirt.

十二月 Twelfth Month

Ox

BaZi Structures & Structural Useful Gods 格局與格局用神

Day Master	Gui 癸 Water		Month	Chou 丑 (Ox)

Additional Attributes

格局 Structural Star	正財 Direct Wealth	劫財 Rob Wealth
用神 Useful God	Bing 丙 Fire	Ren 壬 Water
Conditions	Where Bing Fire and Ren Water are revealed amongst the Hidden Stems or in the BaZi Chart, this Gui Water Day Master shall prosper in life.	
Positive Circumstances	It would be preferable to have a Bing Fire Useful Gods present. Bing Fire should be born in the morning.	
Negative Circumstances	Ding Fire penetrates through the Hidden Stems and combines with Ren Water, to form Wood. Another scenario to be avoided would be when Gui Water penetrates through the Heavenly Stems.	

格局 Structural Star	比肩 Friend	偏財 Indirect Wealth
用神 Useful God	Gui 癸 Water	Ding 丁 Fire
Conditions	Where Ding Fire is revealed in the Year Pillar's Heavenly or Hidden Stem, a Gui Water Day Master born at night shall prosper.	
Positive Circumstances	Where the Earthly Branches form a Water Structure, Fire Qi shall be extinguished. Under such circumstances, Wu Earth and Ji Earth may be used as Direct Officer and Seven Killings Stars, respectively.	
Negative Circumstances	The absence of Fire in the BaZi Chart shall result in this Gui Water Day Master suffering from loneliness and poverty in life.	

Day Master Gui 癸 Water		Month Chou 丑 (Ox)

Additional Attributes

Ox

格局 Structural Star	正官 Direct Officer	七殺 Seven Killings
用神 Useful God	Wu 戊 Earth	Ji 己 Earth
Conditions	Where Earth Qi is present in abundance amongst the Earthly Branches, this Gui Water Day Master may be afflicted with poverty and illness in life.	
Positive Circumstances	Fire present in the chart.	
Negative Circumstances	Presence of Chou (Pig) and Zi (Rat) in the Branches forming full Water frame.	

* *Bing Fire is the most-preferred Useful God.*

** *Ren Water is the second-choice Useful God, although Ding Fire should be prevented from penetrating through to the Heavenly Stems.*

BaZi Structures & Structural Useful Gods 格局與格局用神

| Day Master | Gui 癸 Water | Month | Chou 丑 (Ox) |

Summary

- Where no Wealth penetrate through to the Heavenly Stems of the BaZi Chart of a Gui Water born in a winter month - a male Gui Water Day Master may find it difficult to find a suitable companion or spouse in life. Wealth is Fire element. Needed for warmth and happiness.

- Where Bing Fire is absent from the Four Pillars of Destiny, any Structure formed within the BaZi Chart would still be considered a substandard.

- Ding Fire is merely a secondary choice as it's light is insufficient to bring warmth.

- Where Eating God and Hurting Officer Stars are found but there is no Metal to serve as a Resource Star, this Gui Water Day Master may be afflicted with a disability or handicap in life. Presence of Fire may mitigate this.

- Where Bing Fire comes into play as a Useful God, it should be rooted in the Earthly Branches of Yin (Tiger), Si (Snake) and Wu (Horse). Otherwise, Bing Fire would still be unable to play its role as a Useful God, effectively.

About Joey Yap

Joey Yap is the Founder and Master Trainer of the Mastery Academy of Chinese Metaphysics, a global organization devoted to the teaching of Feng Shui, BaZi, Mian Xiang and other Chinese Metaphysics subjects. He is also the Chief Consultant of Yap Global Consulting, an international consulting firm specialising in Feng Shui and Chinese Astrology services and audits.

He is the bestselling author of over 25 books, including *Stories and Lessons on Feng Shui, BaZi – The Destiny Code, Mian Xiang – Discover Face Reading, Feng Shui for Homebuyers Series*, and *Pure Feng Shui*, which was released by an international publisher.

He is also the producer of the first comprehensive reference source of Chinese Metaphysics, *The Chinese Metaphysics Compendium*, a compilation of all the essential formulas and applications known and practiced in Chinese Metaphysics today. He has since produced various other reference books and workbooks to aid students in their study and practice of Chinese Metaphysics subjects.

An avid proponent of technology being the way forward in disseminating knowledge of Chinese Metaphysics, Joey has developed, among others, the *BaZi Ming Pan 2.0 Software* and the *Xuan Kong Flying Stars Feng Shui Software*. This passion for fusing the best of modern technology with the best of classical studies lead him to create one of the pioneer online schools for Chinese Metaphysics education, the Mastery Academy E-Learning Centre (www.maelearning.com).

In addition to being a regular guest on various international radio and TV shows, Joey has also written columns for leading newspapers, as well as having contributed articles for various international magazines and publications. He has been featured in many popular publications and media including *Time International*, *Forbes International*, the *International Herald Tribune*, and Bloomberg TV, and was selected as one of Malaysia Tatler's 'Most Influential People in Malaysia' in 2008.

A naturally engaging speaker, Joey has presented to clients like Citibank, HSBC, IBM, Microsoft, Sime Darby, Bloomberg, HP, Samsung, Mah Sing, Nokia, Dijaya, and Standard Chartered.

Joey has also hosted his own TV series, *Discovering Feng Shui with Joey Yap*, and appeared on Malaysia's Astro TV network's *Walking the Dragons with Joey Yap*.

Joey's updates can be followed via Twitter at **www.twitter.com/joeyyap**. A full list of recent events and updates, and more information, can be found at **www.joeyyap.com** and **www.masteryacademy.com**

EDUCATION

The Mastery Academy of Chinese Metaphysics:
the first choice for practitioners and aspiring students of the
art and science of Chinese Classical Feng Shui and Astrology.

For thousands of years, Eastern knowledge has been passed from one generation to another through the system of discipleship. A venerated master would accept suitable individuals at a young age as his disciples, and informally through the years, pass on his knowledge and skills to them. His disciples in turn, would take on their own disciples, as a means to perpetuate knowledge or skills.

This system served the purpose of restricting the transfer of knowledge to only worthy honourable individuals and ensuring that outsiders or Westerners would not have access to thousands of years of Eastern knowledge, learning and research.

However, the disciple system has also resulted in Chinese Metaphysics and Classical Studies lacking systematic teaching methods. Knowledge garnered over the years has not been accumulated in a concise, systematic manner, but scattered amongst practitioners, each practicing his/her knowledge, art and science, in isolation.

The disciple system, out of place in today's modern world, endangers the advancement of these classical fields that continue to have great relevance and application today.

At the Mastery Academy of Chinese Metaphysics, our Mission is to bring Eastern Classical knowledge in the fields of metaphysics, Feng Shui and Astrology sciences and the arts to the world. These Classical teachings and knowledge, previously shrouded in secrecy and passed on only through the discipleship system, are adapted into structured learning, which can easily be understood, learnt and mastered. Through modern learning methods, these renowned ancient arts, sciences and practices can be perpetuated while facilitating more extensive application and understanding of these classical subjects.

The Mastery Academy espouses an educational philosophy that draws from the best of the East and West. It is the world's premier educational institution for the study of Chinese Metaphysics Studies offering a wide range and variety of courses, ensuring that students have the opportunity to pursue their preferred field of study and enabling existing practitioners and professionals to gain cross-disciplinary knowledge that complements their current field of practice.

Courses at the Mastery Academy have been carefully designed to ensure a comprehensive yet compact syllabus. The modular nature of the courses enables students to immediately begin to put their knowledge into practice while pursuing continued study of their field and complementary fields. Students thus have the benefit of developing and gaining practical experience in tandem with the expansion and advancement of their theoretical knowledge.

Students can also choose from a variety of study options, from a distance learning program, the Homestudy Series, that enables study at one's own pace or intensive foundation courses and compact lecture-based courses, held in various cities around the world by Joey Yap or our licensed instructors. The Mastery Academy's faculty and make-up is international in nature, thus ensuring that prospective students can attend courses at destinations nearest to their country of origin or with a licensed Mastery Academy instructor in their home country.

The Mastery Academy provides 24x7 support to students through its Online Community, with a variety of tools, documents, forums and e-learning materials to help students stay at the forefront of research in their fields and gain invaluable assistance from peers and mentoring from their instructors.

MASTERY ACADEMY
OF CHINESE METAPHYSICS

www.masteryacademy.com

MALAYSIA
19-3, The Boulevard
Mid Valley City
59200 Kuala Lumpur, Malaysia
Tel   : +603-2284 8080
Fax   : +603-2284 1218
Email : info@masteryacademy.com

SINGAPORE
14, Robinson Road # 13-00
Far East Finance Building
Singapore 048545
Tel   : +65-6494 9147
Email : singapore@masteryacademy.com

Australia, Austria, Canada, China, Croatia, Cyprus, Czech Republic, Denmark, France, Germany, Greece, Hungary, India, Italy, Kazakhstan, Malaysia, Netherlands (Holland), New Zealand, Philippines, Poland, Russian Federation, Singapore, Slovenia, South Africa, Switzerland, Turkey, U.S.A., Ukraine, United Kingdom

MASTERY ACADEMY
E-LEARNING CENTER

Introducing...
The Mastery Academy's E-Learning Center!

The Mastery Academy's goal has always been to share authentic knowledge of Chinese Metaphysics with the whole world.

Nevertheless, we do recognize that distance, time, and hotel and traveling costs – amongst many other factors – could actually hinder people from enrolling for a classroom-based course. But with the advent and amazing advance of IT today, NOT any more!

With this in mind, we have invested heavily in IT, to conceive what is probably the first and only E-Learning Center in the world today that offers a full range of studies in the field of Chinese Metaphysics.

Convenient   Study from Your   Easy Enrollment
Own Home

The Mastery Academy's E-Learning Center

Now, armed with your trusty computer or laptop, and Internet access, knowledge of classical Feng Shui, BaZi (Destiny Analysis) and Mian Xiang (Face Reading) are but a literal click away!

Study at your own pace, and interact with your Instructor and fellow students worldwide, from anywhere in the world. With our E-Learning Center, knowledge of Chinese Metaphysics is brought DIRECTLY to you in all its clarity – topic-by-topic, and lesson-by-lesson; with illustrated presentations and comprehensive notes expediting your learning curve!

Your education journey through our E-Learning Center may be done via any of the following approaches:

www.maelearning.com

1. Online Courses

There are 3 Programs available: our Online Feng Shui Program, Online BaZi Program, and Online Mian Xiang Program. Each Program consists of several Levels, with each Level consisting of many Lessons in turn. Each Lesson contains a pre-recorded video session on the topic at hand, accompanied by presentation-slides and graphics as well as downloadable tutorial notes that you can print and file for future reference.

Video Lecture

Presentation Slide

Downloadable Notes

2. MA Live!

MA Live!, as its name implies, enables LIVE broadcasts of Joey Yap's courses and seminars – right to your computer screen. Students will not only get to see and hear Joey talk on real-time `live', but also participate and more importantly, TALK to Joey via the MA Live! interface. All the benefits of a live class, minus the hassle of actually having to attend one!

How It Works

Our Live Classes

You at Home

3. Video-On-Demand (VOD)

Get immediate streaming-downloads of the Mastery Academy's wide range of educational DVDs, right on your computer screen. No more shipping costs and waiting time to be incurred!

Instant VOD Online

Choose From Our list of Available VODs!

Click "Play" on Your PC

Welcome to **www.maelearning.com**; the web portal of our E-Learning Center, and YOUR virtual gateway to Chinese Metaphysics!

Mastery Academy around the world

United States
Canada

United Kingdom
Denmark
Czech Republic
Austria
Switzerland
Poland
Netherlands
Germany
Solvenia
France
Italy
Cyprus
Hungary
Croatia
Greece

Russian
Federation

Ukraine

Turkey

Kazakhstan

India

South Africa

China

Philippines
Kuala Lumpur
Malaysia

Singapore

Australia

New Zealand

YAP GLOBAL CONSULTING

Joey Yap & Yap Global Consulting

Headed by Joey Yap, Yap Global Consulting (YGC) is a leading international consulting firm specializing in Feng Shui, Mian Xiang (Face Reading) and BaZi (Destiny Analysis) consulting services worldwide. Joey - an internationally renowned Master Trainer, Consultant, Speaker and best-selling Author - has dedicated his life to the art and science of Chinese Metaphysics.

YGC has its main offices in Kuala Lumpur and Australia, and draws upon its diverse reservoir of strength from a group of dedicated and experienced consultants based in more than 30 countries, worldwide.

As the pioneer in blending established, classical Chinese Metaphysics techniques with the latest approach in consultation practices, YGC has built its reputation on the principles of professionalism and only the highest standards of service. This allows us to retain the cutting edge in delivering Feng Shui and Destiny consultation services to both corporate and personal clients, in a simple and direct manner, without compromising on quality.

Across Industries: Our Portfolio of Clients

Our diverse portfolio of both corporate and individual clients from all around the world bears testimony to our experience and capabilities.

Virtually every industry imaginable has benefited from our services - ranging from academic and financial institutions, real-estate developers and multinational corporations, to those in the leisure and tourism industry. Our services are also engaged by professionals, prominent business personalities, celebrities, high-profile politicians and people from all walks of life.

YAP GLOBAL CONSULTING

e (Mr./Mrs./Ms.):

act Details

_____ Fax: _____

le : _____

il: _____

Type of Consultation Are You Interested In?
☐ eng Shui   ☐ BaZi   ☐ Date Selection   ☐ Yi Jing

e tick if applicable:
Are you a Property Developer looking to engage Yap Global Consulting?

Are you a Property Investor looking for tailor-made packages o suit your investment requirements?

Please attach your name card here.

Thank you for completing this form. Please fax it back to us at:

Singapore	Malaysia & the rest of the world
Tel : +65-6494 9147	Fax: +603-2284 2213 Tel : +603-2284 1213

Feng Shui Consultations

For Residential Properties
- Initial Land/Property Assessment
- Residential Feng Shui Consultations
- Residential Land Selection
- End-to-End Residential Consultation

For Commercial Properties
- Initial Land/Property Assessment
- Commercial Feng Shui Consultations
- Commercial Land Selection
- End-to-End Commercial Consultation

For Property Developers
- End-to-End Consultation
- Post-Consultation Advisory Services
- Panel Feng Shui Consultant

For Property Investors
- Your Personal Feng Shui Consultant
- Tailor-Made Packages

For Memorial Parks & Burial Sites
- Yin House Feng Shui

BaZi Consultations

Personal Destiny Analysis
- Personal Destiny Analysis for Individuals
- Children's BaZi Analysis
- Family BaZi Analysis

Strategic Analysis for Corporate Organizations
- Corporate BaZi Consultations
- BaZi Analysis for Human Resource Management

Entrepreneurs & Business Owners
- BaZi Analysis for Entrepreneurs

Career Pursuits
- BaZi Career Analysis

Relationships
- Marriage and Compatibility Analysis
- Partnership Analysis

For Everyone
- Annual BaZi Forecast
- Your Personal BaZi Coach**Personal Destiny Analysis**
- Personal Destiny Analysis for Individuals

Date Selection Consultations

- **Marriage Date Selection**
- **Caesarean Birth Date Selection**
- **House-Moving Date Selection**
- **Renovation & Groundbreaking Dates**

- **Signing of Contracts**
- **Official Openings**
- **Product Launches**

Yi Jing Assessment

A Time-Tested, Accurate Science

- With a history predating 4 millennia, the Yi Jing - or Classic of Change - is one of the oldest Chinese texts surviving today. Its purpose as an oracle, in predicting the outcome of things, is based on the variables of Time, Space and Specific Events.

- A Yi Jing Assessment provides specific answers to any specific questions you may have about a specific event or endeavor. This is something that a Destiny Analysis would not be able to give you.

Basically, what a Yi Jing Assessment does is focus on only ONE aspect or item at a particular point in your life, and give you a calculated prediction of the details that will follow suit, if you undertake a particular action. It gives you an insight into a situation, and what course of action to take in order to arrive at a satisfactory outcome at the end of the day.

Please Contact YGC for a personalized Yi Jing Assessment!

INVITING US TO YOUR CORPORATE EVENTS

Many reputable organizations and institutions have worked closely with YGC to build a synergistic business relationship by engaging our team of consultants, led by Joey Yap, as speakers at their corporate events. Our seminars and short talks are always packed with audiences consisting of clients and associates of multinational and public-listed companies as well as key stakeholders of financial institutions.

We tailor our seminars and talks to suit the anticipated or pertinent group of audience. Be it a department, subsidiary, your clients or even the entire corporation, we aim to fit your requirements in delivering the intended message(s).

CHINESE METAPHYSICS REFERENCE SERIES

The **Chinese Metaphysics Reference Series** is a collection of reference texts, source material, and educational textbooks to be used as supplementary guides by scholars, students, researchers, teachers and practitioners of Chinese Metaphysics.

These comprehensive and structured books provide fast, easy reference to aid in the study and practice of various Chinese Metaphysics subjects including Feng Shui, BaZi, Yi Jing, Zi Wei, Liu Ren, Ze Ri, Ta Yi, Qi Men and Mian Xiang.

The Chinese Metaphysics Compendium

At over 1,000 pages, the *Chinese Metaphysics Compendium* is a unique one-volume reference book that compiles all the formulas relating to Feng Shui, BaZi (Four Pillars of Destiny), Zi Wei (Purple Star Astrology), Yi Jing (I-Ching), Qi Men (Mystical Doorways), Ze Ri (Date Selection), Mian Xiang (Face Reading) and other sources of Chinese Metaphysics.

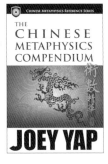

It is presented in the form of easy-to-read tables, diagrams and reference charts, all of which are compiled into one handy book. This first-of-its-kind compendium is presented in both English and the original Chinese, so that none of the meanings and contexts of the technical terminologies are lost.

The only essential and comprehensive reference on Chinese Metaphysics, and an absolute must-have for all students, scholars, and practitioners of Chinese Metaphysics.

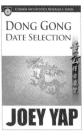

Dong Gong Date Selection

Xuan Kong Da Gua Ten Thousand Year Calendar

Xuan Kong Da Gua Reference Book

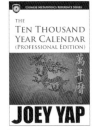

The Ten Thousand Year Calendar *(Professional Edition)*

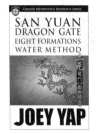

San Yuan Dragon Gate Eight Formations Water Method

Plum Blossoms Divination Reference Book

Qi Men Dun Jia 1080 Charts

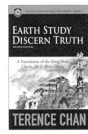

Earth Study Discern Truth Volume Two

Educational Tools & Software

Xuan Kong Flying Stars Feng Shui Software
The Essential Application for Enthusiasts and Professionals

The Xuan Kong Flying Stars Feng Shui Software is a brand-new application by Joey Yap that will assist you in the practice of Xuan Kong Feng Shui with minimum fuss and maximum effectiveness. Superimpose the Flying Stars charts over your house plans (or those of your clients) to clearly demarcate the 9 Palaces. Use it to help you create fast and sophisticated chart drawings and presentations, as well as to assist professional practitioners in the report-writing process before presenting the final reports for your clients. Students can use it to practice their Xuan Kong Feng Shui skills and knowledge, and it can even be used by designers and architects!

Some of the highlights of the software include:
- Natal Flying Stars
- Monthly Flying Stars
- 81 Flying Stars Combinations
- Dual-View Format
- Annual Flying Stars
- Flying Stars Integration
- 24 Mountains

All charts will be are printable and configurable, and can be saved for future editing. Also, you'll be able to export your charts into most image file formats like jpeg, bmp, and gif.

The Xuan Kong Flying Stars Feng Shui Software can make your Feng Shui practice simpler and more effective, garnering you amazing results with less effort!

Mini Feng Shui Compass

This Mini Feng Shui Compass with the accompanying Companion Booklet written by leading Feng Shui and Chinese Astrology Master Trainer Joey Yap is a must-have for any Feng Shui enthusiast.

The Mini Feng Shui Compass is a self-aligning compass that is not only light at 100gms but also built sturdily to ensure it will be convenient to use anywhere. The rings on the Mini Feng Shui Compass are bi-lingual and incorporate the 24 Mountain Rings that is used in your traditional Luo Pan.

The comprehensive booklet included will guide you in applying the 24 Mountain Directions on your Mini Feng Shui Compass effectively and the 8 Mansions Feng Shui to locate the most auspicious locations within your home, office and surroundings. You can also use the Mini Feng Shui Compass when measuring the direction of your property for the purpose of applying Flying Stars Feng Shui.

Educational Tools & Software

BaZi Ming Pan Software Version 2.0
Professional Four Pillars Calculator for Destiny Analysis

The BaZi Ming Pan Version 2.0 Professional Four Pillars Calculator for Destiny Analysis is the most technically advanced software of its kind in the world today. It allows even those without any knowledge of BaZi to generate their own BaZi Charts, and provides virtually every detail required to undertake a comprehensive Destiny Analysis.

This Professional Four Pillars Calculator allows you to even undertake a day-to-day analysis of your Destiny. What's more, all BaZi Charts generated by this software are fully printable and configurable! Designed for both enthusiasts and professional practitioners, this state-of-the-art software blends details with simplicity, and is capable of generating 4 different types of BaZi charts: **BaZi Professional Charts, BaZi Annual Analysis Charts, BaZi Pillar Analysis Charts and BaZi Family Relationship Charts.**

Additional references, configurable to cater to all levels of BaZi knowledge and usage, include:
• Dual Age & Bilingual Option (Western & Chinese) • Na Yin narrations • 12 Life Stages evaluation • Death & Emptiness • Gods & Killings • Special Days • Heavenly Virtue Nobles

This software also comes with a Client Management feature that allows you to save and trace clients' records instantly, navigate effortlessly between BaZi charts, and file your clients' information in an organized manner.

The BaZi Ming Pan Version 2.0 Calculator sets a new standard by combining the best of BaZi and technology.

Joey Yap Feng Shui Template Set

Directions are the cornerstone of any successful Feng Shui audit or application. The **Joey Yap Feng Shui Template Set** is a set of three templates to simplify the process of taking directions and determining locations and positions, whether it's for a building, a house, or an open area such as a plot of land, all with just a floor plan or area map.

The Set comprises 3 basic templates: The Basic Feng Shui Template, 8 Mansions Feng Shui Template, and the Flying Stars Feng Shui Template.

With bi-lingual notations for these directions; both in English and the original Chinese, the **Joey Yap Feng Shui Template Set** comes with its own Booklet that gives simple yet detailed instructions on how to make use of the 3 templates within.

• Easy-to-use, simple, and straightforward
• Small and portable; each template measuring only 5" x 5"
• Additional 8 Mansions and Flying Stars Reference Rings
• Handy companion booklet with usage tips and examples

Accelerate Your Face Reading Skills With
Joey Yap's Face Reading Revealed DVD Series

Mian Xiang, the Chinese art of Face Reading, is an ancient form of physiognomy and entails the use of the face and facial characteristics to evaluate key aspects of a person's life, luck and destiny. In his Face Reading DVDs series, Joey Yap shows you how the facial features reveal a wealth of information about a person's luck, destiny and personality.

Mian Xiang also tell us the talents, quirks and personality of an individual. Do you know that just by looking at a person's face, you can ascertain his or her health, wealth, relationships and career? Let Joey Yap show you how the 12 Palaces can be utilised to reveal a person's inner talents, characteristics and much more.

Each facial feature on the face represents one year in a person's life. Your face is a 100-year map of your life and each position reveals your fortune and destiny at a particular age as well as insights and information about your personality, skills, abilities and destiny.

Using Mian Xiang, you will also be able to plan your life ahead by identifying, for example, the right business partner and knowing the sort of person that you need to avoid. By knowing their characteristics through the facial features, you will be able to gauge their intentions and gain an upper hand in negotiations.

Do you know what moles signify? Do they bring good or bad luck? Do you want to build better relationships with your partner or family members or have your ever wondered why you seem to be always bogged down by trivial problems in your life?

In these highly entertaining DVDs, Joey will help you answer all these questions and more. You will be able to ascertain the underlying meaning of moles, birthmarks or even the type of your hair in Face Reading. Joey will also reveal the guidelines to help you foster better and stronger relationships with your loved ones through Mian Xiang.

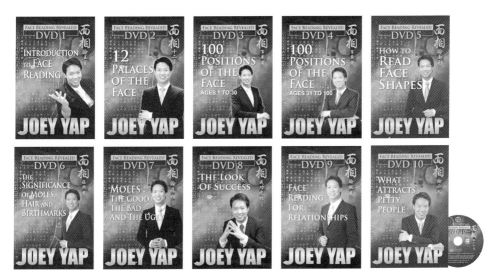

Feng Shui for Homebuyers DVD Series

Best-selling Author, and international Master Trainer and Consultant Joey Yap reveals in these DVDs the significant Feng Shui features that every homebuyer should know when evaluating a property.

Joey will guide you on how to customise your home to maximise the Feng Shui potential of your property and gain the full benefit of improving your health, wealth and love life using the 9 Palace Grid. He will show you how to go about applying the classical applications of the Life Gua and House Gua techniques to get attuned to your Sheng Qi (positive energies).

In these DVDs, you will also learn how to identify properties with good Feng Shui features that will help you promote a fulfilling life and achieve your full potential. Discover how to avoid properties with negative Feng Shui that can bring about detrimental effects to your health, wealth and relationships.

Joey will also elaborate on how to fix the various aspects of your home that may have an impact on the Feng Shui of your property and give pointers on how to tap into the positive energies to support your goals.

Discover Feng Shui with Joey Yap (TV Series)

Discover Feng Shui with Joey Yap: Set of 4 DVDs

Informative and entertaining, classical Feng Shui comes alive in *Discover Feng Shui with Joey Yap!*

Dying to know how you can use Feng Shui to improve your house or office, but simply too busy attend for formal classes?

You have the questions. Now let Joey personally answer them in this 4-set DVD compilation! Learn how to ensure the viability of your residence or workplace, Feng Shui-wise, without having to convert it into a Chinese antiques' shop. Classical Feng Shui is about harnessing the natural power of your environment to improve quality of life. It's a systematic and subtle metaphysical science.

And that's not all. Joey also debunks many a myth about classical Feng Shui, and shares with viewers Face Reading tips as well!

Own the series that national channel 8TV did a re-run of in 2005, today!

Annual Releases

Chinese Astrology for 2009

This information-packed annual guide to the Chinese Astrology for 2009 goes way beyond the conventional `animal horoscope' book. To begin with, author Joey Yap includes a personalized outlook for 2009 based on the individual's BaZi Day Pillar (Jia Zi) and a 12-month micro-analysis for each of the 60 Day Pillars – in addition to the annual outlook for all 12 animal signs and the 12-month outlook for each animal sign in 2009. Find out what awaits you in 2009 from the four key aspects of Health, Wealth, Career and Relationships…with Joey Yap's **Chinese Astrology for 2009**!

Feng Shui for 2009

Maximize the Qi of the Year of the Earth Rat for your home and office, with Joey Yap's **Feng Shui for 2009** book. Learn how to tap into the positive sectors of the year, and avoid the negative ones and those with the Annual Afflictions, as well as ascertain how the annual Flying Stars affect your property by comparing them against the Eight Mansions (Ba Zhai) for 2009. Flying Stars enthusiasts will also find this book handy, as it includes the monthly Flying Stars charts for the year, accompanied by detailed commentaries on what sectors to use and avoid – to enable you to optimize your Academic, Relationships and Wealth Luck in 2009.

Tong Shu Diary 2009

Organize your professional and personal lives with the **Tong Shu Diary 2009**, with a twist… it also allows you to determine the most suitable dates on which you can undertake important activities and endeavors throughout the year! This compact Diary integrates the Chinese Solar and Lunar Calendars with the universal lingua franca of the Gregorian Calendar.

Tong Shu Monthly Planner 2009

Tailor-made for the Feng Shui or BaZi enthusiast in you, or even professional Chinese Metaphysics consultants who want a compact planner with useful information incorporated into it. In the **Tong Shu Monthly Planner 2009**, you will find the auspicious and inauspicious dates for the year marked out for you, alongside the most suitable activities to be undertaken on each day. As a bonus, there is also a reference section containing all the monthly Flying Stars charts and Annual Afflictions for 2009.

Tong Shu Desktop Calendar 2009

Get an instant snapshot of the suitable and unsuitable activities for each day of the Year of the Earth Rat, with the icons displayed on this lightweight Desktop Calendar. Elegantly presenting the details of the Chinese Solar Calendar in the form of the standard Gregorian one, the **Tong Shu Desktop Calendar 2009** is perfect for Chinese Metaphysics enthusiasts and practitioners alike. Whether it a business launching or meeting, ground breaking ceremony, travel or house-moving that you have in mind, this Calendar is designed to fulfill your information needs.

Tong Shu Year Planner 2009

This one-piece Planner presents you all the essential information you need for significant activities or endeavors…with just a quick glance! In a nutshell, it allows you to identify the favorable and unfavorable days, which will in turn enable you to schedule your year's activities so as to make the most of good days, and avoid the ill-effects brought about by inauspicious ones.

Continue Your Journey with Joey Yap's Books

Walking the Dragons

Walking the Dragons is a guided tour through the classical landform Feng Shui of ancient China, an enchanting collection of deeply-researched yet entertaining essays rich in historical detail.

Compiled in one book for the first time from Joey Yap's Feng Shui Mastery Excursion Series, the book highlights China's extensive, vibrant history with astute observations on the Feng Shui of important sites and places. Learn the landform formations of Yin Houses (tombs and burial places), as well as mountains, temples, castles, and villages.

It demonstrates complex Feng Shui theories and principles in easy-to-understand, entertaining language and is the perfect addition to the bookshelf of a Feng Shui or history lover. Anyone, whether experienced in Feng Shui or new to the practice, will be able to enjoy the insights shared in this book. Complete with gorgeous full-colour pictures of all the amazing sights and scenery, it's the next best thing to having been there yourself!

Your Aquarium Here

Your Aquarium Here is a simple, practical, hands-on Feng Shui book that teaches you how to incorporate a Water feature – an aquarium – for optimal Feng Shui benefit, whether for personal relationships, wealth, or career. Designed to be comprehensive yet simple enough for a novice or beginner, *Your Aquarium Here* provides historical and factual information about the role of Water in Feng Shui, and provides a step-by-step guide to installing and using an aquarium.

The book is the first in the **Fengshuilogy Series**, a series of matter-of-fact and useful Feng Shui books designed for the person who wants to do fuss-free Feng Shui. Not everyone who wants to use Feng Shui is an expert or a scholar! This series of books are just the kind you'd want on your bookshelf to gain basic, practical knowledge of the subject. Go ahead and Feng Shui-It-Yourself – *Your Aquarium Here* eliminates all the fuss and bother, but maintains all the fun and excitement, of authentic Feng Shui application!

The Art of Date Selection: Personal Date Selection

In today's modern world, it is not good enough to just do things effectively – we need to do them efficiently, as well. From the signing of business contracts and moving into a new home, to launching a product or even tying the knot; everything has to move, and move very quickly too. There is a premium on Time, where mistakes can indeed be costly.

The notion of doing the Right Thing, at the Right Time and in the Right Place is the very backbone of Date Selection. Because by selecting a suitable date specially tailored to a specific activity or endeavor, we infuse it with the most positive energies prevalent in our environment during that particular point in time; and that could well make the difference between 'make-and-break'! With the *Art of Date Selection: Personal Date Selection*, learn simple, practical methods you can employ to select not just good dates, but personalized good dates. Whether it's a personal activity such as a marriage or professional endeavor such as launching a business, signing a contract or even acquiring assets, this book will show you how to pick the good dates and tailor them to suit the activity in question, as well as avoid the negative ones too!

The Art of Date Selection: Feng Shui Date Selection

Date Selection is the Art of selecting the most suitable date, where the energies present on the day support the specific activities or endeavors we choose to undertake on that day. Feng Shui is the Chinese Metaphysical study of the Physiognomy of the Land – landforms and the Qi they produce, circulate and conduct. Hence, anything that exists on this Earth is invariably subject to the laws of Feng Shui. So what do we get when Date Selection and Feng Shui converge?

Feng Shui Date Selection, of course! Say you wish to renovate your home, or maybe buy or rent one. Or perhaps, you're a developer, and wish to know WHEN is the best date possible to commence construction works on your project. In any case – and all cases – you certainly wish to ensure that your endeavors are well supported by the positive energies present on a good day, won't you? And this is where Date Selection supplements the practice of Feng Shui. At the end of the day, it's all about making the most of what's good, and minimizing what's bad.

(Available Soon)

CHESHIRE

Edited by Carl Golder

First published in Great Britain in 1999 by
POETRY NOW YOUNG WRITERS
Remus House,
Coltsfoot Drive,
Woodston
Peterborough, PE2 9JX
Telephone (01733) 890066

HB ISBN 0 75430 407 8
SB ISBN 0 75430 408 6

FOREWORD

This year, the Poetry Now Young Writers'
Kaleidoscope competition proudly presents the best
poetic contributions from over 32,000 up-and-coming
writers nationwide.

Successful in continuing our aim of promoting
writing and creativity in children, each regional
anthology displays the inventive and original writing
talents of 11-18 year old poets. Imaginative,
thoughtful, often humorous, *Kaleidoscope Cheshire*
provides a captivating insight into the issues and
opinions important to today's young generation.

The task of editing inevitably proved challenging, but
was nevertheless enjoyable thanks to the quality of
entries received. The thought, effort and hard work
put into each poem impressed and inspired us all. We
hope you are as pleased as we are with the final result
and that you continue to enjoy *Kaleidoscope Cheshire*
for years to come.

CONTENTS

Matthew Davidson	20
Mark Pickering	21
Daniel Avery	21
David Burgon	22
Matthew Kellett	22
Nicholas Jackson	23
Jenny Rainford	24
Louise Mooney	24
Kelly Barnes	25
Hannah Whittaker	25
Katie Campbell	26
Kimberley McBride	26
Sarah Bartoli	27
Robyn Pulvertaft	28
Katie Newall	28
Anthony Bird	29
Ciara Sholl	29
Thomas Griffiths	30

All Saints Catholic College

Meera Gohil	30
Alice McGreevy	31
Carmine Circelli	31
Joseph Greenhalgh	32
Scott Texeira	33
Darren Clay	33
Martin Howard	34
Patrick Manley	34
Katie Aylett	35
Ciaran Crombie	36
Andrew Wareham	36
Heather Wilshaw	37
Joe Kowaltschuk	38
Jennifer McCall	38
Kelly Whiteside	39
Katrina Booth	39
Lindsay Bryce	40
Jenny Lowe	40

Katie Jones	41
Heather Turner	41
Frances Powrie	42
Patrick Jones	42
Claire Pollitt	43
Joanne Meakin	43

Bridgewater High School

Nikki Daniels	44
Rosie Grensinger	44
David Jones	45
Ben Mellers	45
Jasmin Brady	46
David Lloyd	46
Holly Quin-Ankrah	47
Hazel Jane Thomas	48
Samantha C Smythe	48
Ben Fawcett	49
Hannah Gibson	49
Justina Bridge	50
Helen Whitehead	50
Michael P Stevens	51
Rachel Harvey	51
Helen Thompson	52
Katrina Patrick	53
Jonathan Butterworth	53
Katie Lang	54
Helen Broughton	55
Mark Rowley	55
Kenneth Lomas	56
Paul Holmes	57
Joanna Tosh	58
Kate Hackett	58
Jenny Catterall	59
Daniel Davidson	59
Helen Smith	60
Michael Hackney	60
Alex Smith	61

Gareth Roberts	61
Daniel Lindsay	62
Nicola Payne	62
Felicity Webb	63
Holly Louise Jones	64
Panna Malik	64
Jenny Owens	65
Claire Bridger	66
Emma Moorcroft	66
Beth Isherwood	67
Amie Bennett-Price	67
Abigail Thompson	68
Elizabeth Henshaw	68
Peter Myall	69
Philip Galsaworthy	70
Daniel Peake	71
Hayley Banner	72
Natalie Whewell	72
Lisa Parkinson	73
Christine Boardman	74
Helen King	74
Andrew McDermott	75
James Carter	76

Hartford High School

Hayley Cox	77
Jodie Withnell	77
Nicola Ruston	78
Nicola Catherine Poole	78
Tiffany Mains	79
Chris Steele	79
Rebecca Mitchell	80
Constance Baker	80
Andrew Morgan	81
Pearl Shallcross	81
Jenny Clarke	82
Claire Darbyshire	83
Rebecca Oakes	83

Victoria Massey	84
Daniel Buckley	84
Emma Collinge	85
Katharine Jones	85
Hayley Kinning	86
Kate Stone	86
Rebecca Mason	87
Helen Walker	88
Mary Gerrard	89
Alyce Giles	90
David Clarke	91
Paul Clarke	92
Lucy James	92
Melissa Rodwell	93
Nick Wilson	93
Richard Payne	94
Ashley Reid	95
Becky Worrall	96
Nikita Ponda	97
Fiona Rudkin	98
Oliver Newman	99
Caroline Hammond	99
Kim Nield	100
Holly Moncrieff	100
Gemma Else	101
Sara Cole	101
Rachel Lockett	102
Carla Whittaker	102
Donna Taylor	103
Nathan Rathbone	103
Natalie Austin	104
Oliver Hynes	105
Rebecca McDean	106
Lois Blower	107
Carole Boag-Munroe	107
Jessica Woodman	108
Donna Kryger	109
Caroline Evans	109

Mark McWha	110
Laura Plumb	110
Jenny Johnson	111
Claire Martin	111
Laura Yates	112
John Harding	112
Shelley Alder	113
Victoria Astles	113
Daniel Bell	114
Iain Bellis	114
Liz Grossman	115
Jonathan Gaze	115
Victoria Gardner	116
Laura Chesterson	117
Donna Archibald	117
Michelle Dutton	118
Richard Tolley	118
Sophie Preece	119
Karen Brotherton	119
Rachel Sayle	120
Ryan Beaumont	120
John Corker	121
Josh Dean	121
Paul Goulden	122
Emma Stockton	122
Nicky Stephenson	123
Joanne Hayes	123
Kelly Taylor	124
Alaina Bexton	124
David Wade	125
Sarah Rutter	125
David Flood	126
Amy Stone	127
Louise Eslick	127
Kerry Atkinson	128
Ben Davenport	128
Jenny Clarke	129
Alanna Rose	130

Oaklands School

James Kracke	175
Elizabeth Broad	176
Philip Murphy	177
Christopher Lloyd	177
Selina Rimmer	177
Christopher Heeks	178
Samantha Bayley	178
Lisa Neild	178
David Llewellyn	179
Shaun Brinksman	179
Kevin Stevens	179
Kimberley Cotton	180
Mark Cressey	180
Katie Holliday	180
Christopher Walters	181
Stuart Carless	181
Craig Wilkinson	181
Lee Humphries	182
Peter Jackson	182
Alex Perks	182
Emma Wilson	183
Rebecca Evanson	183
Mark Barnett	183
Lyndsey Luscombe	184
Gavin Judson	184
Jane Clark	184
Paul Emmison	185
James Jeffries	185
Richard Higgins	185

Sir Thomas Boteler High School

Daniel Solan	186
Sharon Fitzpatrick	186
Kim Vernon	187
Azzita Darani	188
Nicola Birmingham	188
Craig Morgan	189

Kelly Lafferty	189
Kevin Daniels	190

The County High School

Joanne Minton	190

The Grange School

Hannah Tharmalingam	191
Luke Ashall	192
Phil Clancy	192
Richard Hutchinson	193
Jenny Winter	194
Lucy Bate	194
Lisa Bramwell	195
Mark Burton	196
Rajiv Tandon	197
Peter Tipler	197
Stephen Willis	198
Guy Campbell	198
Ross McDyre	199
Debjani Talukder	200
Andrew Taylor	201
Gina Percy	202
Katie Ferry	202
Natalie Johnson	203

Verdin High School

Andrew Hulme	203
Fiona Ellison-Smith	204

Wilmslow High School

Jenny Maddock	205
Emma Varney	206

The Poems

JAILBIRD

Behind the bars I wait
My home is like a jail
The warden comes and goes
He's getting old and frail.

He sometimes lets me out
To get some exercise
I know this pleases him
By the sparkle in his eyes.

He brings me food and water
And calls my name out loud
He gently holds me in his hand
As if I were a cloud.

I love this jail I'm in
I love the warden dearly
I love the life I lead
As a caged canary.

Clare Williams (12)

SMOKING

Smoking, do you know the score?
I wish I was told before.
When I was young, I didn't care,
Of the damage going on in there.
Now here I am, I'm forty three,
They say I'll die eventually.
I've got cancer now you see,
Ending life in misery.
So just go on and have that fag,
And die like me, a withered hag.

Kelly Warburton (14)

A FEAR OF SPIDERS

Webs, webs, webs
Creep, creep, creep
Spiders make me weep
Crawl, crawl, crawl
Spiders make me bawl
Run, run, run
I always call my mum
They have a black body and eight hairy legs
They eat flies and spin webs
I don't know why I am scared of them, I guess it's just a phase
My mum thinks that I am stupid, she says it's just my age.

Kimberley Slack (13)
All Hallows High School

A HAIRY SCARE!

I stood there in the bathroom,
About to wash my hair,
But when I picked up the shampoo,
I had a frightening scare,

For stood there underneath me,
Was a spider with long hair,
So I threw down the bottle and screamed
With despair,
Because after all that,
I was scared to wash my hair!

Rachael Birchall (13)
All Hallows High School

MY LIFE

I was born next to the Potala in the forbidden country of Tibet.
I have crossed the Himalayas - that I will never forget.
My mother and I starved in our effort to flee the Chinese
Fortune and cruelty I have seen in my life,
And now in this alien country
I plead to you to be kind to me.
My life is based on love and respect for all sentient beings.
I believe a religion can be judged by the actions of the practitioners.
I was taught every day to say others before self.
That life is based on things more important than wealth
My wealth is my beliefs,
I breathe them and
Absorb them in my life.
Unkindness and mockery can only bring me strife.
I am proud to have seen so much in my tender years.
But unkindness by others only brings tears.
May your lives be as rich as mine.
As they say in India,
I hope you are very fine.

Sonam Choden (14)
All Hallows High School

MR WILLSON

Mr Willson going for his morning paper.
It was a warm and sunny morning.
Catching the sun in his eyes.
He couldn't see where he was going.
At the end of the street he had to stop or
Else he would be run over.
Lorries swerving, crashing and bashing.

Sean Scroop (13)
All Hallows High School

THE FAIR

Mr Airman man,
Man of the air
Awakes to find a fair,
Outside his window,
It shines bright,
As if the sun is there.
The screams of laughter,
The sounds of fun,
They even eat ice-cream buns.
The bumper cars crash and bang,
As little children run around,
They scream and bellow,
'Arr Mum, why can't we stay longer
For we long to ride the coaster?'
'Not now children, time to go,
We will come again another day.'

You'll see.

Iain Woodhouse (13)
All Hallows High School

POEMS

What is a poem?
Is it just a bunch of words?
Why are poems so important in the world?
I see that some are feelings and they rhyme just like a song,
But now I come to think of it,
I think I might be wrong.
Poems may look boring and you feel you could fall asleep,
But once you hear this poem you will see that it's unique.

Samantha Cummings (13)
All Hallows High School

MY DAD'S A CHAMPION BOXER

My dad's a champion boxer
he's the greatest of them all
he's never lost at all

I can't see why
he's not the tallest of them all
in fact he's the shortest of them all

It might be
because he's built like a wall
or because he's the strongest of them all

But after all
he's still the greatest of them all
because he's never lost at all!

Don't ask me because I just don't know at all!

Nick Eardley (13)
All Hallows High School

DIRECTIONS

This way, that way,
Up and down,
Left and right,
Round and round,
Forwards and backwards.

In and out,
Stop and go,
Under and over,
Fast and slow.

These are the way directions go.

Emma Brandrick (13)
All Hallows High School

OUTER SPACE!

Outer space
Where does it end?
Where is the beginning?
Who is its friend?

Sharing its time
Between the sun and moon
Each in their element
Till one comes too soon.

Ice-blue days
Pitch-black nights
Sparkles of stardust
Fit in just right.

Its extraordinary kingdom
A haven in its own
Wonders never cease to amaze
The dwellers of this home.

Laurie Kershaw (14)
All Hallows High School

NONSENSE

Nonsense is a weird thing,
Sometimes it makes me want to sing.
Then people say, 'What utter nonsense.'
So I walk away and say,
'What happens if it rains some hay?'
But then the adults say, 'What utter nonsense.'
I may have to say
That it is perfect in every way.
Nonsense.

Thomas Bailey (13)
All Hallows High School

CHAMPION SKATER

I'm a champion skater
I'm the best of them all
I do all the greatest tricks and flicks
But sometimes bailed or failed

I do amazing spins and flips
And all the greatest of the tricks.
I've won competitions
I've been on the box.

But I don't want to die
So I think I'll give up
Have a rest but always
Be the best.

Joe Gutkowski (13)
All Hallows High School

SPIDER

Creep!
Creep!
In the night
across the carpet
along the wall.
Hairy legs and little body.
In the morning you come
downstairs,
and he will be gone
until another night.

Jason Ridgeway (13)
All Hallows High School

DESOLATION

A clear pool's reflection,
A past echo alone in the night,
Sorrow's dismal complexion,
Faith evaporates from sight.

The gloomy grey bleakness of morn,
Choked emotions, strangled silence,
The sombre ritual of dawn,
The murky smog of remorse too overwhelmingly dense.

That resilient fortress of hope,
Whose stronghold's too steadfast to submit,
In immortal darkness, sorrows mope,
Bitter memories before, behind me ever flit.

The icy glare of nothingness,
Which stares me in the face,
Ever into empty bleakness I shall gaze,
Yet eyes that behold beauty I cannot place.

The sunrise seemed to me once so sweet,
Frosted cobwebs graced with diamond dew,
But now their bleak shadows bitterly speak,
Imprisoned, divorced from my senses they flew
And never in this sorry lifetime are they to return,
And never then shall my tear-stained eyes discern.

Rosie Trafford (13)
All Hallows High School

THE DARK

The dark is like a stranger
Enclosing all around me.
The dark is like a stranger
Just trying to frighten me.

When I am in bed at night
And I see the dark close in,
I shut my eyes and try to dream
So that the dark can't creep in.

I try to dream of good sweet things
Like chocolate or money.
But in the end the dark sweeps in
And I have nightmares that really are not funny.

So now I sleep with my bedroom alight
And it doesn't seem as scary.
It takes my mind off the deep dark night
And now I dream of fairies.

Georgina Lomas (13)
All Hallows High School

GREEN

Green is for grass, radiant in the sun,
Green is a colour that makes you run, run, run,
Green is the best,
Green beats the rest.

Green is the colour that lets you rest.

Robert Barker (13)
All Hallows High School

FOOTBALL

Football is good
Football is fun,
But broken bones and injuries
Are not much fun.
You kick the ball
In the back of the net.
The crowd roars,
You think you're the best.
You're through to the finals,
You're so tense,
You're into penalties and you're
up next.
What's that noise?
You've just won us the
Cup!

Ryan Smith (13)
All Hallows High School

THE WEARY HOUSE

The weary house
Set upon by the black night.
The creeping door.
The wooden floor.

What will happen to the night?
The house will set upon the black night.
The gaping windows.
The mist with no face.

The black night will be set upon
By the haunted house.

Christian Cartwright (13)
All Hallows High School

THE RAINY DAY

As I looked through the window,
All I could see was rain,
It was coming down quite slowly,
As it splashed on the windowpane.

Two small children ran by,
Splishing and splashing in the puddles,
One of them started to cry,
Because the other one had splashed her in the eye.

It reminded me of a sad film,
With the dull, dark sky,
And the small children wailing,
But I ask myself why?

Gemma Harrison (13)
All Hallows High School

BONFIRE NIGHT

People make me out of straw
Putting me on the dusty floor
I cannot see my feet or toes
So I look for my ugly nose.

Seeing fireworks in the sky
Watching them with my beady eye,
My heart is full of sadness,
Ready to be turned into ashes.

Throwing me on the bonfire
Fireworks going higher
Soon I will be lying dead,
On the floor without a head.

Kirsty Leech (13)
All Hallows High School

LEAVING HOME . . .

As the train pulls away from the station,
She is left on the platform alone;
And I wave 'til I no longer see her,
As I travel a long way from home.

On a journey before never travelled,
While the engine grinds under my seat,
I look down to my small, battered suitcase
Sitting silent and still at my feet.

Inside is a clingfilm-wrapped sandwich,
A bottle of Coke - and a book;
A small pile of clothes packed so neatly:
A sign of the trouble she took.

The train ride will take quite a long time,
To take me away from my home;
From the town that I've known since my childhood;
To a place I'm completely unknown.

It's a strange kind of feeling, this leaving
To go into the world on my own,
But I know when I'm homesick or lonely,
There she'll be - on the end of the phone.

I'm excited and scared all together.
Just a mixture of feelings - it's true;
But it's time, and I know that I'm ready
To start life in my own pastures new.

Meagan McNish (13)
All Hallows High School

THE FORMULA ONE DRIVER

You're on pole, the crowd cheering happily
Is today the day you cross the line first?
You rev the engine smoothly and off you go
But it's only the formation lap so keep calm
Lining up on the grid and you're there first
The red lights come on, one after another
Foot to the floor and you're away
The first corner decides it, so get through first
You're still first and pulling away
The first lap ends and you're two seconds up
Everybody is waiting for the pit stops
But how many do you need to make?
Twenty laps gone, many more to go
You're away in the lead enjoying the race
Over the radio at mid-distance *'pit-in'*
Everybody else has stopped for fresh rubber
Into the pit lane, play easy with the throttle
Your mechanics are ready and now it's up to them
The fuel goes in, new tyres are added
'Go!' You floor the power and you're back in the race
First position is still yours, keep calm
You're nearly there over the finish line
Only a couple of laps to go, so be careful
The last lap and you're cruising
Your lead dwindles, but it doesn't matter
You have won, you have beaten the best
What can stop you now?

Michael Lea-O'Mahoney (14)
All Hallows High School

ROBYN'S DREAM

I
sat
waiting
anxiously
surrounded
by other people
with high hopes.
I looked around at them, confident looks on
their faces, but they didn't fool me. I knew that
inside they felt exactly like I did. I knew
they were sat there, palms sweating,
cracking their knuckles, shaking.
Then . . . it was time . . . the moment
we were all waiting for . . . I
could see my name in lights
already . . . 'And the award
for the best new
actress . . . snaps open
envelope) . . . goes to . . .'

Miss Fletcher: 'Robyn, Robyn, it will do your acting career
no good if you fall asleep in the lesson.'
Robyn: Sigh . . . ! What did she know about anything!

Lucia Jimenez (13)
All Hallows High School

AUTUMN

Autumn is here now,
and the leaves begin to fall.
A carpet of orange begins to form.

Autumn is here now,
the frost, the wind and rain,
driving us all insane.

Autumn is here now,
and I wrap up warm,
as the cold days seem to dawn.

Autumn is here now,
the summer is long gone.
The season of many colours
has now begun.

Sarah Foden (13)
All Hallows High School

THE WORK OF SUNLIGHT

In the morning up I jump,
Hitting the floor with a thump.
The sun comes up like a ball of flame,
The rays of power spraying on my window frame.
The strong scent of a new day,
Hits me like I'm its prey.
To me it is bright,
Is this the work of the sunlight?
The shrill of a voice,
With its choice,
Piercing through the air,
From where?
The colours splashed,
They also lashed,
Whipping our eyes,
Like a thousand flies.
Down everything goes,
Where nobody knows.

Hannah Cutler (13)
All Hallows High School

PLAYTIME

Cat sat on the mat,
Watching the devious rat,
Taking food without permission,
But he must make a quick decision,
To run or stay or find his way,
Back to his hole,
Disappearing like a mole.

Quietly sitting on the mat,
The cat watches the rat,
Winding, weaving thereabouts,
Not stepping on the louse,
Cat's tail waving gracefully,
Purring, purring intensively

A sudden leap from the mat,
The cat makes for the rat,
The race is on,
Under tables, under chairs,
Under doors and under stairs,
He hits the floor with a bounce and a bang,
The rat takes cover,
The cat bares his fangs,

Hark, the cat hears footsteps,
Coming from the hall,
He leaps back on the mat,
As if he's done nothing at all.

Lindsay Ciupak (13)
All Hallows High School

WHY?

Why can't I fly?
Why can birds fly?
I wonder why?

Why is the sky so high?
And why is it called the sky?
I wonder why?

Why do we have to die?
I don't want to die,
I want to live forever,
And never say goodbye
But I have to go now,
Goodbye!

Jordan Hitchen (13)
All Hallows High School

FISHING DAYS

Fish jump
Into the air
Strike the rod, no
Hint of fight, reel
It in, then a nudge
Yes, a fish!
Going for it
Diving down
And jumping
Yes, nearly in
Snap!

Chris Ford (13)
All Hallows High School

THE BOY

He follows you round, striding about
'Just go away,' all the other kids shout
He laughs it off but deep down inside
He just wants to burst out and cry.

'You can't do anything' one boy said to him
He looks at another, just a cheesy grin
He tries his best all the time
No justice, he failed, he's hurt down inside.

The kids say he lives in a bin
The priest says he's a devilish sin
He has some bad stuff
And wears it all wrong.

He sings a song
All the windows shatter
The teacher claps
But is drowned by laughter.

Richard Ferguson (13)
All Hallows High School

CLAUSTROPHOBIA

Trapped inside a tiny place
My heart begins to bound and race
I close my eyes and try to find
A way out of my silly mind.

I'm feeling really ill
And my chest begins to kill
Then I open my eyes to see
That all of a sudden I'm free.

Bill McCartney (13)
All Hallows High School

BIGFOOT

Bigfoot, Bigfoot, everywhere
Everywhere you go he's always there
Better be careful he's in town
He'll get you down with one big frown.

Bigfoot, Bigfoot, everywhere
Everywhere you go he's always there
Better be careful he's in town
He'll have you running here, running there,
He'll have you crying with one almighty stare.

Bigfoot, Bigfoot, everywhere
Everywhere you go he's always there
Better be careful, he's in town
If you cough he'll blow you down.

Alex Baird (13)
All Hallows High School

THE GIRL

She hates school, can't you tell?
She's always moody and she never smiles
She sits in that same corner every lunch
Giving evils to people who walk past.

I don't really like her and she doesn't like me
Hopefully she will find a friend and stop picking on
me
    me
       me!

Rebecca Dodd (13)
All Hallows High School

MY SECRET LOVE

My secret love, thou cannot be named,
Still I yearn for thy tenderness and sweet grace.

As Romeo loved Juliet, I shall love thee,
With all my heart, for all eternity.

As Polonius once said 'To thine own self be true,'
And I shall be true to you my love.

My heart pounds like rain on a concrete ground,
Whenever I am blessed with your presence.

Mi amour, I shall love you day after day,
For evermore.

Jayne Leversidge (13)
All Hallows High School

CHRISTMAS

Two weeks before Christmas
And there is still no snow
I wait and wait for hour on end
And I'm all aglow.
It's a week before Christmas and
I'm still waiting and waiting
And I'm still all aglow
Oh when will it snow?
Oh when will it snow, snow, snow?
And all of a sudden magic happens
It's snowing and snowing
It snows and snows.

Matthew Davidson (13)
All Hallows High School

THE BULLIED VICTIM

Alone he stands,
Mocked and unwanted,
He just wants a friend
But they push him around.

They are *cool*
But he drools
According to them
He's a big fat hen.

He thinks of dying
But his mum would be crying
He just wants to be left
Alone.

All alone
All on his own
He shouts a yelp
And it spells out *help*.

Mark Pickering (13)
All Hallows High School

WINTER

W   hen I'm cold and dull inside
I   have to run away and hide
N   ever, ever do I think what pain my mum and dad are in.
T'   is Christmas I do know.
E   ver to wonder about the snow
R   iver flowing, icicles drop, people starve without their crop.

Daniel Avery (13)
All Hallows High School

THE ROAD OF LIFE

The road of life does reach so far
Impossible to reach by train or car
To get to the end of the road of life
You pass through forests of happiness,
And the deserts of strife,
The road is long.
Long is the road of life.

I'm only part-way down the road of life,
A long way to go, so many strides to take.
I think I see the end, the doorway to death
The staircase to Heaven and Hell.
How many people have come this way so death can ring its bell?
The road is long,
Long is the road of life,
Long is the road of life
Large are the deserts of strife
Deep are the chasms of death
Steep are the steps between Heaven and Hell,
Many travel the road of life so death can ring its bell.

David Burgon (13)
All Hallows High School

THE WIND

Wind is like a thrashing whip
Sometimes fast
Sometimes slow
It will just blow and blow

Wind is sometimes cold
Wind is sometimes hot
Wind will sometimes blow leaves off trees
And other times it will not.

Matthew Kellett (14)
All Hallows High School

GLITTERING, RING OF GLITTER, DEEP SHIMMER OF ICY BLUE

As I look up into the dark night sky
I see a thousand silver glittering stars
Shining back at me,
Like crystals they glint in deep shimmering blue.
I look further into that huge piece of gaping space
And what do I see?
I see multicoloured balls,
A blazing, raging inferno of fire
And rings of glitter, a solar system.
Shooting stream of light, glittering bright,
Is a shooting star shining in the night.
Flying through the dark, faster than light,
Everything seems so bright
Then into the dark
I plunge into a pool of everlasting dark,
Everything swirling, sucked into a glittering hole.
Then I look back and see a thousand silver
Glittering stars glittering, glittering, glittering . . .

Nicholas Jackson (11)
All Hallows High School

A PUTT FOR A WIN

As I tee off,
I stand to the ball with confidence,
Swing back,
Swing through,
My ball shoots off like a speeding bullet . . .
Into a bunker!
Annoyed!
How am I going to get that little ball out?
Keep calm . . .
Head down . . .
Swing back,
Swing through . . . onto the green.
I have this five-foot putt for a win.
I stand to the ball,
I take my putter back and through
Like a swinging pendulum.
Yes! . . . I hole the putt!
I win the championship!

Jenny Rainford (13)
All Hallows High School

DREAM FLIGHT

Soaring high, waving the world goodbye,
Feeling free,
Feeling alive.
Wind blowing through my hair,
Wondering what it's like back there.
It's turning dark,
I must return,
Back to where I sleep unturned.

Louise Mooney (13)
All Hallows High School

SPRINTING

Zooming, slipping, gliding through the air,
Moving, running, skipping fast around.
The school we go past.
I go fast, they go fast.
I know I won't be the very last.

We do cross country, but I like sprinting,
I know one day I'll be going round the country.
I run down the road and go past the church,
And I stop and have a little lurch.

Looking left, and looking right,
I must take care when traffic's in sight.
I mustn't forget the green cross code
I'm about to cross the road.
I'm nearly there, I'm nearly back,
I've done my best, so I'm gonna hit the sack.

Kelly Barnes (11)
All Hallows High School

GETTING OUT OF BED IN THE MORNING

I hear my mum
Shouting, 'Get out of bed.'
I snuggle the covers over my head.
I hear my mum coming up the stairs.
I suddenly jump out of bed and hide behind the door.
When my mum comes in,
I scare her and rush downstairs
To where my breakfast is sitting
Waiting to be eaten.

Hannah Whittaker (12)
All Hallows High School

IN MY IMAGINATION

In my imagination I can go anywhere I like.
I can to up into space,
I can go to a magical land,
I can go back how far I like.

In my imagination I can be anything I want.
I can be a butterfly with glorious wings,
I can be a nightingale with a sweet voice,
I can be a dolphin in the deepest oceans.

In my imagination I can see anything I like.
I can see beautiful cocoons opening,
I can see brilliant kingfishers perching,
I can see sleek killer whales swimming.

In my imagination I can hear anything I want.
I can hear the waves clashing in the wild seas,
I can hear birds singing on a spring morning,
I can hear the voice of silence,
I can hear exciting music,
Just in my imagination.

Katie Campbell (12)
All Hallows High School

THE BEACH

Blue beach waves,
Crashing on the sand,
With the sun and seagulls above our heads.

People eating picnics pleasantly,
In the company of the blue, beach waves.

Swimming in the sea,
Sunbathing in the sun,
Eating with the seagulls,
And playing in the sand.

I am at the beach.

Kimberley McBride (11)
All Hallows High School

MY BODY

People say my blood is red
I say it's green

People say my bones are white
I say they're pink

People say my liver is grey
I say it's yellow

People say my eyes are brown
I say they're orange

People say my skin is white
I say it's blue

People say that I'm not normal
But I say I'm normal, are you?

Sarah Bartoli (11)
All Hallows High School

BULLIES

Mean, nasty, must be cold-hearted
Why are they here, we should be parted.

They've got minds of disgrace
Get them out of this place!

Just why, just why do they do it?

Rough, tough and nobody's friend
I don't think this will ever end.

Spiteful, teasing
Always pleasing themselves
But nobody else.

Just why, just why do they do it?

Robyn Pulvertaft (11)
All Hallows High School

HALLOWE'EN

H aunting Hallowe'en comes round again
A s children set out to scare.
L ots of money and
L ots of sweets as
O ur neighbours give out the treats.
W itches, devils and wicked beasts
E veryone's dressed to look the piece.
E veryone creeps from house to house
N obody knows who will turn up next.

Katie Newall (13)
All Hallows High School

OLD JOHNNY CLARK

He slowly walked through the park
But for all he knew he was in the dark
He had a dog and a blind man's stick
But for him the dog was walking too quick

He arrived at his old tatty council house
The phone sat there as quiet as a mouse
He hated himself, he hated life
He wished he had back his loving wife

The next day he didn't walk through the park
But anyway, who cared about old Johnny Clark?

Anthony Bird (11)
All Hallows High School

STARLIGHT

Stars are for gazing at,
in the night sky.
Stars are so sparkly,
their beauty shines around.
Stars are out there,
they are watching us.
Stars are guarding us,
while we're snuggled up in bed.

Ciara Sholl (11)
All Hallows High School

MY GRANDAD

My grandad was like a big brother to me
He liked all nature and all living things
He had a BMW and let me sit in the front
He would take me into town and ask me
To pick some sweets
I hope you are kinder towards your
Grandparents because you only get one chance!
For my grandad is no longer with me.

Thomas Griffiths (11)
All Hallows High School

DROPLETS OF WATER

Droplets of water trickling down,
Droplets of water make me frown,
Down from the sky is where they fall,
Racing down strong and tall.

As the precious droplets fly,
High up in the sky,
Dripping off the green leaves,
In the cold wintry breeze.

These droplets are made of H_2O,
They crash down fast and slow,
Each one a different size,
Falling there in front of your eyes.

When the droplets begin to tumble,
And the bees begin to bumble,
When the sun beams through the rain,
This whole cycle begins again.

Meera Gohil (12)
All Saints Catholic College

MY MOONLIGHT MARE

Your slender body I see,
running through the mist of the meadow;
With delicate strides,
you strut towards me;
Your golden mane close behind you flows,
and your eyes suit well the name I have chosen.

My moonlight mare is with me now,
yet only in my dreams.
But long awaited is the night,
when my moonlight, will in my dreams come,
Then not just vanish at the rise of the sun.
I know deep in my heart that this will never be.

My moonlight mare, will always have a meadow inside of me!

Alice McGreevy (11)
All Saints Catholic College

FAST CARS!

F earless racers rev up their engines at the start, an air of
A nticipation fills the pits and the stands, the
S tart!
T he cars fly down the track as they pile into the first

C orner, then round the track as the cars jockey for
A position
R acing oh yes, the home
S traight. The winner is praised, the loser is dazed in a tyre wall.

Carmine Circelli (12)
All Saints Catholic College

THE DEVIL'S TALE

It was a dark and misty night,
I was in the garden.
I heard a rustling sound
In the bushes.
I went to investigate -

Suddenly a dog-like creature
Hit me from behind.
The creature had a brilliant grip.
His red eyes were glowing.
It was slavering and foaming at the mouth.
It was growling at me.

Suddenly I thought it was
A black hound who had come to
Take me to the devil.
Baring its teeth,
It had black shaggy fur.
It grabbed me by the neck.
I felt a cold shiver
Falling down my spine.

Suddenly the ground opened up.
I fell down with the dog-like creature.
I saw flames all around me.
I went to him.
He threw me into a deep dark tunnel.

Joseph Greenhalgh (13)
All Saints Catholic College

HALLOWE'EN NIGHT

On a very dark night
You're guaranteed a fright
Witches cackling
Ghosts moaning
Cauldrons bubbling

Children watch out
Monster about
Tricks and treats
Lots of sweets

Pumpkins clattering
Children's feet pattering
Scary night
Very big fright

Candy snacks
Broomstick snaps
Devil's night only
Till light.

Scott Texeira (13)
All Saints Catholic College

A SPECIAL NIGHT

There is a special night in October.
It comes one time in each year,
Witches, werewolves and vampires.
Kids dressing as monsters
And shouting 'Trick or treat'
At a door and getting candy.
This night is called Hallowe'en.

Darren Clay (12)
All Saints Catholic College

THE NIGHT

Howling was the wind,
Bouncing was the rain,
The night was so scary scary scary
Scary as could be.
It's found me,
It's found me, its hands all big and furry.
Oh it's my teddy bear.
The night was so scary scary scary,
Scary as could be.
Banging was the door,
Footsteps on the floor,
Oh it's morning, morning, morning, morning.
Morning is cheerful.

Martin Howard (12)
All Saints Catholic College

THE HALLOWE'EN POEM

One misty night, October 31st
A lot of noise and a lot of kids.
More sweets than you've ever seen,
And a witch like a horrible queen.
You've never seen nor smelt
Anything like this before.

The devils will be out at midnight
With their ghosts and witches.
The witches will have black cats
And devils with black hats on.
I see a black cat chasing and eating a black bat.

Patrick Manley (12)
All Saints Catholic College

THE WITCHES

Witches fly around in the sky,
Looking for people who will die,
On the back of a broom is a black cat,
The witch wears a pointed hat.

They make up spells,
And horrible smells,
They use toes, fingers, noses and bones,
And all in powerful tones.

Witches have green faces,
Some, different races,
They have square toes,
As well as a pointed nose.

They find their supper,
Who pray it will all be over,
They suck out people's lives,
Of husbands, children and wives.

Witches come from everywhere,
Looking for people to tear,
As all the witches disappear,
People have nothing left to fear.

Katie Aylett (12)
All Saints Catholic College

MY BROTHER THE ALIEN

My new brother's an alien,
And soon you'll find out why,
My Mum was on a stroll one day,
And he fell from the sky.

He has a long green spiky tail,
And one big beady eye,
Along with two gigantic ears,
He has learnt how to fly.

He has no table manners,
For he eats food with his nose,
He is too big for a bathtub,
And so uses a hose.

So he's my little brother,
My little alien friend,
And we are hoping that he won't
Return back to the sky.

Ciaran Crombie (12)
All Saints Catholic College

SNAKES!

Snakes slimy, wriggling everywhere,
With their forked tongues hissing in and out.
Cobras standing up straight,
Pythons squeezing their prey,
Adders injecting venom into their prey.

Andrew Wareham (12)
All Saints Catholic College

HALLOWE'EN

Spooks, freaks, ghouls,
Hallowe'en is really cool.

As midnight strikes,
Get ready for a real fright.

Spooks, freaks, ghouls,
Hallowe'en is really cool.

All the ghouls come out to play,
They all disappear during the day.

Spooks, freaks, ghouls,
Hallowe'en is really cool.

They make people scream,
Who hope it's all a dream.

Spooks, freaks, ghouls,
Hallowe'en is really cool.

As dawn draws near,
All the ghouls start to fear.

Spooks, freaks, ghouls,
Hallowe'en is really cool.

As all the ghouls disappear,
People have nothing left to fear.

Heather Wilshaw (12)
All Saints Catholic College

BIG BAD BROTHERS

Big bad brothers,
In my room all the time,
Big bad brothers,
Why does he have to be mine?

Big bad brothers,
He says he'll pay me back,
Big bad brothers,
Please give me some slack!

Big bad brothers,
Plays practical jokes on me,
Big bad brothers,
Why is it always me!

Big bad brothers
Stealing my things all the time
Big bad brothers
He made my eye shine.

Joe Kowaltschuk (13)
All Saints Catholic College

THE OCEAN

Dolphins swim in the deep,
On the bottom turtles sleep,
Crabs crawl and seagulls fall,
Searching for food,
Whales in a happy mood,
Penguins dive,
The eels are alive.
      The ocean.

Jennifer McCall (11)
All Saints Catholic College

SCHOOL SUBJECTS!

French is boring,
So it maths,
Art is creative,
And music is class.

IT is interesting,
It is fun to do,
But I don't like woodwork,
Because I get covered in glue.

English is great,
German is brill,
Geography is good,
But PE is skill.

Kelly Whiteside (12)
All Saints Catholic College

WITCH'S SUPPER

Witch's spells,
Dong of bells,
Wing of a bat,
Tail of a rat,
Woof of a dog,
Stench of a bog,
Look of grime,
Sin of a crime,
Look of soup,
Tastes like puke!

Katrina Booth (12)
All Saints Catholic College

Trick Or Treat, Pumpkin Pie ...

Trick or treat, pumpkin pie,
Ghosts shout *boo!* And witches fly.
It's a full moon tonight, the children are scared.
They're out trick or treating, and sweeties are shared.

Trick or treat, pumpkin pie, ghosts shout *boo!*
And witches fly.
The children are in costume, they all look really good.
Werewolves howl, witches cackle and
Vampires drip with blood.
Trick or treat, pumpkin pie,
Ghosts shout *boo!* and
Witches fly ...

Lindsay Bryce (13)
All Saints Catholic College

Ghost

G ruesome ghouls
   from the grave

H aunted houses
   in the hills

O ooooo! is the
   spooky sound they make

S cary spirits in
   the sky

T errible creatures
   of the night.

Jenny Lowe (13)
All Saints Catholic College

THE WITCH

On Hallowe'en night
She makes her flight
Down to the old dark house

She takes out her book
To take a look
At the spells which transform a mouse

She then goes out upon her broom
To spread her doom and gloom
Oh no! She's over my house!

She'll probably watch you
For she's nothing to do
So beware if you see a black mouse!

Katie Jones (12)
All Saints Catholic College

I HATE WITCHES

I hate witches.
I hate their tall pointed hats,
I hate their wicked black cats.
I hate their cauldron that smells,
And I hate their stupid silly spells.
I hate witches.

Heather Turner (12)
All Saints Catholic College

WENDY WAS A WITCH

I once knew a witch named Wendy,
I knew she was a witch because
My grandma told me so!
I saw the purple gleam in her eyes,
Oh Wendy was a witch all right!
Once, although she doesn't know it,
I saw her wig fall off.
Her head was bald, just like it should be.
Yes, Wendy was a witch all right!
Once, in the dark of the night,
I crept into her house,
I pulled off her bed covers,
And saw her square feet with no toes,
Oh Wendy was a witch all right!

Frances Powrie (12)
All Saints Catholic College

HALLOWE'EN

H allowe'en
A ll the scary witches' stories
L ikely to be scared with a full moon
L oveable children trick 'n' treating in scary masks
O h! Don't say boo, I get scared to death
W e'll be chased by the pumpkin head
E ating the inside of the pumpkin after making it light
E verybody is scared on Hallowe'en
N obody gets away without twitches from the witches.

Patrick Jones (12)
All Saints Catholic College

CREATION

God created a place called Earth,
He gave us humans, our birth.
He made the Earth, the sea and sky,
He taught the birds how to fly.

He created a vast amount of land,
He did it all with his own hands.
He created mammals, fish and birds,
He created lots of wonderful words.

He made man to live in this place,
He put the planets into space.
We should treat this world with care,
Because we haven't got a spare!

Claire Pollitt (13)
All Saints Catholic College

BONFIRE NIGHT

Hooray, hooray it's Bonfire Night,
The fire is burning so bright.
Crowds of people standing around,
Noisy children making lots of sound.
The fireworks are nice, red, blue and green,
The brightest fireworks I've ever seen.
The people are all wrapped up,
It's the cold autumn air,
All they can do is stand and stare.
Balls of colour and flashing light,
Orange and yellow, oh so bright.
Now the dead fireworks are left alone,
All the people have gone home.

Joanne Meakin (12)
All Saints Catholic College

MUSIC

Music.
Is it classical, folk or pop?
Or is it the Spice girls singing 'Stop?'
It could be Five getting down
Or Pavarotti singing out loud.
It might be 911 or even Space
Maybe it's Steps dancing with a pace.
When I hear music, I can't sit still
Because music like pop, gives me a thrill.
Whatever it is, dance along
'Cause there's nothing like a good old song.

Kelly's favourite music is probably rap,
Her foot always goes tap, tap, tap.
Matthew's favourite music is definitely rock
Dancing away, around the clock.
My favourite music always has class,
Especially when I roll over the grass!

Nikki Daniels (13)
Bridgewater High School

ROSEMARY, THAT'S FOR REMEMBRANCE

Rosemary, that's for remembrance
For when my dog died
Rosemary, that's for remembrance
For when my brother got married
Rosemary, that's for remembrance
For when I got my pony
Rosemary, that's for remembrance
For when my grandad died
Rosemary. That's for remembrance.

Rosie Grensinger (11)
Bridgewater High School

FRIENDS

Friends are a wonderful thing
They're very kind and helpful
They're always there for you
Whatever happens
To talk to or even share things
They can be big or little
Strong or weak
Chubby or skinny
Black or white
Don't treat them differently
Treat them like you want to be treated
As a friend.

David Jones (11)
Bridgewater High School

WAR!

Why do we fight?
We fight for our freedom
We fight for our lives
We fight for each other
We fight for our leader
We fight for our family
We fight
We battle
We kill
Who wins?

Ben Mellers (13)
Bridgewater High School

GLUTONOUS GOBBLING GRUB I LOVE . . .

I love cake,
I make it,
I bake it,
I also love biscuit.

I love sweets,
They are treats,
Bonbons I love to eat.

Ice-cream,
Of I dream,
To the extreme.

Cherries make me merry,
As do berries.

Jasmin Brady (11)
Bridgewater High School

FEAR

Fear is here getting weird
Going around in my head,
Bouncing around in my bed.
Never leaving, never stops,
I'm going to call the cops.
When I call the cops
There's nothing here,
It's all stopped.
So now I know why people fear
The all night fear.

David Lloyd (13)
Bridgewater High School

ODD SHOELACES

Me   I was worried about going to school,
I would be the odd one out,
The only one with odd shoelaces,
(Tut, *hummph*) without a doubt.

Mum   'No one will look at your shoes love.'
'I look at others all the time,
Nelson has Bootleg, Martin has Kickers
And Fred's are the same as mine.'

Me   'Can we drive to school today Mum?
We never go in the car.'
Mum   'Walking is good exercise love,
And school isn't really that far.'

Me   We are walking up to school now
I really do not like this.
I know, I thought, I know what I'll do
I'll tie my laces like Chris.

Me   So down I went on one knee,
And tucked my laces under my heel.
Oh no I thought, that still won't do
This just can't be real!

Me   I walked into school neat and smart,
Well I was apart from my laces.
Teacher 'Come on children drama time,
Shoes off and sit in your places.'

Me   Drama was a bit of a relief,
The rest of the lessons went OK too,
But no one did notice my shoelaces,
So let's just say it's a secret between me and you.

Holly Quin-Ankrah (11)
Bridgewater High School

FRIENDS

Friends are very important
And they care for you
Friends are very helpful
And they look after you

Friends are very loyal
And they don't lie about you
Friends are very kind
And they don't steal from you

Friends you couldn't live without
And they will protect
Friends are very good to gossip with
And won't gossip about you.

Friends are good to talk to
About things that are private
Friends are very reliable
And they invite you to things they do

Are you a good friend?

Hazel Jane Thomas (12)
Bridgewater High School

THE MOON, THE STARS AND MARS

The moon is a silver sphere, in an ebony space.
Some people say that the moon has a face.
Around the moon are twinkling diamonds, called Stars.
There are lots of them around the planet Mars,
The planet Mars is big and red.
'I am an alien from Mars,' a boy once said.

Samantha C Smythe (12)
Bridgewater High School

RUGBY

Rugby is the game for boys
it keeps us trim and fit
we play our matches on Sundays
and with pride we wear our kit.

Woolston Rovers wear yellow and greens
we start our matches looking new
The whistle blows, we kick the ball
before we know it we have muddy knees.

Tackling is the name of the game
we try to take the lead
we run the ball in hard and strong
a win is what we need.

Ben Fawcett (11)
Bridgewater High School

IN THE GARDEN

In the garden
A world of moss
So soft and green
A world of insects
Crawling all over me
A world of grass
So long it comes to my knees
A world of trees
As tall as houses
Oh what a world that we live in!

Hannah Gibson (13)
Bridgewater High School

FOOTBALL FEVER

The game's between Liverpool and Manchester United
People who got the tickets are all delighted
The whistle's blown, Beckham's got the ball
The subs wish they were playing, don't we all?
The ball's passed to Giggs
What are the crowd doing, they're acting like pigs
Giggs is coming up to score, will he? He missed!
Liverpool cheered and kissed
Redknapp on the ball now
He's blocked, no he's not, he can still get it past
He passes to Owen, he's got the ball, I must say he's not very tall
But wait, he's going to score, Schmeichel out of the net and it's a goal!
We have to see that again, the way it flew through the air
and hit the pole
Half-time, one-nil to Liverpool
They've had their tea and biscuits which isn't very cool
Giggs is back on the ball, but I've just noticed he's rather titch
Passed to McManaman, he's running down the pitch
Will it be a miracle? Yes he's scored!
The whistle blows for the end of the game
The crowd go wild and there is a magnificent roar.

Justina Bridge (13)
Bridgewater High School

FIREWORKS

I am no fool,
But I bent the rules.
My name was Fred,
But now I am dead.
I played with fireworks,
And then they blew off my head.

Helen Whitehead (13)
Bridgewater High School

A FORGOTTEN CHILD

A forgotten child,
A lone refugee
Walking the road
Of wasted dreams.

War to a child
Is like an endless dream,
An endless hell
Of broken glass
Reflecting a perfect
Life it seems.

Being chased is like a game
An evil game with many
Losers and loss of life.

They'll all be a forgotten child,
A young loner in this world of fear.
Don't allow the evils of this world
Harm a little child.

Michael P Stevens (13)
Bridgewater High School

SISTER, SISTER

Sister, sister, I love you,
You're always there when I need you,
You're kind and gentle,
Clever and smart,
And always so kind of heart,
I'll love you always, you know that's true,
Sister, I love you!

Rachel Harvey (11)
Bridgewater High School

WHAT A LIFE!

I've travelled more than a mile today,
Within this cage of wire,
I get bashed around from side to side,
I wish I could retire.

I get served at ninety miles per hour,
Onto a tarmac floor,
I'm bruised and cut all over,
Cruelty's against the law!

My friends have been on live TV,
They play a vital part,
Our furry, yellow coats we wear,
Really do look smart.

Sometimes they spin me round and round,
I do get rather ill,
Once they left me out all night,
I nearly caught a chill.

I don't deserve all this,
No one cares at all,
I'm lost, hit and thrown about,
It's hard being a tennis ball.

Helen Thompson (13)
Bridgewater High School

MEN!

Who can ever rely on men?
For example my last husband's name was Ken.
Well Ken was bright and always looked smart,
He never was late and looked the part.
But something unusual happened one day,
My Ken got stuck in a traffic delay!
Dearest Ken was travelling west,
For that's the way he travelled best.
He was going to collect me from the station,
Because I had a very important invitation.
My invitation was to a ball,
Where little infants would play and crawl.
My poor Ken knew he was going to be late,
As it was already half past eight.
That night I was too late for the ball,
So I got a bus home from Tatten Hall.
Later that night I switched on the news,
On and on, it was talking about two fools.
Until it started to talk about Ken,
He had jumped into the Mersey, oh poor Ken!

Katrina Patrick (13)
Bridgewater High School

THE OLD MAN FROM SPAIN

There was an old man from Spain
Who was in a lot of pain
So he went to the doctor
Whose name was Mike Foster
Who discovered he had swallowed a chain.

Jonathan Butterworth (12)
Bridgewater High School

DON'T YOU JUST HATE IT . . .?

Don't you just hate it when your parents say No?
No to going out,
No to those special trainers,
No to anything you want.
No, No, No!

Don't you just hate it when you can't choose yourself?
No vote,
No decision,
No voice,
No, No, No!

Don't you just hate it when your age won't fit?
No, you're too young,
No, you're too tall,
No, you can't drive.
No, No, No!

Don't you just hate it when there's nowhere to go?
No disco,
No youth club,
No cinema,
No, No, No!

Don't you just hate it . . . No!

Katie Lang (12)
Bridgewater High School

ALL IN A DAY'S WORK!

Today I went to Marbury Park
But I didn't get home before it was dark!
Or to be truthful I never got home at all
People have still seen me here at fall!

Through winters of cold snow,
I have camped here all nights,
Where foxes and badgers roam,
And I got frozen to the bone!

So now you see
It's not just me,
I really have been here.
If you dare, come near!

Helen Broughton (11)
Bridgewater High School

THE GIPADORE

The gipadore is the most amazing of creatures,
Its gigantic tail, its scaly features.
Its sharp toenails, its giant claws,
(Which were not made for everyday chores).
The way it wraps around its prey,
Would you like to meet him night or day?
His nimble limbs, he's muscle-bound,
When he's here things don't hang around.
If this creature is giving you the flinches,
Did I tell you he has a height of two inches!

Mark Rowley (11)
Bridgewater High School

MY NAME POEM!

K enny is my name,
   karaoke is my game.
E xtremely funny
   and soft as a bunny.
N intendo 64
   lover, you'll never
   get me under
   the cover!
N eighbour friendly,
   that's me!
Y esterday was in
   the past, tomorrow
   will come very fast.

L oves playing football,
   why don't you give
   me a call?
O riginality is me,
   Hey, have you got
   my key?
M ags are oh so cool,
   but not as good
   as pool.
A lways playing pool,
   it is really cool.
S leek as a panther,
   sly as a fox.

Kenneth Lomas (11)
Bridgewater High School

Name Poem

P aul's my name
and football's my game
A lways doing homework
not!
U nusual
organisation
habits
L oves to eat
chocolate eclairs

H ates doing
history
O n and off
goes the television
L ikes to go
rollerblading
M akes *eggcellent* eggs
on toast
E xcellent at getting
away with murder
S uperb sense
of humour.

Paul Holmes (11)
Bridgewater High School

IT'S NOT FAIR!

Every day I know you'll be there,
Why pick on me, it's just not fair,
What did I ever do to you?
Is it just because I am new?

I can't tell anyone how unhappy I feel,
I try to convince myself it's not a big deal,
You'd just beat me up even more,
If I happened to knock on the staff room door.

Will this nightmare ever end?
Why won't you just be my friend?
You do loads of things like steal my stuff
But that in itself is bad enough.

Every day I know you'll be there,
Why pick on me, it's just not fair.

Joanna Tosh (13)
Bridgewater High School

ROSEMARY THAT'S FOR REMEMBRANCE

I remember me and my friends talking softly over the birds.
I remember me and my friends walking quietly across the playground.
I remember me and my friends hanging out with each other
                                                at weekends.
I remember me and my friends being kind to each other
                                        when we were feeling down.
I remember me and my friends falling out and then feeling upset.
I remember things now, now they don't seem true. Life is changing
                                                as we get older
But I remember!

Kate Hackett (11)
Bridgewater High School

THE FIGURE

Among the heaps of scrapped metal,
Behind the wooden fence,
The figure stands in the shadows,
Like a star in its surrounding darkness,
He makes a sudden, silent move,
Like a cat on a gatepost,
Away from the shadows and up the mountain of scraps,
There he stands in all his glory,
Like an owl ready to take flight,
As the dust settles to reveal a starry sky,
There is an empty space where he used to be,
And all that is left is a memory.

Jenny Catterall (11)
Bridgewater High School

BRIDGEWATER

B rilliant facilities
R ugby training is great
I   t has its own library
D rama Club is superb
G reat technology lessons
E nglish is good as well
W onderful merit system
A lways getting new ideas
T errific with art
E xcitement in PE
R aring to go.

Daniel Davidson (11)
Bridgewater High School

IT'S NOT FAIR

My younger sister
Gets every treat.
People always say
'Oh she is so sweet.'

My younger sister
Is really cute.
My mum says it's
Because she eats fruit.

My younger sister
Is wearing a very nice dress.
She's always neat and tidy
And never in a mess.

My younger sister
Has curly golden hair.
So I always say
It's not fair!

Helen Smith (12)
Bridgewater High School

PEACE

To every face a smile,
To every clock a hand,
To every man an ambition,
To every ruler a land,
To every country a leader,
To every world, peace.

Michael Hackney (11)
Bridgewater High School

POEM ABOUT FOOTBALL

Old King Cole has scored a goal
He's scored a goal has he.
Myhre dived and hit the post
Cole jumped about in glee.

Cantona runs and trips over Myhre and kicks Cole
in the head
'Oh no' says Myhre 'I don't believe it.
Andy Cole is dead.'

They had the funeral there and then.
They buried Cole in the pitch.
Problem is now Old Trafford
Has a great big ditch.

Alex Smith (13)
Bridgewater High School

MY FISHY LOVE LIFE

The humble fish,
Is such a dish,
It flirts with all the crabs.
It walks right by,
With its skirt up high,
And winks while eating kebabs.

The sharks flirt too,
But not with crabs,
They like a bit of whale.
After a hard day swimming,
And eating,
They come home to love mail.

Gareth Roberts (13)
Bridgewater High School

FRANKENSTEIN'S MONSTER

Made by man, from others' parts.
He has strength,
As well as feelings.
His skin, as green as grass,
His face, is covered in scars,
His hair, black as coal.
He lives alone,
No friends at all.
His master gone,
No one to care.

Being lonely,
Makes him mad.
The madness turns to anger.
Then he goes on the rampage,
Destroying anything in his path.
People flee in all directions,
Just to get out of the monster's way.
Then he returns home lonely as ever,
After his anger's passed!

Daniel Lindsay (13)
Bridgewater High School

TO OUR SUPERVISOR

Here lies our dear supervisor.
Whose last drink was a bottle of Budweiser.
He died in the pub,
With his bottle of Bud.
I think Coke would have been wiser.

Nicola Payne (11)
Bridgewater High School

FLUTE

When you're feeling lonely and sad,
Turn to your flute, it isn't bad,
'Cause when you play that sweet mellow tune,
You'll be happy very soon.

When you feel you want to yell,
Play your flute and play it well,
Practise every day and night,
And it will turn out just right.

When I see that long silver shine,
I know the flute is definitely mine,
I always rub it to look its best,
So it looks better than all the rest.

Without my flute I would be sad,
Without my flute I would be bad,
What would I do without my flute?
I would miss its lovely toot.

I love to have my flute to hold,
To me it is more precious than gold,
It's the best thing since sliced bread,
When I play, nice thoughts are in my head.

I think I'll always keep my flute,
And remember its first toot,
Where would I be without you,
Without you for a teacher what would I do?

My flute teacher gives excellent advice,
Because she is both kind and nice,
She is the best person of all,
Without Mrs F, I would fall.

Felicity Webb (11)
Bridgewater High School

ON THE PHONE

As soon as I get home
I phone my friend.
My parents think
I am going round the bend.

'You've had all day to chatter,
Do you have to phone?
Does it really matter?'
They sigh.
'Of course it does'
I reply.

When I phone my friend
The phonecall
Goes on and on
And never seems to end.

When my parents
Get the bill
They go
Very white
And very still!

Holly Louise Jones (12)
Bridgewater High School

A WHITE LIE

I'm burning up like a fire,
I feel as warm as toast,
I'm burning, burning like some wood,
On a bonfire in the night.

My mother says it's just a cold,
I'm sure she must be wrong.
I should be like a Viking bold,
And maybe sing a song.

I'd warble like a singing bird,
But it would come out like a crack,
She wouldn't hear a lark on high,
But more a lowly toad.

Panna Malik (13)
Bridgewater High School

THE TIGER

The last flash of the tiger's smile
The last flick of the sun-kissed tail
The last blink of the diamond eyes
The last heartbeat under the black, blue sky
The sharp loud bang as the bullet is freed
The piercing sound the beast falls to his knees
His last proud roar of anger of pride
The poacher saunters over and takes his hide
This magnificent beast's life is just for a hide
Now he lies inside his eyes sad but proud
None seem to know he was once a glittering beast
Now he's just a rug on the hard stone floor
No heart to tell his story just his eyes so proud, so sore
They follow you round the room
They've faded now, they're not so bright
But they'll always have the glow of the safari
The freedom of the plains
But the thing I remember most
Something still proud and wise
In the dim dark night sky of the plains
Is the look in the pair of the gold-flecked eyes.

Jenny Owens (14)
Bridgewater High School

MY PET HENRY

Henry was my pet,
But I never took him to the vet.
I said one day to my mum,
'Mum he's really dumb,
Can I take him out one day?
I'll promise I'll pay.'
That day I took him to the zoo,
And was nearly eaten by a kangaroo.
Henry saw a fly,
And was stood on by a guy,
He instantly died,
With me by his side.
That poor piece of fluff,
Looked sad enough,
Just sitting on my pillow.
I've never had a piece of fluff,
Like my pet Henry.

Claire Bridger (13)
Bridgewater High School

FOOD

Food, food it's all I eat,
I'll eat it with my feet.
Food is yummy in your tummy,
Chocolate's fun especially in your tum.
Food, food if I'm in the mood,
Food is great on your plate.
Banana sarni is better than salami,
My favourite of all is Pepperami.

Emma Moorcroft (14)
Bridgewater High School

MY PASSION

Chocolate.
If chocolate was a person it would be my
best friend.
Chocolate gives me comfort.
It never lets me down.
Chocolate cheers me up.
It never makes me frown.

Chocolate.
If chocolate was a garment I'd wear it
all the time.
Chocolate is smooth and silky.
It feels nice on my skin.
Chocolate makes me feel good,
Especially from within.

Beth Isherwood (13)
Bridgewater High School

FRIENDS

Friends are such wonderful things to have,
They're there to support you through good and through bad.
They're there to help you have a good time,
They give you a shoulder when you need to cry.
They'll pick you up when you fall down,
They'll take you to discos and a shop around town.
They'll tell you their problems, when you tell them yours,
And they'll talk to you when you do your chores.
They'll make you laugh when you are sad,
They don't mind if sometimes you're bad.
In fact a friend is just what you need
But be a friend back or else they'll leave!

Amie Bennett-Price (13)
Bridgewater High School

REFLECTIONS

I looked in the pond and what did I see?
A gently moving reflection of me
I passed by a window earlier today
And saw someone like me walking my way

On sunny days I have a close friend
Who follows behind 'til I go round a bend
She copies my movements, but she's darker than I
She's a gift from the fiery ball in the sky

Reflections are seen in many places
If we look in a mirror we will see our faces
But reflections don't show what we're like inside
They are only images behind which we can hide.

Abigail Thompson (12)
Bridgewater High School

HALLOWE'EN

Vampires and toads and pumpkin pie,
Witches that fly through the night sky,
Ghosts and ghouls that haunt a house,
Spiders and insects and a disgusting mouse,
This is a recipe for a good Hallowe'en,
This is a recipe for a good night's scream.

Put on a video and take a trip,
On a high tech, alien, freaky spaceship,
Go round a graveyard on a night's walk,
Listen to the owls and the way they talk,
Hallowe'en is a night full of terror,
Especially in the stormy weather . . .

Elizabeth Henshaw (13)
Bridgewater High School

AFTER THE BATTLE

Salem, the rebels' young major,
Had been wounded in the rush,
His troops, deserted from danger,
His leg snapped under the crush.

Oh, Cossette, left back in the camp,
The soldier's sweet, bonny daughter.
Her mother left only a lamp,
The lamp her grandmother bought her.

He lay wounded, a tear in each eye,
The twin tears of despair and loss,
For explosions shattered the sky
And surely, the camp, the cost.

He felt loss, for his beautiful daughter,
Hid in a tent in the camp,
The enemy must have caught her,
And stolen her beautiful lamp.

The lamp worth a sou to be sure,
But for that Salem did not care,
He wept for Cossette, 'til he saw
Her wonderful face in the air.

'Now Daddy, I am with the Lord,'
The fair phantom seemed to say,
'Soldiers took me to my reward,
And they, for their crimes, shall pay.'

All of a sudden, down from the sky,
Came a blinding flash of lightning.
Her final words, the phantom cried,
'Oh, Daddy, the tents are lighting!'

Peter Myall (13)
Bridgewater High School

MAN UTD VS JUVENTUS

The match started hopeful,
But quickly turned to trash,
In came Del Piero,
And our defence did he mash.

The crowd went wild,
When Sheringham leapt,
Then bounced the mighty header,
That Juve's keeper couldn't keep.

In the net again the ball went,
This time it was Scholes,
Then near the end,
Giggs began to make holes.

In the final minute,
Then came the breakthrough,
Giggsy got the ball,
And not even he knew,

That he would do a darting run,
And break into the box,
Unleashed an almighty shot,
And approached it like a fox.

The ball whizzed past the stranded keeper,
And flew into the net,
Juventus got a consolation,
A win they did not get.

Philip Galsaworthy (13)
Bridgewater High School

WHAT A DIFFERENCE A DAY CAN MAKE!

I've had a nice day
So I'm feeling rather gay.
A friend said 'You look happy,'
I said 'Thank you good chappy.'

I carried on walking down the street
I had pins and needles in my feet.
A man was robbing a grocery stall
He must have looked about six feet tall.

I shouted 'Oi you, stop!'
He panicked and said 'Oh no it's a cop!'
I pulled out my gun and shot him in the head,
Before he was down I knew he was dead.

The blood was draining from his body.
All I could think to say was sorry.
My head was full of thoughts of death
And that gunshot bang had made me deaf.

All went silent along the busy road.
You could hear the sound of a noisy toad.
I could feel the glaring eyes
I felt about two foot in size.

Daniel Peake (14)
Bridgewater High School

AFTER SCHOOL

When I get home from school
It is so cool
First I do my homework
Then I have some lemon curd
I like to phone my friends
The call never ends
I have to feed my rabbit
It's just a habit
I always watch TV
Even though it's not good for me
Every night I read my book
It's about a little duck
At last I go to bed
That's enough of using my head.

Hayley Banner (12)
Bridgewater High School

AIR

To air, we are blind but air is visible in movement,
Swishing, swirling through the seasoned leaves,
Air surrounds us everlasting,
Encasing us in a shell of respiration.

We take for granted what material keeps our heart beating,
We go for a 'breath of fresh air' but we have millions already around,
Air ripples through air, making anything in its path shiver,
With a force of kinetic energy showing with its whispers of breeze.

We feel it on our skin, every one of us.
Air considers temperature, air declares temperature.
The Earth lives for air, relies on the presence of mysterious cold.
Unpadlock the fiery wilderness of air and a twister of power will arrive.

Natalie Whewell (13)
Bridgewater High School

POP MUSIC

My poem is about pop music,
So get up and groove it,
When I listen to Five,
I buzz like a beehive,
When I listen to the Spice Girls,
I think that they're nice girls,
When I listen to B*Witched,
I dance and get a stitch,
When I listen to 911,
I think of a special someone,
When I listen to the Backstreet Boys,
I think of how I used to play
With all of my toys,
When I listen to Hanson,
My brother has a tantrum,
That is the end of my poem,
And don't you know it!

Lisa Parkinson (12)
Bridgewater High School

FIRST DAY AT SCHOOL

Nervous and anxious I stand.
Feeling lonely but excited,
Standing nervous but delighted.
The bell sounds, the day has begun,
Everyone moves but I am numb.
Friendly faces to show me the way,
Panic over I've started my day.
The school seems large, everything is new,
I have my book in front of me but what do I do?
The teacher talks to the class,
I sit and listen, should I ask?
Pen in hand, I start to write.
With different lessons, different rooms,
I hope it's completely right.
The bell sounds for the end of the day.
Everyone leaves so I say bye,
I'll come back tomorrow and have another try.

Christine Boardman (13)
Bridgewater High School

IN MEMORIAM

Where did you go?
Why did you leave?
You left me alone.
You left me to grieve.
And now I sit here,
Wondering what I should do.
Whatever I do,
I'm waiting for you.

Helen King (14)
Bridgewater High School

FOOTBALL MAD

Football is a funny game
And I don't know where it got its name
Its tactics can be very hard
And then you need defenders to guard.

It's a game with very skilful tactics
And a goalkeeper can do his silly antics
Strikers need to be ready for the ball
And then they also have to do their call.

The referees are a bit bad
And it can get me upset and very mad
They say things that are very wrong
Then they go off singing a jolly song.

Man Utd are the best
They can beat all the rest
Arsenal are the mighty Gunners
They never lose and are beautiful winners.

I love football and I am football mad
You may think I am very sad
But football, football
Is a beautiful game.

Andrew McDermott (13)
Bridgewater High School

THE PREDATORS AND THE PREY

Running swiftly through the long grass,
Making not a noise as it slips past the stalks,
Its slender body moving across the clearing,
Quickly, but with feline gracefulness.

The prey is in sight,
Stiff, back hunched,
Nose in the air, cautious,
And then it's gone, running towards the trees.

The predator has increased its pace,
Determined to do or die,
Hunter and hunted locked,
Locked in a deadly pursuit.

There is a watcher, peeking through the edge of the trees,
There is a click, and the sound of rustling,
A tube of metal emerges from behind a tree,
Following the predator in its chase.

The predator is gaining now,
Gaining on the prey,
Closer still, teeth bared,
Preparing for the pounce.

The predator increases its speed,
Jaws open, about to pounce,
It leaps . . .
Bang.

The predator smiles.

James Carter (12)
Bridgewater High School

THINGS I LIKE

Netball is a very good game,
Gym is very good too.
I like to swim
In pools of blue,
I like playing games,
Cards, board games and computer
On my Sega,
I try to go faster.
Flopsy my bunny,
Has a furry, silky coat.
Her ears flop down,
Which makes her look cute.
I like to listen to music
That is in the charts.
I can play the recorder and piano,
Especially my favourite parts.
I like reading Top of the Pops,
Eating sherbet,
Lots and lots!

Hayley Cox (12)
Hartford High School

THINGS I LIKE

I like swimming in the pool, diving,
We do art in school, painting, drawing.
I like dancing all the time, leaping across the room.
I like music.

Jodie Withnell (11)
Hartford High School

WHAT I CAN DO

As I swim, I glide through the waves,
as if I am a dolphin leaping,
singing a beautiful song,
or as if I am a graceful whale,
breaking the deep blue sea
with my huge tail.

As I do my gym, I leap like a bird
and do a cartwheel as quiet as a mouse,
just hearing the background bustle,
I can jump off the end of the beam
and pretend I am flying for miles,
with the wind in my face.

When I do my art I use the most
colourful colours ever,
which brighten up the room.
Then at the end of every lesson,
instead of a blank piece of paper,
I have an instant flash of colour
in my face.

Nicola Ruston (11)
Hartford High School

TODAY IS TUESDAY

Today is Tuesday, art to come,
English and maths, what fun.
Walking and talking to school,
We talk about our trip to the swimming pool.
At the weekends we go on bike rides,
Sometimes I watch rugby and people score tries.

Nicola Catherine Poole (11)
Hartford High School

A Poem Of A Cloudy And A Misty Day

The picture makes me feel like the day is uncalm,
like the uncalmness of a hurricane.
The picture has two people in it, a man and a woman.
The man seems to be drawing a picture of the scenery,
he's looking puzzled like an animal thinking
whether to run away from its predator or not.
The woman is waiting patiently
like a fluffy, white cloud in a endless sky.
The front of the boat is a dark, dull colour,
like the darkness of the night sky.
The sky has different shades of blue and speckles of white,
like a misty, cold day, the sea also looks rough, like broken glass.
The shape of the boat is like a banana, cut longways down.
The man's hands are clasped together,
like a pearl securely sealed in a shell.
The sound of the waves is like a little boy
playing on a quiet instrument.
The smell of the smoke from the buildings
is like a fire burning down.

Tiffany Mains (14)
Hartford High School

Rugby

R ugby is a sport,
U nder the posts we stand
G et on down to your nearest club.
B y putting the ball over the line you score,
Y ou get lots of pleasure playing rugby.

Chris Steele (12)
Hartford High School

THUNDERSTORM

T he orange sky turns blue and the pink clouds turn grey
H umidity fills the air,
U nder canal bridges the murky brown water swirls and crashes against
    the sides,
N earby, the thunder rumbles and roars through the towns and villages,
D anger and fear fill everyone's minds,
E verlasting howls and the whistle of the wind in the trees,
R umble after rumble gets louder and louder, at last the storm is here.
S cary and shaking, the unstoppable storm reaches its peak,
T hunderbolts race through the sky,
O verhead the lightning makes windows vibrate,
R aging through the summer night sky,
M ild, cool air seeps through the sky, finally the storm is over.

Rebecca Mitchell (11)
Hartford High School

A POEM ABOUT THINGS I ENJOY DOING

I enjoy riding my bike in the park,
But when it gets dark
I go home.
But it doesn't stop there
I don't despair,
I play on the CD ROM.
Then the very next day
I go out and play
And go swimming with my friends.
I do the back stroke, front crawl
And play with a ball
And then go down the water slide *Wheee!*
Plop!

Constance Baker (11)
Hartford High School

A THUNDERSTORM

Darkness falls
The humidity rises
It begins to meet cold
It starts to make chaos
Stormy rain clouds gather overhead
An atom is split
The heavens explode

An electric charge lights up the sky
Monstrous booms are heard all around
The wind starts to blow like a howling wolf
The rain comes down from a bottomless bucket
For hours and hours the storm creates havoc
And still the anger carries on

Suddenly the bucket gets empty
The golden sun comes out with pride
The electricity runs out
The booms just vanish
And the sky becomes peaceful once more.

Andrew Morgan (11)
Hartford High School

MY FAVOURITE THINGS

My biggest treat is a number five
To be at McDonald's is to be really alive
Large fries and Coke
Make me laugh better than any joke
I have been to many a fast food place
But a Big Mac is the only meal to fill my face.

Pearl Shallcross (11)
Hartford High School

I LIKE . . .

I love reading,
Books are . . .
Exciting,
Sometimes funny.
I like writing
Funny stories,
Imaginative stories,
Practising handwriting.
I love swimming,
Doing . . .
Backstroke,
Breast stroke,
Over arm,
And messing about.
I really like watching TV,
I like to watch . . .
Home and Away,
Neighbours,
EastEnders,
Coronation Street,
And Changing Rooms.
I like drawing,
Cartoon characters,
Landscapes,
Doodles of funny animals.

Jenny Clarke (12)
Hartford High School

THROUGH THAT DOOR

Through that door my dreams come true,
Marshmallow land is in view.
Bouncing up on the mushy hills,
Getting lots and lots of thrills.

Through that door all I see,
The fresh green plants looking at me.
Trees growing up to the sky,
It's so amazing I think I could fly.

Through that door I see the key,
The key in my fantasy.
Shining, shimmering in the sun,
I think my dream has just begun.

Through that door the sun shimmers,
In the lake the water glimmers.
Suddenly *clap!* What a fright.
My dream has come to an end.

Claire Darbyshire (12)
Hartford High School

WHAT I LIKE DOING

Art, art makes me want to start,
drawing all those pictures, art, art.
English makes me wish there were other
good subjects like this.
Football crazy, football mad, if my team
loses, I would be sad.

Rebecca Oakes (12)
Hartford High School

MY JOURNEY THROUGH PAGES

A book is full of mysterious things.
It's waiting to be opened.
An enchanted tale that we can read,
Turning all the pages.
A journey through some written words
Which lead to thrilling lives.
A mischievous life is in front of them,
Eager to see what's on the next page.
I read and read and read.
As I get to the end of the book
I turn the last page.
I leave my adventure.
As I enter another.

Victoria Massey (11)
Hartford High School

FOOTBALL

I like football, it makes me glad
I am in a team so I am not that bad.
I am football crazy
Still it is better than picking daisies.
Rollerblading is so cool
But when I fall I look like a fool.
I go to the ramp at the park
But Mum says 'Get back before it gets dark.'
I like TV but Mum says to me,
'Get your homework done before you watch TV.'

Daniel Buckley (11)
Hartford High School

THUNDERSTORM

The night is cool.
It starts to rumble, the sky is grey, the electric heat is charging.
It starts to get angry, all moody and monstrous.
Flashing, rampaging, booming and powerful
deep rumbles disturbing the town as it sleeps.
Never gets tired, just keeps crashing and booming.
Blasting thunderbolts across the sky as the
lightning starts to light up everything like
somebody throwing a match in the sky.
The rumbling starts to get weaker and weaker
and then it fades away.
The clouds part, the sun is free to shine on the
world again.
It's just cool air and a cold breeze.
The sky has lost all it its tears.

Emma Collinge (11)
Hartford High School

ROLLERBLADING

When I put my blades on
And whiz around the street
I feel as if my body
Has been lifted off my feet.

When I'm blading round and round
My feet, they hardly touch the ground
I get a really great buzz
From doing what I does!

Katharine Jones (11)
Hartford High School

DISMAL DAYS

Grey smoke rising like a hurricane from the dark, brick chimney.
Black umbrellas shelter black-mooded people.
Heavy, dull raindrops like giants' tears.
Racing drips dribble down the cold glass pane.
The misty background of fog suffocates the skyline.
Crisp, white snow converted into trampled, grey slush.
Filthy puddles frozen solid like a hard, dapple-grey rock.
Grey-faced adults huddle by the fire, avoiding the shadowy skies.
A waterfall of raindrops slips down the worn dismal roof tiles -
a mini Niagara Falls.
A heavenly fountain spouts water from the cracked, black drainpipe.
Black clouds fuse together to form a thundering storm.

Hayley Kinning (11)
Hartford High School

A DULL DAY

The picture makes me feel cold.
There's a man and woman sitting quietly like mice.
The sky looks grey, like the sky we get in England.
The boat looks like a melon, chopped in half.
The water is different colours of blue,
like a pair of jeans that have faded.
It's calm, like my mum on a good day.
The sound I would hear is the two people shivering,
watching the day pass by.
The smell of the water would be disgusting,
like putting your head in a dustbin.

Kate Stone (14)
Hartford High School

ARRIMAN'S AWFUL ZOO

A ntelope, admiring each other's artwork
B lind bats, bang against broken bulbs
C aterpillars, climbing up a camel's coat
D aring dragonflies dodge dangerous deer
E mus emigrating to Eastern Europe
F rightened fowl, frantically look for their father
G enerous giraffes give gifts to gorillas
H edgehogs hibernate in hens' hay
I ntelligent iguanas look at an interesting invention
J uggling jaguars juggle pieces of jewellery
K razy kangaroos try to kick a cunning kingfisher
L azy lizards like lazing around
M ischevious monkeys, making marmalade
N asty newt nibbles the nostril of a gnat
O ysters, opening revealing their oval pearls
P arrots patrolling the pelican crossing
Q uarrelling koalas argue about a quick quiz question
R eligious reindeers ride a raging rhinoceros
S creeching seagulls clean their special spectacles
T raining toads try out their new trampoline
U seless unicorns, eating an upside-down catfish
V isiting vultures play a violet violin
W ise walruses are worried about a wounded whale
Y apping youth plays with his yo-yo
Z ebras, studying zoology.

Rebecca Mason (12)
Hartford High School

ARRIMAN'S ZOO

A ngry adders achieve a lot of attacks.
B eastly bears beat up bugs.
C razy cuckoos cook their kids.
D izzy dragons dance daringly.
E lectric eels eat eggs.
F urry ferrets have funny feet.
G iant gorillas eat gooseberries.
H appy hedgehogs hate humans.
I ngenious insects build igloos.
J azzy jaguars jive all night.
K razy kangaroos kick koalas.
L azy lynx likes light.
M agic mongeese munch mangoes.
N utty newts need 'nanas.
O bedient otters eat aubergines.
P eaceful platypus pleases people.
Q uiet quokkas are queens.
R estful racoons eat raspberries.
S low sloths sound silly.
T iny turtles talk Turkish.
U nknown ungulates are ugly.
V icious vultures are like violets.
W acky wombats watch witches.
X enopus expect to have X-rays.
Y ellow yetis yawn a lot.
Z ebras play xylophones

Helen Walker (12)
Hartford High School

ARRIMAN'S ZOO

A dventurous ants, in armies attack angry antelope.

B usy buffalo bite bruised bananas.

C razy cats catch crabs quietly.

D angerous dinosaurs draw disastrously.

E normous elephants eat the entire enterprise of emus.

F iendish frogs fail to fight ferocious fairies.

G alloping gazelles give goblins the goose bumps.

H erds of horrid hyenas haunt humble hares.

I nterfering imps invent illegal ink.

J umping jellyfish chew juvenile Jack Russels.

K icking kangaroos cause chaos doing karate and kung-fu.

L azy lobsters love logic problems.

M enacing mongoose make mysterious magic.

N aughty newts nick nits' nests.

O verweight otters attract awful odours.

P assionate pandas' parties cause pandemonium.

Q uivering quails quarrel about questions.

R adical racoons ramble when reading.

S ensible seals scare selfish squirrels.

T errible tarantulas take termites' teeth.

U ncanny unicorns use ugly umbrellas.

V icious vipers vent their venom.

W hining weasels wobble when wet.

X iphias explodes when X-rayed.

Y ellow yaks yank yarromans' ears

Z ombie zebras zap zones.

Mary Gerrard (12)
Hartford High School

ARRIMAN'S ZOO

A bundant aardwolves attack adolescent animals.
B lood-coloured beadlet anemones bite black mussels.
C asual crocodiles cavort on canoes.
D og whelks adhere decidedly to dark, dangerous rocks.
E gyptian electronic elephants eat eclairs.
F erocious flies fly away from frogs.
G igantic giraffes tower greatly over grouper fish.
H airy hake hastily cause hazards.
I solated iguanas eat ice-cream.
J aguars jump jauntily over jealous jellyfish.
K iwis kick away carrots.
L onely, loathsome lions line up.
M assive manta rays cruise along.
N aughty narwhals need no nourishment.
O range orang-utans leap through orange vines.
P atient penguins persevere with word processing.
Q ueer quaggas enjoy reading the Quran.
R estless rhinos run from the rain.
S limy, sinuous snakes slide silently among shoals of slippery fish.
T errible tarantulas tower over terrified terrapins.
U nusual unaus are unaware of dangerous pythons.
V icious vampire bats vacuum up blood.
W easels whimper whilst waiting for food.
X tremely extinct dodos exert themselves exercising
Y elling yetis yelp alarmingly.
Z any zebras zip along.

Alyce Giles (12)
Hartford High School

ARRIMAN'S ZOO

A ggravated armadillos argue at afternoon break,
B at-eared fox blasts around bickering,
C razy cheetahs chanting curiously,
D aft ducks dangerously disguised as dogs,
E ager emus eating elephants' heads,
F ierce frogs falling in flames of fire,
G rant's gazelles gazing at gorgeous guinea-pigs,
H orrid hedgehogs hitting happy hephalumps,
I gnorant iguanas being idle,
J ellyfish jaunting with jousts,
K angaroos carting around cautiously,
L imping leopards lashing out,
M ean mauling monkeys miserably moaning,
N aughty, nasty newts nosing around,
O ctopuses owing offers,
P artying penguins pondering peckishly,
Q ueen bee quarrelling quietly,
R hinos rushing and running rapidly,
S nakes slithering on ceilings,
T ortoises torching terrible twins,
U nicorns in unique uniforms,
T he viper's vanishing venom,
W hales wandering wilfully,
E xtremely ferocious tigers exceedingly expensive,
Y orkshire terriers yapping uselessly,
Z ebras' zeds snoring.

David Clarke (12)
Hartford High School

THROUGH THAT DOOR

Through that door is a muscular sky,
Where birds are circling by,
And there is a foaming lake
Where mountains and moors suddenly awake.

Through that door shining bright,
The moon's beam gives it light,
Brightening up the dull dark night.

Through that door the cool green sea,
With its beckoning finger waving to me,
Rainbow-coloured fish swim to and fro.

Through that door meadows green and lush,
I hear the welcoming song of the speckled thrush,
Rabbits and foxes pass me by,
Not even a second glance or a friendly 'Hi.'

Paul Clarke (12)
Hartford High School

WATCHING

Watching from down below,
the great big spacecraft too high to show.
Carrying itself without any fuel
the space craft is drifting into the black gloom.
Looking up into space
a group of stars make up a face
Gleaming from the endless black sky.
The stars of space held up in the sky.

Lucy James (13)
Hartford High School

THROUGH THAT DOOR

Through that door
is a moor
of galore
you can share it
if your mind can spare it.

Through that door
is an ocean
of potion
waiting for people
to come and seek it.

Through that door
is the world of your imagination
it's all part of your magical creation.

Through that door
you will peep
play a game of hide and seek.

Melissa Rodwell (13)
Hartford High School

PESCATON POEM

P eople screaming everywhere
E nemies fight together
S aving their country
C ausing craters of damage
A ttacking and being defeated
T heir lives now coming to an end
O nly the lucky live for a few seconds longer
N ot even the fittest survive.

Nick Wilson (13)
Hartford High School

ARRIMAN'S ZOO

A mazing acrobatic ant eating aardvarks from Afghanistan.

B eautiful boomslangs bite blasted beetles.

C ommon carpet vipers catch careless camels.

D esert lark dusts down dropsy donkey.

E gyptian elephant shrews eat enthusiastic elf owls.

F urious fighting fish frolic from Fulham to Fiji.

G iant grey gorillas eat grey gooseberries.

H appy humming birds eat hasty hedgehogs.

I diotic Irish impala travels to Iraq.

J umping jackal gobbles jellyfish.

K illing Komodo dragon crushes koala bear.

L aughing lizards love to lurch at lazing ladies.

M indless mudskippers muddle magic monkeys.

N aughty newts nibble nasty newts.

O ver-enthusiastic opossum overpowers onlooking ostrich.

P owerful pushes playful pea fowl.

Q ueuing quails kick quiet quokkas.

R ampaging rattlesnakes rustle round rowdy racoons.

S limy, slithering salamanders smack sniggering snakes.

T retus thytacine trap troublesome toads.

U nique ultra-coloured unigates eat umbrellas.

V iolet, vibrating vebrata from Vancouver.

W eird wombat washes windows.

X enopus X-ray xylophone.

Y o-Yang yaks yank yachts.

Z ebra called Zac.

Richard Payne (12)
Hartford High School

ARRIMAN'S ZOO

A ngry ants ate apples.
B elly bouncing bees buzz backwards.
C lawing cats claw curiously.
D iving ducks dance daily.
E lephants eat endlessly.
F reaking fizzy fishes flow friendly.
G rumpy goats gallop gratefully.
H ungry hares hop harelessly.
I mportant impalas imagine images.
J umping jellyfish jiggle jellyishly.
K angaroos curiously keep cakes.
L aughing lizards lick leaves.
M oaning monkeys make mates.
N aughty gnats gnaw nectarines
O tters often offer oranges.
P andas plant poisonous potions.
Q uivering koalas kick quickly.
R acing rabbits run round rapidly.
S lithering snakes slide slowly.
T alking terrapins teach terrible tales.
U nbelievable unicorns utter under breath.
V icious vixens view voles.
W ild wolves wander wickedly.
X ploding energetic excited eggs.
Y oung yearlings yawn yearly.
Z oo zebras zealously zig-zag.

Ashley Reid (13)
Hartford High School

ARRIMAN'S ZOO

A stonished alligators awaiting animals.
B elgium bears believe in bats.
C olourful coral commits suicide.
D ogs dive in delicious dirty mud.
E normous elephants elbow each other.
F ighting fish forage for food.
G orgeous gazelles graze in the sun.
H ungry hippos have holiday heaven.
I gnorant iguanas ignore everybody.
J umping jellyfish like eating jelly.
K iddy kangaroos kindly share kidney.
L eopards look longingly at licking lips.
M inute mice munch on mouldy muffins.
N imble newts never need nourishing.
O versized ostrich often oggle owls.
P lump penguins prefer pilchards.
Q uaint quails quiver quite quickly.
R oger Rabbit runs rapidly.
S nakes sometimes slither slowly.
T iny tadpoles turn to toads.
U nusual unicorn upsets understanding uncle.
V icious vultures view a visible vole.
X otic dodos are extremely extinct.
Y oung yapping yaks yawn yearly.
Z any zoo zebra zooms.

Becky Worrall (12)
Hartford High School

ARRIMAN'S ZOO

A rguing avocets with abominable attitudes.
B urly baboons bully bisons
C olourful chameleon with a contagious cough.
D ancing dinosaurs do dirty deeds.
E vil emus with exotic eggs.
F ive fierce frogs fight with fire.
G ruesome giraffes gallivant in the garden.
H orrible hyenas have horrific haemorrhoids.
I nebriated iguanas ignite instantly.
J umping jerboas jive to Jermeraquai.
K angaroos karate-kick koalas.
L oathsome lemurs love leeches.
M assive mongoose makes much manure.
N auseous narwhal need nurses.
O ctopus operating on the occiput of an ostrich
P andas pestering people for presents.
Q uails quarrel in Quebec.
R evolting rhinoceros retches in Rome.
S inging serpents slither silently to San Francisco.
T iger tightropes to Timbuktu.
U nbelievably ugly ungulate with an ulcer.
V ulgar veal vent venom.
W icked weasels work wonders.
X cited extrovert exposes the exhibit of an extinct animal.
Y obbo yaks yodel in Yugoslavia.
Z illion zebras play xylophones.

Nikita Ponda (12)
Hartford High School

ARRIMAN'S ZOO

A ngry anacondas arguing about aging.

B ickering bison beating up baboons.

C rocodiles cracking curious crabs in half.

D ung beetles delivering disgusting droppings.

E nergetic emus elegantly elope.

F rightened ferrets run fast.

G igantic gorillas grilling helpless grasshoppers.

H igh-pitched hyenas haughtily hanging around.

I ntelligent iguanas isolate an idle impala.

J aunting jaguars jeering at giraffes' necks.

K icking kangaroos cleverly cage the kissing bugs.

L ivid lizards lazily lounge around.

M enacing monkeys may migrate.

N aughty-looking nightjars not knowing.

O dd-looking ostriches openly outrage orange elephants.

P in-sharp porcupines play pettily.

Q uiet quails quit quarrelling with the queen.

R unaway rhinoceros romping around in rage.

S currying scorpions seductively tempt selfish spiders.

T errifying tarantulas tempt termites to destroy.

U gly orang-utans unusually upright.

V omiting vipers find toilet thankfully vacant.

W andering wolves waiting for whiffing warthogs.

X cellent X-ray fish exist wanting extra.

Y oung yellowbills yodelling yonder.

Z any zorillas zestily zap zebras.

Fiona Rudkin (12)
Hartford High School

THUNDERBOLT

T he grey clouds draw in.
H ot atmosphere closes in on me.
U nder the blankets I go.
N ervously I look up.
D anger appears.
E rupting clouds race across the sky.
R aging flashes shoot through the night.
S udden clashes and smashes.
T orrential rain pours down.
O pening of the clouds.
R uining of trees and cars, broken and smashed.
M ischievously the storm creeps away from the ruinings it has made.

Oliver Newman (11)
Hartford High School

UNTIL YOU'RE A THROWAWAY

You don't know what you've got till its gone
Till your life has become worthless
Till your heart and mind are filled with nothing but hate
You can't tell where life's heading
Till there's nowhere left to go
Till there's no direction to anything
You won't know what's the point in living
Till there's no life left
Till there's nothing . . .
Until you're a throwaway.

Caroline Hammond (13)
Hartford High School

STILL THEY FIGHT

The screaming and shouting starts,
Now is the time to hide.
Only the very brave stay,
That, and only the very stupid.
They start to push and shove,
Now this is getting more dangerous.
Who'll be the first to get hurt?
Someone's bound to be,
Someone always is.
Please don't let it be me,
Please not my family.
A shot rings out and everyone screams,
Then sigh, grateful it wasn't them.

Kim Nield (15)
Hartford High School

THROWAWAYS

T   he sun rises over the mountain of rubbish.
H   eat and light cast out shadows
R   eleasing life into the sleeping shanty town.
O   pening eyes gaze into the sky.
W   aiting, anticipating, thinking.
A   ll today will bring is more disappointment.
W   ill no one rescue them from their fate?
A   lthough they are living they don't feel alive
Y   esterday's sorrows linger in the air.
S   truggling for freedom in their prison with no boundaries.

Holly Moncrieff (13)
Hartford High School

UNIVERSE

No faces to be seen.
Not a single human smile to be observed by another.
Just the claustrophobic darkness, and the stars.
A sun glints off a gold visor, a suit spinning through space.
Oh, the space - it hits you like a wall, throughout an infinite
Universe, the stars, the cold and the expanse - to which you are nothing.
Just you, in the middle of infinity, alone and worthless and the feelings
of not being a millimetre tall - of not being worth anything.
Oh, so alone.
And at the end, there you will be spinning forlornly through the black
nothing - hopelessly lost - with the Universe saying,
'So now you understand, human? Are you still so sure of your own
superiority?'
And you, nothing but a tiny star in the blackness, say nothing.
You are not worthy
   You
     Never
       Were!

Gemma Else (12)
Hartford High School

THE FATAL MOMENT

Slow, slow, slow we went, passing the victims involved.
With one eye on the event I winced.
There was a cry of shame passing me as I saw it.
A hurt man was walking down the path of death
Into the tunnel of new life.
It went over and over in my mind.
Over, over, over, over . . . *Gone!*

Sara Cole (13)
Hartford High School

Through That Door

Through that door,
Is a great big sea,
Which tosses and turns,
For everyone to see.

Through that door,
Seagulls will fly high up in the sky,
Where fish will swim,
Around the sea's brim.

Through that door,
Is an island that's fantastic,
With a forest of green,
And animals that are magic.

Through that door,
It was dark and dull,
And when I looked up,
The moon was full.

Rachel Lockett (12)
Hartford High School

The Mirror

I look through the mirror and
what do I see?
I see a face gazing at me,
With bright blue eyes,
With bright red lips,
And a nice kind smile.
With skin as soft as a peach
And after all it's only me.

Carla Whittaker (12)
Hartford High School

THROUGH THAT DOOR

Through that door,
Is a room full of luxury,
A relaxed place,
Full of everything
There is even space for a race.

Through that door,
Is a kitchen floor,
Where lunch is cooked,
It's smell is a lure,
And it's definitely fully booked.

Through that door,
Is a school,
That horrible dungeon,
Full of teachers in a whirlpool,
With a policeman and his truncheon.

Through that door,
Is freedom,
At last!
It's like a kingdom,
It's so vast.

Donna Taylor (12)
Hartford High School

AFRICA

Where the golden sun shines,
Shines over the vast fields of roaming wildlife.
In their natural habitats and not encased in metal cages on show
Rejected creatures saddened by loss of family.

Nathan Rathbone (14)
Hartford High School

THROUGH THAT DOOR

Through that door
is where your wildest dreams come true,
where everything you touch turns to chocolate
and toys that are new.
Where you can have a new bike,
do what you like,
everything is up to you!

Through that door
is money,
and bees that make magical honey.
The money floats through thin air,
lands softly on your hair.
So grab that handle,
but it's quite hard to handle.

Through that door
are clothes,
what will happen, nobody knows.
There are shoes, skirts, tops and coats,
pens and paper for writing notes.

Through that door
is a secret,
which nobody knows.
There is a big castle.
There is never any hassle.
You can see the light,
through the door shining bright.

Natalie Austin (12)
Hartford High School

THROUGH THAT DOOR

Through that door
Is a vastness of black
Where no light can shine on the sunniest day
The air is damp and cold
And it smells like something old.

Through that door
When you hear the bell
You all rush through to the sensational smell
You hear lids clang
With a crash and a bang
You can hardly wait as the food's put on your plate.

Through that door
You hear him shout
'You're late!'
And he gives you a clout
You race upstairs
Climb into your bed
And pull the duvet over your head.

Through that door
I can see
The perfect view
Looking back at me
With singing birds and shady trees
And butterflies
And buzzing bees
A peaceful world waiting for me.

Oliver Hynes (13)
Hartford High School

THROUGH THAT DOOR

Through that door,
there are different scenes,
try each one and you'll know what I mean!
Let your imagination go wild,
do whatever you feel,
each little thing is so gentle and mild.

Through that door,
there is a world of snow,
when children want to play,
that's where they go!
With its special sparkle and that little glow,
there's nowhere else you will find,
this world of snow.

Through that door,
is the ocean blue,
flowing there gently waiting for you.
The calming noises let you unwind,
the ocean blue, that's what you'll find!

Through the door,
there is a pleasure dome
for us all to enjoy and see,
it springs to our attention and
grabs our fantasy!
Everything is so beautiful, including
the elegant sun, but now my dream
is definitely done!

Rebecca McDean (12)
Hartford High School

THROUGH THAT DOOR

Through that door
Is a house with,
Shining pans and cutlery,
Knives and forks placed out,
And candles glow and burn furiously.

Through that door
Is darkness
With glittering stars,
And the moon with the beaming face.

Through that door
Are the fountains
Which trickle and weave through trees for eternity
And the creepers make their way
Up a tree twisting and turning.

Through that door,
Is joy and happiness
With laughs and fun,
Children playing everywhere
Making the world a happy place.

Lois Blower (12)
Hartford High School

AFRICA

A   dventure in Africa.
F   lying birds in the fluffy blue sky.
R   hinos charging at their prey.
I   ncredible numbers of wildebeest in their herds.
C   ats roaming from tree to tree.
A   n afar place too far to be true.

Carole Boag-Munroe (14)
Hartford High School

THROUGH THAT DOOR

Through that door,
Is a very big bedroom,
Where people sleep but they can't be poor,
It is full of drawers and wardrobes too,
Lots of pictures, every kind,
This makes it look nice if you never knew.

Through that door,
Are a dozen trees,
Big ones, small ones, all sizes will do,
All these trees have little knobbly knees,
Which sway to and fro,
In the breeze.

Through that door,
Is a gigantic wall,
Which has ivy on it,
Creeping big and tall.
Adding the hollyhocks that
Are beginning to bloom in all of the gloom.

Through that door,
Is a good imagination,
Where you can wander,
And look in,
You can find a place that hides,
If you find it then peer inside!

Jessica Woodman (12)
Hartford High School

ALONE

Loneliness creeps over them
Like a blanket of fear
Covering their bodies
Taking their breath away
Their loneliness is an unusual feeling
Something both children never wished to experience
But something they had to take into their lives
Something they had to accept
Something they had to fear
A new life is forced upon them
Without any warnings or signs
Without any meaning
Without any love
Without anyone.

Donna Kryger (13)
Hartford High School

THE THUNDERSTORM

The humid evening draws in,
Deep rumbles can be heard in the distance,
The sky turns a shade of black.

A bombshell roar erupts into the night sky,
Thunder bellows, making the earth shudder.
A flash of lightning leaps through the sky,
Trees collapse to the ground.

Thunderclaps die down until all is silent and still,
The air is hot and clammy.

Caroline Evans (11)
Hartford High School

COLOURS OF WINTER

Winter sounds the time of death
Like a coffin going to the graveyard
The screeching sound of the wind
Blowing through the tree is like the
Scream of a thousand dead warriors
When the leaves fall off the tree it's
Like the tears falling from the face of
A mourning friend, and the colours that
Light the ground are like the flames
on hell's floor, and the howls that you
Hear at night are like the cries for
Help from a dead man's son. When
Autumn appears it's like the world
Has a new beginning.

Mark McWha (13)
Hartford High School

HOW CAN I LIVE WITHOUT HER?

I don't know if I can live without her, if I can ever survive,
If I can carry on living, without her here by my side
Maybe I'll just give up trying, what have I got to forfeit?
With just one drink of this poison, Juliet and I shall once again meet.
The very first time that I saw her, I knew that
                                she'd stolen my heart,
But without her here in my life, my world has been torn apart.
Goodbye cruel world, goodbye my blood.
I would have told you we were married, I'd have told you if I could.

Laura Plumb (14)
Hartford High School

THESE I HAVE LOVED

The smell of fresh bread
A blown-out match
Birds in the morning
Dew on the grass.

Snow on the church roof
Carols at night
The cold sea water
And the silky soft sand.

Ice-cream and chocolate
Sunset at night
Rain on the window
New buds on the trees.

Crisp autumn leaves
Floating from trees
The smell of Mum's perfume
The cat on my knees.

These I have loved!

Jenny Johnson (13)
Hartford High School

AFRICA

A   frica, a place of dreams.
F   ierce lions lurking on the plains of land.
R   hinos charging.
I   maginative landscapes.
C   alm settings until extinction.
A   nd then you wake up.

Claire Martin (14)
Hartford High School

ONE EVENING BACK IN '38 . . .

One evening back in '38
Five innocent victims met their fate
They were all famous in their own way
But none of them lived to see another day
It was the opening of a Grand Hotel
The owner was a Mr Schnell
He was so proud as he entered that lift
And the following events had everyone miffed
Four others followed on his heels
They could even smell the 12th floor meals
A Mr and Mrs Sminter were
Delighted to have been invited there
Little Sally and her Nanny too
When the lift doors closed they both gave a *'coo'*
The lift, it whirred, it jittered and jarred
It lished and lashed and finally crashed
The mystery was that no bodies were found
No heaps of corpses lying in a mound
So now every year the ghosts pile in
To that lift that crashed and made such a din
They can even hear the party on the 12th floor
And are doomed to remain on the ground evermore!

Laura Yates (14)
Hartford High School

THE EAGLE

The eagle it is a wonderful bird
its feathers widely spread.
It waits for its prey.
It swoops down for the kill
Then takes it to its nest.

John Harding (13)
Hartford High School

HOTEL BY A RAILROAD

Smoky like an old-fashioned pub
Silent in deep thought
Hazy with the warm summer breeze
The sunny cream walls add warmth to the room
The free green wallpaper in next door's window
gives the feeling of independence
The clear blue sky covers the world
The man, smoking, dressed in waistcoat,
shirt and trousers
The woman sitting reading,
dressed in fine summer dress
Peace overcomes them
The old-fashioned decor sets the room as well kept
Outside sits a railroad unused
The creamy walls give a summery look
No words are spoken
The only voices are the faint happy laughs
from the beach
The power of concentration
Silence gives them time to think.

Shelley Alder (13)
Hartford High School

AFRICA

A   nimals racing across the desert.
F   amily waving goodbye.
R   oaring lions frightening their prey away.
I   n the plane high in the sky.
C   ircles of birds surrounding the sky.
A   ll day every day in the hot sun.

Victoria Astles (14)
Hartford High School

ROLLERBLADING

Rollerblading is
The best
I wear baggy
Jeans and a vest
I put my new
Skates to the
Test
And did a big rail
It was the best
I looked at my
Jeans they were a
Mess
So I went back
Home and assessed
My rollerblades
Are the best.

Daniel Bell (13)
Hartford High School

MY OBJECT

It's like an insect walking
It's like a spider but bigger
It's like there are caves under it
It has mixed colours
It has very sharp ends. They are like needles
It would be found on the floor because it is dead
It has fallen from where the rest came from
They were all attached together by lots of poles
And a big one in the middle.

Iain Bellis (14)
Hartford High School

THE LEAF

The leaf is like . . .
A man on a hill, his eyes like a razor-sharp knife.
His hands are as rough as sandpaper.
Sweating like a damp cloth, black and brown from
being beaten by the sunshine
to put the gloss on as a finishing touch.
He's been held so tight that veins are beginning to burst
from under his skin.
His back is as soft as a silky smooth face.
Falling down on his knees, he's not alone.
Next year new buds will grow on the trees.

Liz Grossman (13)
Hartford High School

MOON LANDING

The moon's in sight,
Looks like night.
Space module landing
Legs expanding
Sucking drinks from a spout
Astronaut getting out
Putting a flag in the ground
Bouncing all around
In slow motion
Alien spaceship . . .
Causes commotion.

Jonathan Gaze (13)
Hartford High School

BAGS I

Bags I the space shuttle
Raring to go
5, 4, 3, 2, 1
And off we go.

Bags I the solar system
See the spaceship fly
Soaring through the Universe
Passing planets by .

Bags I the landing
Smooth and fast
'Is anyone here?'
The frightened astronaut asked.

Bags I the astronaut
Stepping out the craft
'You are now my prisoners,'
One alien laughed.

Bags I the finish
Of our astronaut friend
He is taken to be executed
Is this really the end?

Victoria Gardner (13)
Hartford High School

LEAF ON FIRE

A leaf lay on the floor
Burning like a house on fire
Lying still
Like a dead bird.
It flew across the sky
Like an eagle in a rush
Then slowly it drifted down to Earth
Like a milkman drifts down the street in winter
Then landed quickly with a bump
Like a plane when it lands on the runway
Then floated along
Like a ferry going across the sea
Floating slowly then it bolts to the ground
Like a flash of lightning hitting Earth
Then it loses its colour
Like a jumper in the wash
Then the fire goes out, not a flame's left.
As if a fireman had been working all night
Then the leaves wait quietly waiting to be trampled on
                              like a baby in its bed.

Laura Chesterson (13)
Hartford High School

DAY

How the day just slips by watching
the clouds float in the sky.
How the birds sing in June.
How the leaves rustle at noon.
And how does man walk on the moon?
For when the days pass by I wonder if I could ever just
go out and fly in that wonderful clear blue sky.

Donna Archibald (13)
Hartford High School

A Response To Edward Hopper's
Rooms For Tourists

The welcoming smell of coffee
Like Granny's house on holidays
The zoom of an odd car
Like a dragonfly in a race
Mellow light yellow bold against shadows
Sharp green moulding round cool cream
Standing back is a r ather large window
Revealing the wonders inside
In the middle ground is a small doorway
Protecting the house from the outside
I can hear a light snoring and knocking
Like the wind gently carrying old leaves.

Michelle Dutton (13)
Hartford High School

Moss On A Rock

It is like a little mountain full of mini rabbit holes.
The moss is like the furry soft touch of the normal household hamster.
The holes are miniature tunnels dug by extremely tiny moles.
On one side the stone may be rough just like a piece of sandpaper,
But on the other side it is shiny like an ancient Pharaoh's jewels.
The moss is like the grass on top of the mountain which is the stone.
The rock may be too small for us humans to climb
But it may be quite a task for a newborn baby ant.
The rock may be on a drive full of gravel
Or a back garden of a house where the children come
And play, with their voices full of joy.

Richard Tolley (13)
Hartford High School

WAITING
(Inspired by Edward Hopper)

Waiting alone like a memory being forgotten,
The repeating sound of someone sipping coffee
like the bouncing of a ball,
A strong smell of coffee like the smell of petrol,
The pale sky being stained with black ink,
A green coat hiding the woman like a child in
tall green grass,
The blue table as cold as an ice rink,
A table blocking your way like a jail guard,
The woman distant from the world like a man
asleep in his grave,
A window dark and cold like a power cut in a
warm and friendly house,
Lonely and distant like a star far away from the world.

Sophie Preece (13)
Hartford High School

FOOD FLIGHT

The canteen is silent, only the sound of munching can be heard.
When suddenly a large spatter of jelly occurs.
Then from out of the blue in a dark corner the words
'Food fight!'
are heard.
Custard here! Mustard there! Then, *splat!*
I accidentally threw a custard pie at the headmaster.
'Right!
Detention
for you Ryley Watts!

Karen Brotherton (12)
Hartford High School

MY DOG

My dog's glowing brown eyes
staring at me.
Her small legs jumping at me
as I shake her food box.
Her loud snappy bark when
she sees another dog.
Flashes of brown and white
as she rushes past me.
Running towards me when
I rattle her lead.
Lying in front of the fire in
the cold winter months.
Soft shiny fur shining in the sunlight
That's my dog, Ellie.

Rachel Sayle (12)
Hartford High School

MY POEM

The green and brown piece of wood,
Sits on its own in the wood.
Little cracks and little holes,
Make this twig look very old.
It's got a bend in the middle,
Like a pipe going around a corner.
If it had a much stronger smell,
It would smell like an old wooden cupboard.
At first sight it looks as though it could be alive.

Ryan Beaumont (13)
Hartford High School

FINAL DAY EMOTIONS

The final day of the football season
the final game deciding survival
or despair of the drop
from the top flight
disaster strikes as rival opponents take the lead
the destined hard-hitting drop comes ever closer
caution thrown to the wind
a last-ditch fight for survival
all-out attack!
shots cleared off the line
crashing against the bar
off the outside of the post
Until . . .
. . . the final minute
two against one
two-nil behind and no fuel left in the tank
a season full of emotional highs
but finishes on a low
silent but for the cries of relegation.

John Corker (14)
Hartford High School

THE LEAF

The leaf falling from the tree
You take a look at the leaf
You notice the fur on the leaf like a dog's furry coat
The leaf's like a snake
The roughness is a snake's scaly back
The scales join up like the segment of the leaf.

Josh Dean (13)
Hartford High School

THE HEAVENLY WOOD

The sight of glory, the paint ran to make a perfect sight.
The lilies floating slowly along the top of the lake,
The swing crafted slowly and perfectly, made for a princess,
And the beautiful sound of wildlife.
The footsteps crackling on the leaves
Like a plunge of milk hitting the Rice Krispies,
The green leaves like a mountain of sponge.
It's as hot as the flames of hell, with a slight draught.
The mirror image reflects the lake into a perfect picture
Following every move.
The trees like angry spikes, the overhanging oaks like curtains.
The water, lilac like a dream in a holiday brochure.
The grass as soft and furry as a panther's back.
The angel-like lady swinging to and fro with a dress made for a queen.
Voices of joy and happiness tell how peaceful and
Immaculate is the heavenly wood.
This is like an island where no one can disturb me.
If anything was moved this would definitely be ruined.
This is without doubt the heavenly wood.

Paul Goulden (13)
Hartford High School

MEDUSA

M y power is to create
E yes turn you to stone
D angling from my head
U se my powers to get you
S nakes in my hair
A fter all, I am Medusa.

Emma Stockton (13)
Hartford High School

MY ONE TRUE LOVE IS MY ONE TRUE HATE

My one true love is my one true hate,
my family are at war with hers,
since we were young it's always been
known as Capulets versus Montagues.

My one true love is my one true hate,
I am told 'We hate the Capulets' and
she is told 'We hate the Montagues,'
soon our love will be torn apart by our families at war.

My one true love is my one true hate,
our families will die hating each other
our lives are slowly being destroyed as they
are filled with hate, and one by one we are being slain.

My one true love is my one true hate,
my one true love is Juliet.

Nicky Stephenson (14)
Hartford High School

MY CAT

A flash of black and white goes past me.
I hear a fierce hiss and see two golden eyes
with a black dot in the middle.
Her ears stand on end and her tail shoots up.
I slowly put my hand out and touch her soft fur
and she bites me with her sharp teeth.
Her paw pads are so muddy, I know
she has been in the nearby field.
I then realise she is my pet cat, Merlin.

Joanne Hayes (13)
Hartford High School

MY DOG

Have you seen my little brown dog?
His name is Matt and if you have a hat
you will never get it back.

Have you seen my little brown dog?
He chases bunnies and thinks he's funny
but all he is, is a little dummy.

Have you seen my little brown dog?
He's fun to play with, he makes me laugh,
you should see the mess when he has a bath.

Have your seen my little brown dog?
His nose is always cold
and he never does as he is told.

If you know where he is, please let me know
I do miss him, terribly so.

Kelly Taylor (14)
Hartford High School

RIDE

I dance all night on the creature's back,
As she flies gracefully in the silk sky.
It seems as if we can go anywhere.
I see dolphins leaping and playing in the crystal blue sea.
I see, as the birds fly, the wind gushes past them
As my ride comes to an end
For my creature is tired
She takes me back to my sleep
For my creature is a . . . ?

Alaina Bexton (12)
Hartford High School

ALONE

Alone, alone in a field on a winter's day
footprints crunched into the frosty grass
haze drifting all around
A breeze freezing your fingertips like an icy hand
reaching for you.
Alone at night in your home
darkness stretching into every corner closing in on you
pipes rapping continuously.
Your mind controls you as you
hear footsteps on the stairs.
Alone in the rain outside, soaking, seeping through your clothes.
Warmth disappears as the water drips down your face
Isolation becomes a realisation as you stare at the roadway,
silent and empty.
All alone.

David Wade (11)
Hartford High School

STRESS

'Bleep, bleep' down my ear,
The alarm clock wakes me up to another stressful day,
The bathroom light explodes as I turn it on,
A blast of water gushes up in my face as
I turn the tap on,
The kettle whistles, screaming for help,
I pour the water in a cup, it spills and burns my hand,
But when I drink it, it's cold,
I try to find my shoes, I find one under the bed
And the other in the cupboard,
I hate these stressful days.

Sarah Rutter (12)
Hartford High School

THE DANDELION

The dandelion is like a jagged icicle
hanging from a cave roof
waiting to fall or
to melt and
disappear.

Hollow like a burnt-down tree
smelling like the dandelion
has been thrown in a bog
and just been caught
before it went
under.

Ripped off its roots like a knife
going through some butter
from top to bottom
will it ever grow
again?

As people touch the bud it is like
a newly-born teddy bear
people tread on the bud
like a nail going through
a piece of
wood.

David Flood (13)
Hartford High School

GOOSEBUMPS

Your eyes glued to the page as all the chilling
thoughts get mixed up inside your mesmerised mind.
You enter the world of the optical fantasy among the characters.
Your wild imagination takes you places you have
only dreamt of in your nightmares.
Hideous faces,
bulging eyes,
repulsive teeth,
sagging skin.
monsters,
mummies,
vampires,
ghouls,
are all I can see in my weird illusion.
My heart pounding as I slam the book shut
and put an end to my freakish delusion.

Amy Stone (12)
Hartford High School

THE RISING OF THE PHOENIX

The fire roared,
The flames swayed,
Then, from the heart of the orange blaze
Rose the golden crest of the phoenix.
He stood in a nest of fire,
His graceful wings spread out,
His head arched in a majestic manner,
The flames danced around him,
A figure of dignity.

Louise Eslick (12)
Hartford High School

WHY IS IT?

Why is it
that
in our bathroom
it's not the dirtiest
or the strongest
who stay longest
but it always seems to be
the one who gets there
just ahead
of me?

Why is it
that people fret
when they're wet
with loud cries
and soap in their eyes
and agonised howls
because they forgot
their towels?

Why is it?

Kerry Atkinson (13)
Hartford High School

WARTIME

Jewish people in the street getting
shot in the heat.

German soldiers' machine guns too
killing people like me and you.

Hitler, Churchill, like to fight
through the heat of the deadly night.

English, American, French, to fight
against the Germans and their might.

Ben Davenport (12)
Hartford High School

THE UNKNOWN

In the field where hay grows tall,
There are things that people don't understand at all,

Crop circles are all around,
They've punched the hay towards the ground,

Some are big and some are small,
Sometimes they're not circles at all,

They're squares, ovals and sometimes swirly,
Some are small and some are curly,

A place where UFOs have landed?
The work of teens, some have been branded,

But no one knows what happened for sure,
How the hay got to the floor.

Jenny Clarke (12)
Hartford High School

JET

He roams through the field
so wild but beautiful
His black coat is so shiny
He canters towards the fence
And is over with a jump.

He slows down
And walks beside the road
A car comes round the corner
And *toots* its horn
He is startled by the noise
And starts to gallop
He sees an opening in the fence
And goes through it
He stops and watches
As the car goes past
And lies down to rest.

Alanna Rose (12)
Hartford High School

FAIR LADY WILL YOU MARRY ME?

You Juliet are the
sun and I am the
east. You light up
my world with your
beautiful eyes and
your soft sweet skin
touching my face.

Can you learn to love
me with your tender
loving heart?

I give thee my heart
and soul in hoping
you shall comfort me.

Juliet will you marry
me till death do us part?
Where pilgrims are
pilgrims and names
mean nothing.

Nicola Martin (14)
Hartford High School

TITANIC

A cold and
Mysterious night,
With mist covering the sky
Like a blanket,
With candle-like stars
Pricking the fog,
Drifting in the middle of what
Seems to be nowhere,
In a deep freeze,
Shimmering like clear glass,
Brilliant white shining in the moonlight,
Like a gloomy, invisible danger,
A doomy chill creeps over the
Midnight-blue sky,
With a touch of death,
Till the end of time.

James Ashley
Hartford High School

THE BACKSTREET CAFE

(A response to a painting by Edward Hopper)

The musky aroma from a cigarette fills the air
A cold clean atmosphere of a cave
Small windows outside watch you like forlorn faces
Quiet murmurs like the television downstairs
A calm yellow illuminates the inside
A dog's constant barking
Like a recorded message played again and again.
The pepperpot shaped like an overweight man
A woman staring deep in thought
The bright green foliage of the occasional plant
A dull grey overtakes the view from the window
People thinking in the deafening, tense sound of silence
A silence too dense to bridge with words.

Joanne Wallace (14)
Hartford High School

THE NEVER-ENDING DAY

People talk, people stare
It's like you are in a cage
Can't get out.
No friends
People are embarrassed at the sight of you
I am like a fly with no wings,
A leopard with no spots
I am cornered
Trapped
People walking past, whispering
It's not my fault I am like this
Why?

Dominic Hagerty (14)
Hartford High School

IT ALL STARTED WITH A BRANCH

That lonely old branch,
On that lonely old tree,
At the end of the garden,
Never visited, never seen,
Like a hopeless old bean,
Shrivelled and green,
What a terrible scene,

No branch,
No tree,
Can't be visited, can't be seen,
That poor old tree,
Shrivelled and green,
Just like that hopeless old bean,
But this bean was never seen,
What a horrible dream!

Lara Caffery (13)
Hartford High School

THE OLD TIMES
(A poem based on a painting)

The flag has lost its pride in the wind.
The tree in the distance like a feather duster in the wind.
The man's hat on his head like a king in his tower.
The houses surrounding them like faceless squares.
People standing on the ground
Like it is a big brown sheet.
People looking around and seeing
The colours of the rainbow.

Adam Bown (14)
Hartford High School

NOTHING TO LIVE FOR

It's hopeless now,
nothing to live for,
everything's gone.
There's nothing left worth fighting for,
worthlessness lurking over me
like a tree's reflection in a still, dark lake.
The earth's breath whispers around me.
My dark, dismal face jumps back into my cold, lonely eyes.
The sounds cascade around me into a pool of thought.
I'm left wondering, the breeze rushes past my ears,
my numb, lifeless body stands in the silver moonlight.
A chill goes through me, like a wolf
howling from the highest mountain.
The fiery desire burned in my heart, glowing like eternal flames.
Will I ever love again?

Sally Wright (15)
Hartford High School

THUNDERSTORM

The sky was dark and gloomy,
The lightning came
Then a rumble, it started to rain.
The lightning was hitting the tops of trees.
Then a crashing noise, trees were falling down.
Some were on fire.
The noise of the rain hitting the window.
The crash of the lightning and thunder was hideous.

Christopher Woodward (11)
Hartford High School

THE PIECE OF STRAW

Blowing in the wind,
Like a feather from its bird,
As long as a small ruler,
As thin as a matchstick.

Smooth like a bird in flight.
Soft like a kitten's fur,
A mixture of yellow and brown,
Like when desert sand mixes with soil.

Growing in a field,
Or in a pony's stable,
It still smells like a farmyard,
Or the countryside around it.

Blowing in the wind,
As light as a feather,
The straw blows freely,
Like a wild bird in flight.

Sarah Wilson (13)
Hartford High School

SEASIDE

S pectacular waves, curved like a swan's neck
E veryone turning sunburnt, like toast.
A ngry people as the wave hits their patch.
S urfers looking like penguins
I n their glistening wetsuits.
D anger signs stop people in their tracks!
E very day goes past with people on the beach.

David Jacks (13)
Hartford High School

TITANIC

An icy chill drifts over the choppy sea,
Stars twinkle like millions of eyes
in the vast emptiness of the black night sky.
A huge white shape lurks behind
the black curtains of mist,
A deadly sea god sitting on
his ocean throne looms ahead,
An enormous iceberg like
a perfectly carved piece of crystal
floats on the freezing water,
He stands tall as the ship crawls round him
trying to escape her doom.
It rips the ship's side like a thousand knives,
She sails on, a wounded soul,
awaiting her final fate.

Rebecca Chitty (14)
Hartford High School

THE SNAKE

Still like a dead man
Watching over the world
Its left black beady eye has spotted something
It is a rat scattering about like an ant as its nest has been
disturbed
Slowly it begins to move like water ripples in the sea
Then with a wink of an eye the rat has gone
It has successfully caught its prey
Slowly its camouflage returns and it slithers up a tree
It closes its eyes for another day
Tomorrow it will catch more prey.

Zac Hazlehurst (11)
Helsby High School

A Helpless Baby

Lying upon a filth-ridden bed
a small baby lies alone,
trying to flick a fly off his head,
as he quietly manages a moan.

One hand is still, as the other one moves,
all of his strength mustered up
he's trying to move, he's desperate to prove
pleading they shouldn't give up.

He hears the guns, they make him jump,
as he cries, he cries out loud,
upon his leg there grows a lump,
as he breathes into another dust cloud.

He desperately wants, he desperately needs,
someone to cuddle, someone to hold,
someone willing to rid him of the cold.

As daylight fades and night-time dawns,
there lies a small baby dying of AIDS.

Sara Houghton (13)
Helsby High School

The Bear

Fuzzy fur still in the wind,
Reflected by the trickly stream,
The fish is seen as is the pounce and *plop!*
The fish is caught,
Chopped and chewed as he eats unmannerly,
Then it slips and slides down his long tubed neck.

Philip Richards (11)
Helsby High School

SPIDERS

Eight thin legs run through the hall,
Then quickly scuttle up the wall.
Who is watching me at night?
A great big spider, what a fright!

The spider stares with beady eyes,
As if trying to stay in disguise.
I think, oh please go away,
But old spider, no he's here to stay.

He waves his long legs about,
But with no one here to hear me shout,
I'm going to be brave, I know what to do,
I'm going to flush him down the loo!

I catch the spider in a tin,
Put the lid on, seal him in.
I calmly walk to the door,
I chuck the spider on the floor.

The spider runs down the path,
'Oh thank God he's gone at last.'
I'm very glad, I heave a sigh,
The spider's gone, farewell and goodbye.

I go back into the room,
My heart skips a beat.
Just guess what's sitting on my seat!

Sarah McGing (13)
Helsby High School

THE CHASE

Silently, she stalks her prey
Silently, her large paws splay
And as she wanders through the gloom,
Her prey, she thinks, will meet its doom.

And as she tails this quarry fine,
Moving in, preparing to dine,
I turn, and there what do I see?
My deranged pet about to attack me!

I bolt, and make it through the door
She runs, haphazardly 'cross the floor
I try to run, my strides are vast
But she is closing on me fast.

She propels herself into the air,
Catching my head by the hair.
She's got me now, she's pinned me down,
Ensnaring me in a single bound.

She can smell the fear
I can feel her breath
As she prepares
To lick me to death.

Rachel Ball (13)
Helsby High School

BEAUTY

Beauty is more than 'skin deep'
Places, people,
Everyone's unique!
The view from a window,
Rustling trees,
Breathtaking flowers,
Animals, creatures, everywhere.
Different people, different smiles,
Beauty is different to everyone.
Who cares what others think?
Smiles, happiness, peace and plenty
That's beauty!
Not skin deep
Natural beauty is all we see,
Look further in the eyes,
Windows opened wide.
Glowing colours, pretty scenes,
These are the insides.
Some of us don't see,
In people's eyes past the flesh,
You'll see what they possess.
Beauty is everywhere,
Inside us,
Outside us,
Open eyes everywhere and search.

Charlotte Dobson (13)
Helsby High School

I Don't Like The Cupboard In The Hall . . .

I don't like the cupboard in the hall,
It's full of bogeymen and cobwebs,
What are those spooky shadows?

Bulging eyes are all over the wall,
Looking at me,
Watching me,

I only popped in here for my coat,
Closed the door to hide from my mum,
Now I'm spooked, transfixed by those eyes,

Bulging eyes are all over the wall,
Looking at me,
Watching me.

OK, here is the ironing board,
That's the Hoover, here's the duster,
What are those glinting in the light?

Bulging eyes are all over the wall,
Looking at me,
Watching me.

'Oh Mum! You made me jump
You've found me!'
'Yes, now I'll do the washing up.'
Firstly I will see what it was
Phew! Only wine bottles resting in the racks.

Helen Davies (13)
Helsby High School

RECIPE FOR LIFE

When making a batch of life,
You need joy, love and care,
Look in the cupboard of your heart,
You never know what you could find there.

Start with a kilo of common sense,
Then a dash of learning,
If things start to get nasty,
Then it definitely needs turning.

Add a pinch of inspiration,
And a slice of fun,
But don't forget some humour,
Or the mixture could run.

Take the dough in your hands,
Then knead and fold,
Add flour, so life won't stick,
And then put into a mould.

When putting in the oven,
Remember to be wary,
For if life gets too hot,
It could turn out to be scary.

When following this recipe for life,
Don't give up,
Through trouble and strife,
Let your emotions out,
And don't keep in what you feel.

In the end it will produce a *brilliant* meal.

Elizabeth Pearce (13)
Helsby High School

ALONE

I'm all alone,
There's no one about
I hear a noise,
Is it a bang or a shout?

I look around,
What's that over there?
The curtain moved,
Something touched my hair

I reached up,
To switch on the light
It wouldn't work,
That gave me a fright

I fell asleep,
But was awoken by a bleep
My eyelids were heavy
And I fell back to sleep

Morning's here,
Gone is my fear
I wasn't as brave last night
When the spirits were near.

Debra Ford (13)
Helsby High School

MY TOY SHOP

As I walked into my shop,
I saw my favourite toy.
It was a large, brown teddy bear,
And it filled me with such joy.

Then I saw behind the door,
My old Eeyore,
With its blue coat,
And old sad look,
It was just like the story book.

Sitting on the counter,
Looking at an old book,
Was my green puppet,
Looking at the picture
My mum and dad took.

Victoria Louise Clutton (13)
Helsby High School

SUNRISE AFTER THE FIRE

I sat on the grass and watched the sun rising slowly,
Majestically, over the cold horizon.
Though the sky was brightening,
The moon and stars could still be seen,
Their light glistening on the frozen dewfall of the night before.
The air was cold, and I shivered in the pale dawn.
The bare trees cast shadows over the burnt fields around me,
Their branches twisting jaggedly over themselves
Like the many stems in a rose bush.
All was silent as the sun rose over the barren landscape,
The destruction of the day before.

Thomas Smith (13)
Helsby High School

A WINTER WONDERLAND

Snowflakes drift slowly down from a frozen sky,
Carpeting the ground like a crisp blanket,
Icicles hang high from snow-covered rooftops,
Their melting residue lightly hits the frosty paths.

Ice-cold winds whistle against a lone robin's tune,
It makes me shiver,
I wrap up warm in my hat and scarf,
As I look down at the frozen puddles on the icy paths.

Animals scavenge for food,
They leave their footprints on a carpeted surface,
The foggy sky seems to swallow the misty hilltops,
Far, far in the distance.

Families join together to celebrate the season of goodwill,
A lonely fir tree stands proudly in the corner,
Of a beautifully decorated room,
Covered with glinting tinsel and flashing lights.

Chestnuts roast on a blazing orange fire,
Sending serpents of thick black smoke,
Contrasting with the pure white,
Of the ever falling snow.

But despite the dull and dreary days,
People's happiness and love shines through,
Winter weather may be wet and cold,
But joy and love warm people's hearts.

Amy Richards (13)
Helsby High School

THE AFRICAN MAN

My belly is empty,
Haven't eaten in days,
I'm dying on the coast,
Listening to the African waves,
I smile because my stomach is like a pot bellied pig's,
I smile because my legs are like twigs,
I smile at the photographers from the west,
That shame people into giving money to the dying rest,
But not me,
I'm past it,
The doctor said so himself,
So I'm dying like a beached whale,
And I'm dying because I failed,
I failed to be born in a rich country,
Come on all you people in the west, look at me,
Repulsive as I am,
Can you spare some of your change for a dying man?

Peter Ingram (17)
Helsby High School

WHY?

Why does rain fall from the sky
Why do sad films always make me cry
Why do I hate my nan's pumpkin pie?
Please, someone tell me, why?

Why did my rabbit have to die
Why do I sometimes tell a lie
Why do I hate apple pie?
Please, someone tell me, why?

Why is the sun so high in the sky
Why do nosy people have to pry
Why do I hate meat and potato pie?
Please, someone tell me, why?

Why is it only birds that fly
Why don't planes fall from the sky?
OK, Mum I'll eat that pie
But please Mum just tell me, why?

Ami Louise Mathieson (13)
Helsby High School

THE SNAKE

Swaying from side to side,
Like a tree in the wind.
It has tiny black eyes,
Peering through the long grass.
Its ruby red body slithers silently towards the water-hole.
It glides like a slippery serpent into the cool water,
Then in one quick quivering movement it is out of the water
And back on the hot desert ground.
It coils its huge body,
And bares its venomous fangs.
A small desert beetle scuttles slowly along the sand,
The snake lifts its tiny head.
It slowly moves towards the prey.
The beetle is caught and swallowed
And the snake closes its eyes and waits
For its next prey to come.

Ashley Slater (11)
Helsby High School

GAGA!

She isn't an ordinary grandma,
In fact she's not all there,
She wouldn't wear socks on her head,
Or walk around quite bare,
But then again she might do,
There's no predicting Gaga,
She's more into giving herself facelifts,
With Vaseline and Bonjela.

No Gran, it's not Sunday,
Yes, all the animals are fine,
We never get homework,
Well anyway I've done mine!
Everything must be perfect,
Everything must be straight,
If not we end up with,
A granny in a state.

She mustn't know the cat's died,
She mustn't know there's been a flood,
She mustn't know that we have
Homework,
Or that the field's a bog of mud.
If she did, she would go into depression,
But then forget why,
So we would have to tell her over
Again,
And end up making her cry.

Her case is really quite sad,
You only know a bit,
But as I'm running out of space,
You'll never know all of it!

Lee Slimming (13)
Helsby High School

THE MILLENNIUM DOME - 1998-2000

Anthurium
Bacterium
Cymatium
It's getting near

Datium
En dometrium
Francium
I can't wait

Gynoecium
Hymenium
I'm getting ready

Indusium
Jabium
Kickium . . . Labium
All my friends will be there

Millennium
Will you be there?

Helen Richards (13)
Helsby High School

THE RAT

Lovely soft fur
Eyes look mysteriously for prey,
As they scurry along the floor,
Like an ant whose nest has been disturbed
Their teeth as sharp as razor blades
Claws sharp at the end like pinpoints
Its great scaly tail swifts in the moonlight.

Laura Hassan (11)
Helsby High School

THE ELEPHANT

Its eyes are a pool of darkness,
With a slight sparkle in one tiny
Corner
It plods peacefully around,
Its ears flapping in the wind
Like a gentle giant
Its grey, wrinkled skin rough and
Dry
With a long trunk,
It sways from side to side hungrily
So clumsy, so gentle
Its teeth are not like a cheetah's
Or a lion's
They chomp up and down continuously
It slowly, steadily, lowers itself to
The ground
It eventually drifts off to sleep
All is quiet
Except all the wildlife in the
Background.

Ashley Kennedy (11)
Helsby High School

MY LOCAL FOOTIE TEAM

My football team is rubbish
We've never won a game
We try our hardest every week,
The manager's to blame.

He lies down on the touch-line
Sleeping while we play,
He says he'll watch it if we win
That'll never happen the fans say.

Then one game we were winning
And all was going cool
We'd eventually won a football game
But it was against the blind school.

We then played top of the table
But we were confident still
All was going brightly
But then we lost ten nil!

David Roberts (14)
Helsby High School

LOSING HIM

The time I lost him was so bad,
I was destroyed, just so sad.
I never talked to anyone again,
My life without him was so plain.

Being with him was so great,
Now it's all just too late.
Looking at him and knowing he was mine,
Made the days in my world shine.

On my own for such a while,
Nothing seemed to make me smile.
Endless day in a world so bleak,
An hour seemed to last a week.

Wind and rain and so much gloom,
Sat alone in a dreary room.
Perhaps one day the sun will shine,
And once again he'll be mine.

Sarah Hollyhead (12)
Helsby High School

MY FRIEND JO

I have a friend called Jo,
Who has way too many problems,
I am surprised that she hasn't already,
Hired herself an agony aunt.

Her brother is going mad,
Her sister is insane,
Her dad has gone and left them all,
Her mum's the one to blame.

When it comes to school work,
She's bottom of the class,
She can't add, take or multiply,
Read, write or spell.

She gets 0/10 for everything,
Her parents really don't care,
She never gets a merit,
And her self-confidence is low.

It's very boring to talk to her,
It really is a shame
That I'm her only friend in the world,
Well . . . she is only in my mind!

Rachael Wojtala (13)
Helsby High School

FOOD AND DRINK

There are many different types of food and drink
What should I eat? Let me think
Tomatoes? Crisps? Cheese?
Can I have some chips please?
What could I have to quench my thirst?
I'll have to find something first.
If only I could have some wine or beer,
But I'm under-age - oh dear!
I've got an idea of what I can eat!
Golly gosh, I'm in for a treat.
I'll have all of my favourite things,
I could invite my friends, I'll give them a ring.
'Oh great you can come!
We will have so much fun.'
Crisps, cakes, sausages on sticks,
We could even have a Haribo star mix.
Orange, lemonade and Coke
Better watch that I don't choke.
None of this food is good for us,
My mother will make a very big fuss.
This party is going to be great!
It starts in an hour, I can't wait!

Rebecca Thomas (14)
Helsby High School

My Favourite Animal

Is it . . .
Eagle, majestic, lord of the sky,
Angelic golden feathers, but cruel dark eye.
Stag, the ruler of the fell,
Fleet of foot, but tends to smell.
Magical hare, without compare,
Or 'twould be with more brain cells spare.
Badgers, black and white
Hidden in the shadows of the night -
Whose cutesy characters hide one shame,
For to dine on worms is their night's aim.
Hedgehog, like the prickled mouse
Nice to see, but has many a flea or louse.
Fox, to sing his ode, many a poet has taken up pen,
But potters say he has a smelly den.
Pandas are cuddly and eat bamboo,
But they are omnivorous and would eat you.
Bonny polar bears from Manitoba,
Who eat tramps when they're not sober.

No
Long ago in ancient days
A creature such as this
Rolled the sun across the sky.
But fie!
Nowadays my praise
Is all the dung beetle's going to get.

Rose Jones (13)
Helsby High School

MUM

Why is the sun always yellow Mum?
Why do you always kiss Dad?
Why do you make me have baths Mum?
Why do you always get mad?

Why does it snow in December Mum?
Why is Dad always rude?
Why can't I stay up late Mum?
Why are you always in a mood?

Why is the grass always green Mum?
Why is my brother a pain?
Why do you send me to school Mum?
Why do you jog in the rain?

Why are you always so kind Mum?
Why do you cook lovely teas?
Why do you give me pocket money Mum?
Why do you put up with me?

Debbie Parker (12)
Helsby High School

THE LION

Eyes focused on its prey
Its long bushy tail
Waggling from one side
To another like a snake
In the Sahara,
Its long mane brushed
To one side by a cool
Breeze.

Toby Mutton (11)
Helsby High School

A PIG

A rounded body like a ball
A snout coming from its face
With trotters on its legs
And a tail turning round
It sees something brown
It runs, it jumps
Mud everywhere
It rolls around having a lovely time
An hour gone
It gets tired
And goes to its sty
It gets on the hay and falls asleep
To start the day,
The same way
Tomorrow.

Helen Ireland (12)
Helsby High School

THE LEOPARD

Sharp claws scratching
Carefully camouflaging
Follows its prey around like an eagle.
Launches from a tree,
Pounces from a bush,
Kills like a lion,
Viciously attacks.
Tremendous teeth chomp,
Sleekly goes to find some other prey,
Spotty body gets ready to be a fright again.

Sarah Smith (11)
Helsby High School

THE EAGLE

Looking down at his prey,
Opening his wingspan wide,
His claws stretching.
His colours he shows as he swoops down,
He just misses and lands back on his branch,
Waiting patiently, quietly,
As he tries again the scattering of his prey stops.
His beak opens wide and shuts just as quick.
His wingspan pulls back in
And he's caught his catch for tonight.
He squawks his evil laugh
And flies towards the moon.

Sam Healing (11)
Helsby High School

THE SNAKE

Slimy like green gunge
Scary like a werewolf,
As fast as a bullet
Being shot from a gun.
It slowly moves when it sees its prey,
Then makes its move
Which makes its day.
Its tongue flicks out as fast as an arrow,
And eats its prey by swallowing it whole.
Its black long body slithers along the floor,
Looking for a hiding place, waiting for more.

Tom Hodgson (12)
Helsby High School

THE FALCON

The falcon is sitting on a branch,
Looking for its prey,
The falcon takes flight like an aeroplane.
It hovers,
It sees its prey; it does not take its eyes off it
For even a split second.
Like a sniper aiming for its shot,
It goes higher then stoops at 155mph
It comes down like a bullet.
It lifts up its wings and out come the claws.
It hits the rabbit with great force,
The rabbit is dead.
The beak is as sharp as a *razor*.
The falcon rips the flesh off the rabbit and eats it.
The falcon takes off with its prey back to its family.

Adam Dean (12)
Helsby High School

THE FLY

Small like a pebble the fly sitting on the window frame.
Its two thousand eyes fixed on only *food!*
It buzzes towards its dinner
Flying towards its food
It lands on the plate
But then something glistens in the sun
A fly swat.
The fly buzzes frantically out the window,
Away from the house,
Now gone.

Alastair Chadwick (11)
Helsby High School

A HAWK

Eyes filled with mystery
Soaring like a rocket through the sky
He calls for a mate which he longs for
Then suddenly he looks down
His vision like a telescope
Then he silently swoops down
The mouse had no chance
It ran like a jet but it was all over
The beak of the hawk tore at the mouse
Blood flowing like a river
Then he took off
Again soaring away with no trace
But he will not be gone for long.

Lee Thornhill (12)
Helsby High School

HAWK

Flying like an aeroplane,
Hunting for prey,
With scanning black eyes,
Peaceful wings and sharp claws,
A bear's lovely brown fur colour,
Looking around for something juicy,
Maybe it will find something tasty,
Wwwooossshhh!
A little field mouse for its prey,
In the nest young chirp for food,
They eat the juicy mouse,
Now it's time to find some more.

Mark Antrobus (11)
Helsby High School

THE EAGLE

Watching the wilderness below
Searching soundlessly like a soldier on watch
Sun scorching its plume of feathers
Electrified by a movement below
Something scurrying below
For a split second it stares
Then
It spreads its wings and soars into the sky
As quick as a gunshot its prey moves away
But the king of the sky is on it
In its talons it carries it home
For the eagle is the jewelled emperor of the sky.

Graham Harrison (11)
Helsby High School

THE TAWNY OWL

Eyes sharp and squinted,
Like a spinning blade.
Distant hooting and howling,
Filling the night sky with noise.
As it swoops down silently,
Disturbing branches and leaves,
A mouse pops out of a drainpipe,
And gets gripped by small piercing teeth.
The owl catches its prey,
Devouring it slowly, silently,
And with the wind howling away,
The mouse does not see another day.

Jim Yearley (11)
Helsby High School

THE FALCON!

Long sharp claws to grab its prey,
A long wide, wingspan to fly through the
air with,
Excellent flyers,
Gliding gradually through the sky,
Small, black, beady eyes to see its prey
with,
Its prey is seen,
Speeds down to catch it,
The prey is caught,
Slowly takes it back to its nest,
And feeds it to her young ones.

Jennifer Hayes (11)
Helsby High School

TIGER

Hear the soft sound of purring
As he slowly sneaks up on his prey.
His fur striped and sleek,
Big ears pricking up at every sound.
Huge paws pounding on the ground
Bright eyes flashing
Suddenly he leaps into the air,
Sharp claws releasing,
Teeth bright and gleaming
As he lands, his teeth bite into flesh.
Filled with happiness,
He sneaks away to the trees.

Kristen Ellison (11)
Helsby High School

THE CHEETAH

Still like a hard brick wall
Claws shining brightly like a star,
Its spotty coat like a million dots
Sees its prey and ready to pounce
The teeth sharp like a knife or dagger
Its feet run like a train on a track.

Prey has been caught,
Lying dead on the ground
All is quiet and very still like an empty house.
Its great sharp teeth start to eat
It's a dinner party for hundreds
It's all soon gone and bones on the floor
The day is gone
And it walks off into the jungle.

Stephanie Payne (12)
Helsby High School

THE JAGUAR

Fast as a sports car it chases its prey,
Creeping carefully to his food,
Prowling, pouncing on his meal,
Reaching speeds up to forty miles per hour,
Its food will not get away.
His beady eyes watching every move
Like a statue in a park.
Panting after a fast chase he patrols his land
His beautiful skin startling everything that sees him.

Ryan Maloney (11)
Helsby High School

LEOPARDS

The big furry body covered in spots
He looks as though he's got chicken pox.

If you scare him he will roar,
He might even scratch you with his claw.

He comes up to you, gives you a scare,
You don't want to run anywhere.

You see his teeth and think oh no!
But he just wants to be friends with you.

His dark beady eyes move around the room,
You just feel like you're in a room of gloom.

Elizabeth Ellams (11)
Helsby High School

THE CHEETAH

It speeds through the grass as fast as a swift arrow,
Slowing down as it sees its prey.
Stands still and watches it,
Then it starts to creep with its claws digging in the ground.
It lies still,
As still as a frozen lake it watches its prey.
Heart beating fast and furious
The prey has seen it.
As fast as a shotgun the prey has gone.
The cheetah starts to run,
Then it pounces - thump!
The cheetah's caught it,
The sharp teeth devour the buffalo.

Helen Millington (11)
Helsby High School

THE BOX

When you look inside my box
There's amazing things, lots and lots
The sun, the moon and the stars
All the planets including Mars.

A photo of my family and friends
A road which never ever ends
A dream of flying on a cloud
A great big tunnel underground.

A day's trip around the world
The nicest song I've ever heard
Being small like a mouse
Living in a chocolate house.

Snow on a summer's day
A playground where the children play
A green dog and a purple fox
This is what's inside my box.

Sophie McGrogan (12)
Helsby High School

THE EAGLE

Tall and still like a statue,
Wings stretched out wide.
Snow-white feathers gleaming in the sun,
While its prey waits aside.
Suddenly its eyes catch sight,
Of a little mouse creeping around.
It swoops down like a rocket,
Watching its prey all the time.
Then, its victim is caught and quickly devoured.

Natalie Dash (11)
Helsby High School

THE LION

Playful like a tabby cat
His tail sways from side to side.
As he leaps through the meadow,
He spots a deer
Through the long green grass.
He quickly slides to the ground
As fast as lightning.
His razor-sharp claws
Twinkle in the sunlight.
He pounces! His dinner is caught.
He eats the deer hungrily
And then settles down for a nap in the shade
And sleeps like a log.

Rachel Horsefield (11)
Helsby High School

THE VULTURE

Gliding like a hang glider looking for food
Turning his bald head this way and that
Suddenly he sees its food and swoops down
He lands without the slightest thud.

He walks up to the carcass and waits
for the king vulture and all the other
scavengers to open the carcass
Once the carcass is open they eat like
they have never eaten before.
The mothers go back to their high nests
and feed the baby vultures.

Adam Ryder (11)
Helsby High School

A HORSE'S SEED OF WISDOM

The horse is as swift as the seeds flying in the wind,
picking up on their scented smell.
But, come planting time
all might not be well.

For as the seeds find their ground, starting their fresh, new roots
the mouse and slug are quite nearby.
Beware, for there is a feast ahead,
starting when the seeds begin to fly . . .

Ah, back to the horse, my friend,
as their manes do fly.
All is well? I don't think so, my lord
for they begin to die.

Heidi Roberts (11)
Helsby High School

THE WHALE

The smooth slick whale grabbing its prey
Diving, ducking under the sea
The whale moving slick as a slither
Devours its prey like water.
Swimming off into the lonely sea,
Off to find another victim it can take.
It speeds up and takes a little fish in its huge jaws,
All down in one.
Finds another and another until its hunger
Is beaten.

Tony Charles (11)
Helsby High School

I WONDER WHAT IS OUT THERE

I wonder what is out there
I wonder who is there
I wonder if they wear their cats
And stroke their underwear.

I wonder what is out there
I wonder what they eat
I wonder if they eat Chinese
Or maybe eat their feet.

I wonder what is out there
I wonder what they do
I wonder, do they play football
Or jet-ski in the loo.

I wondered what is out there
But now I don't think I care.

Christopher Clarke (12)
Helsby High School

THE DOG

Bounding through the fields of gold,
Goes a puppy, three months old.
He's full of joy, and dark as night,
And all he sees is in black and white.
He looks around to see his master,
Catches his sight, and then runs faster.
Now he's far . . . far, far away,
He's been running all through the day.
He finds a corner to rest his head,
But then he finds out it's his own warm bed.

Hollie Wilson (11)
Helsby High School

FISHES IN THE SEA

Fishes, fishes,
Big and small,
To them, the world above is a wall.
Harder for fishes to cross the line,
But easier for a fishing line.

Shallow waters,
Deep seas,
Fish can be found
Wherever they please.

Coral can be colourful,
Coral can be bright,
But not in the dead of night.

Gina Walker (12)
Helsby High School

MY GRANDAD

You will find my grandad
Sitting in that chair
God only knows
How long he has been there
His eyes closed tight
As if it was night

You reach for the remote
He calls out
'I'm watching this.'

David Hawes (12)
Helsby High School

BIRTHDAY THOUGHTS

It's my birthday tomorrow
And I can hardly wait
All that I must do now
Is go to sleep . . . and then wake.

My mum and dad usually surprise me
But do they know I'd like a money tree?
Sister Rebecca always hides something away
Brother Richard gives me a game to play.

Will there be a party with lots of things to do?
Or perhaps a visit with my friends to the local zoo!
A trip on an aeroplane would make my day complete
Or even a famous pop star I would love to meet.

Laura Mullin (12)
Helsby High School

TWO FAT BEETLES

One fine day in the middle of May
Two fat beetles caught some prey,
Three years later it got away,
Which turned the beetles white and grey.
They bought a badger in its place
And put it in the fireplace.
The badger went all green and mouldy
But the beetles liked it just the same.
They took it to the supermarket
But a spider ate them up straight away.

Darren Hodgeman (12)
Helsby High School

FEAR

It was a lovely warm night and exciting until
We turned off the light and lost the big thrill.
Then all of a sudden a rustling sound
Like a little peep, nothing could be found.
Adrenaline was pumping as our heads hit the floor,
But no one would dare to open the door.
Then a howling noise like a new baby's cry,
Worried in case something would fall from the sky.
Then a gust of wind rushed through our tent
Now I would rather be paying the rent.
Then a claw reached out to take us away,
Turn on the torch to keep it at bay.
The zippers drew open, slowly we glare,
It's only Dad but he gave us a scare.

Jade Mao-Moraghan (12)
Helsby High School

PUDDLES

I looked in a puddle,
And what did I see?
This funny face,
smiling back at me.

It was kind and happy,
the face I saw,
a big smiling face,
from on the floor.

The teeth that looked back,
were crooked and bent.
It made me sad,
that they just hadn't grown
as they were meant.

The mirror in the puddle,
made me see,
what was right and wrong with me.
It showed me that I'm not perfect and,
I shouldn't be.

Robert Tust (12)
Helsby High School

MAGICAL BOX

Magical Box contains things about me.
It's buried in the deepest blue ocean,
So that no-one can see.
Magical Box contains an enormous roller-coaster,
For only I have the key,
Which lets the fun run free.

I'll have my sister's blow-up chair
And my teddy 'Snowy Bear'.
My friends and family will be there too,
My hamster 'Levi' and my cat named 'Sue'.

To be a famous singer, with a number one hit,
Or sail around the world on a great sailing ship.
To fly on Concorde across to New York,
And join Leonardo on a long romantic walk.

Miranda Newey (12)
Helsby High School

SEASONS

Spring comes with
animals from
hibernating,
flowers come in
bright colours.

Summer brings
children out to play in
their shorts and
T-shirts. Getting
cooling ice-creams and
lollies off the ice-cream man.

Autumn is when
brown and yellow
leaves drop onto the
floor and make a bed
for animals to
start hibernating.

Winter brings
snow and children
out on their sleighs,
throwing ice-cold
snowballs at friends and family.

Kirsty Lorimer (12)
Helsby High School

COLOURS

Colours of so many shades,
How we wonder how they're made.
Colours warm, colours cold,
Colours new, colours old.
The colour yellow *bold* and bright,
The colour of the moon at night.
The colour blue like the sky,
The colour of tears in my eye.

Colours bright, colours dim,
Where shall I begin?
The colour grey,
Which spoils the day,
The colour green,
Which makes the scene,
And the colour red,
The shade of my bed.

Colours of so many shades,
How we wonder how they're made.
Colours warm, colours cold,
Colours new, colours old.
The colour purple, my favourite of all,
The one I'd like on my bedroom wall.
The colour black, not a colour at all,
But colour of sky after sun falls.

Terri Wade (12)
Helsby High School

A BOX FULL OF NOTHING

A box full of nothing,
Let's go and see
How many horrible things inside there could be.
Elephants' toenail clippings, a poisoned rat
A tortured rabbit from a magician's hat.
All this in a box full of nothing.

A box full of nothing,
Let's go and see
How many wonderful things inside there could be.
A sweet shop filled with candy, a hot sunny day
And a thousand children out to play.
All this in a box full of nothing.

A box full of nothing,
Let's go and see
How many dreamy things inside there could be.
A castle of sunflowers, in a cloudy sky
How many pretty angels will fly by.
All this in a box full of nothing.

Katy Selby (12)
Helsby High School

PARENTS

Mum is very very kind
When my kit I cannot find.
She puts it in the washing machine
For me to take to school
Nice and clean.

Dad is helpful all the time
Assisting me in making words rhyme.
He's always relaxed and quite calm,
Ensuring that we don't come to harm.

Squeaks is a noisy girl
I really think she's in a whirl.
In her bedroom late at night
Singing dancing, it's quite a fright.

Grandma and Grandad really care
They fuss when I don't brush my hair.
Uncle Neil and Auntie Sue
They'll always be there for you.

Nick Gilbody (12)
Helsby High School

FEAR

My name is Mr Clarke
I jump every time I hear . . .
A dog bark.

I am such a nervous lad
I feel so gloomy . . .
And sad.

When people stop and stare
I stand still . . .
And glare.

My face goes bright red
So I go upstairs . . .
To bed.

James Kracke (14)
Oaklands School

THE DOLPHIN

Elegant and graceful these marine mammals
glide through warm turquoise waters,
where tropical fish in rainbow colours
flash through an ageless coral kingdom.

Leaping, splashing, an excited school
playful and adventurous explode from the waves,
tumbling somersaults, arching through the air
one by one they submerge into the ocean.

Sonar clicks warning of danger,
shadow cast by iron-grey hull with churning motor
terrorising drag-net, imprisoning, caging,
wounding fragile dorsal fin.

Escape to freedom, desperate dive
searching for security in peaceful dark waters,
cautiously surfacing, breathing deeply,
seeking tranquil friendship.

An intelligent trusting creature
the dolphin, lesson learned,
joyfully explores its translucent environment,
a beautiful magical specimen.

Elizabeth Broad (13)
Helsby High School

ON THE BEACH

The sand is yellow
The water is blue
Out come the seagulls
All clean and new
The lifeguard watches the children swim,
While Mum and Dad are lying in.
In the shop a little boy spends
Lots of money on his friends.

Philip Murphy (15)
Oaklands School

FISHES

F ishes have fins and some have hairs on their faces
I   n a pond they are good swimmers/
S whim in a river on their own,
H ungry all the time
E very time they go alone,
S omeone tries to catch them.

Christopher Lloyd (13)
Oaklands School

LIMERICKS

There was a young girl called Michelle,
She didn't feel very well,
She went straight to bed
And her teacher said
'Stay in bed till you hear the bell.'

Selina Rimmer (13)
Oaklands School

THE SCHOOL CARETAKER

My name is Mr Breaker
I am the school caretaker
I scrub the floors
And clean the doors
The kids are brats
And hide the mats
I'm really a fool
For working in a school.

Christopher Heeks (14)
Oaklands School

HORSES

H orses jump
O ver fences
R ivers
S treams
E ating grass
S tanding looking.

Samantha Bayley (13)
Oaklands School

FROGS

F rogs are slimy
R ibbit-ribbit they croak
O n the rock they sit
G azing
S taring.

Lisa Neild (13)
Oaklands School

ROY KEANE

My name is Roy Keane
I always look mean.
I want to score goals
and plug all the holes
My team will stay up
We will win the cup
We will go out on the town
and never go down.

David Llewellyn (14)
Oaklands School

MONKEY

M erry monkeys
O n trampolines
N ever fall off
K ind and gentle
E at grass and peanuts
Y ou will love them.

Shaun Brinksman
Oaklands School

ODD ONE OUT

My name is Kevin Stevens
I always have good reasons
To stay up late and watch TV
To see the wrestlers go crazy
The next day when I go to school
The others have all watched football.

Kevin Stevens
Oaklands School

LIMERICKS

There was a young lady called Kim
Who was badly in need of a pin
Her skirt was so big
When she did a jig
It dropped and we all had a grin.

Kimberley Cotton (14)
Oaklands School

LIMERICKS

There was a good boy called Mark
Who liked to play in the park
He swung so high
He flew in the sky
And he only came back when it was dark.

Mark Cressey (13)
Oaklands School

LIMERICK

There was a young girl called Kate
Who came to school very late
She would not get dressed
She was such a pest
That naughty young girl called Kate.

Katie Holliday (13)
Oaklands School

BIRDS

Birds fly
They have wings made of beautiful feathers
They make nests in trees
They lay lovely, smooth eggs
Some swoop down and eat worms
Some circle and eat insects
Some perch and eat seeds
But they are all fascinating.

Christopher Walters (12)
Oaklands School

LIMERICK

There was a young lad called Stu
Who always knew what to do.
He'd go out each day
To the farm and play
But ran when the cow went 'Moo!'

Stuart Carless (13)
Oaklands School

MY NEW SCHOOL

I like woodwork,
It is good,
I make models,
And I can take them home.

Craig Wilkinson (11)
Oaklands School

MR ROSS

My name is Mr Ross
I am the computer boss
I teach all day
And never play
Kids tap the keys
And bang their knees
They drive me mad
I get so sad.

Lee Humphries (14)
Oaklands School

LIMERICK

There was a young lad called Peter
Who could high jump more than a metre
He went so high
He touched the sky
And landed *K'plonk* on Anita.

Peter Jackson (14)
Oaklands School

THE ZEBRA

Z oos have zebras
E ating grass
B lack and white stripes
R oaming and running
A round and around.

Alex Perks (13)
Oaklands School

HAMSTERS

Hamsters are snuggly
Hamsters are cuddly
They run a lot
Kick a lot and
Eat a lot
Hamsters are snuffly
Hamsters are lovely.

Emma Wilson
Oaklands School

CATS

C uddly, friendly pets
A lways on your lap
T apping and playing
S leeping in the sun.

Rebecca Evanson (12)
Oaklands School

FISH

F ishes always swimming
I n rivers, seas and tanks
S ome of every colour
H elp to keep them safe *from pollution.*

Mark Barnett (12)
Oaklands School

MISS BROWN

My name is Miss Brown
I live in a town
I went to meet my man
We met in the street
Had something to eat
And left in a caravan.

Lyndsey Luscombe (14)
Oaklands School

HOT SHOT!

I go to Oaklands School.
They treat me like a fool.
But I am not
I'm a real hot shot
Whenever I play football.

Gavin Judson (14)
Oaklands School

MONKEY

Monkeys climb up high
They jump up from tree to tree
With long thin tails
They hang from the branches
And stare with their big brown eyes.

Jane Clark (12)
Oaklands School

FROGS

Frogs are green
Frogs are slimy
When you put one in your hand
It will slip out
Be careful
Or it will hit the ground hard
Splat.

Paul Emmison
Oaklands School

MRS CHRISTY

My name is Mrs Christy
I go out when it's misty
I work at school
And watch football
I stay out late
For bed I hate.

James Jeffries (14)
Oaklands School

DOGS

Dogs are pets
Our best friends
Going for walks
Staying at home.

Richard Higgins (12)
Oaklands School

AUTUMN AND THE CAT

A leaf twirls around
And drops to the ground,
Another shade to the pile.
A leaf goes crunch
Another in the bunch
A wrecked shade to the pile.

The tree's limbs are dead
There's the shade of brown to the bed,
Lying on the floor.
The wind blows the leaves away.
Now there's less leaves than yesterday.

Next year will there be more?
On a path a cat scurries across.
On its feet is dark green moss.
It's been climbing up a tree.
Will there be more leaves next year
Blowing right here?
I'll find out, and I'll see.

Daniel Solan (11)
Sir Thomas Boteler High School

EXQUISITE STAR

The exquisite star floats gracefully
through the deep dark sky.
The other stars go floating by,
But this star stands out from the rest,
Gracefully, peacefully doing its best
To shine all night,
Clear, crystal, bright.

The Earth is a unique place,
Yet lonely somehow,
With an isolated face.
Deep down it is filled with joy and charm,
Even deeper you will find the anger and harm.

Sharon Fitzpatrick (12)
Sir Thomas Boteler High School

OH, MORNINGS

Get up, get out of bed
Wake up, sleepy head
Don't run down the stairs
Do it anyway because no one cares.
Open the door
Fall on the floor
Oh, mornings!

I have my breakfast
And think about the awful test
Forgot to revise
Oh my life
Such a strife
Oh, mornings!

Brush my teeth
They start to bleed
I pressed too hard
Oh I feel so tired
Wash my face
Oh I'm late
Oh, mornings!

Kim Vernon (11)
Sir Thomas Boteler High School

I Can't Sleep

I went to bed last night
and I couldn't sleep.
I tried counting backwards and
I tried counting sheep.

I looked out of the window
and looked up at the moon.
Its beams of moonlight,
Were shining into my room.

I tried to count the stars,
Twinkling way up high.
After counting 500, I really,
Had to sigh.

I think I'm getting tired now
and I really want to yawn.
So I'll get back in bed
and get up when it's dawn!

Azzita Darani (11)
Sir Thomas Boteler High School

Polar Bears In The Snow

I painted a brilliant picture,
The greatest ever seen.
It's hung in the National Gallery
and was published by the Queen.
This greatest ever picture,
Was called 'Polar Bears in the Snow'.
And in case you didn't believe me.
I've hung it here below.

Nicola Birmingham (11)
Sir Thomas Boteler High School

A FEATHER FROM AN EAGLE

A feather is so light and delicately floats around
A feather when dropped slowly falls to the ground
When I look at a feather I stare at its golden colour
I like feathers the way they are
It would be awful if they were duller.

The eagle is a mighty bird,
Flying through the air
Soaring high in the pale blue sky
Without a thought or a care.
The eagle with its beady eyes makes a perfect hunter
It stalks its prey with extreme care
Always turns out the victor.

Craig Morgan (12)
Sir Thomas Boteler High School

ACORNS

Who would have thought it, a tiny little acorn,
Could bring such beauty in the spring,
But now it's an acorn in the autumn season,
Rolling around on the floor for a reason,
To make an oak tree years from now.
We'll all be old,
It'll be standing proud,
With its roots firmly placed in the ground.
With its crown of leaves on its head,
Ready to make the acorns spread.

Kelly Lafferty (12)
Sir Thomas Boteler High School

THE PEN

The pen glides swiftly across the paper,
Up and down looping the loop.
'All the work finished before you go home class'
It hears.
The pen speeds up.
The clock strikes 3:09.
The pen changes into a blur of speed.
It hears a bell ringing.
'Stay behind Daniel' it hears.
It slows down again.

Kevin Daniels (12)
Sir Thomas Boteler High School

MOTHER

Though I often say I love you,
And couldn't mean it more,
I know there are many things
I haven't thanked you for.
For instance there's the
Love you show,
The understanding too,
In accepting me for who I am
And caring as you do.
I may not speak my gratitude
As often as I should,
But like the love I have for you,
I hope it's understood.

Joanne Minton (13)
The County High School

THE ANIMAL

Small, yet lethal,
Slowly, it spins the web
Of deceit.

Darkness
follows its every step.
Shuddering, I stare into its
empty eyes.
It makes my skin crawl.

A smile so sickly-sweet.
The king of destruction
and death.

I watch,
as it tightens its grip.
The Earth trembles
at its feet.

Its poisonous stench
fills the air.
Venomous vibes
forming around me.

A world,
once at peace.
Torn apart, ripped to shreds,
by one vicious,
vile animal.

So wrong yet
so powerful,

The animal
is man.

Hannah Tharmalingam (13)
The Grange School

THE CAT AND THE SQUIRREL

She hunts in the garden,
Looking for her prey,
Then she sees a squirrel,
Ascending up the tree.

Unaware of the menace
It jumps between the branches;
Then it sees the table beneath the tree;
It climbs down the tree;
It runs up the tree and collects the nuts.

Suddenly she sees the squirrel on the table.
She crouches down waiting to pounce
As if she is camouflaged into the green grass.
She waits there like a statue waiting for it to come down.

The squirrel has bundled all the nuts together.
She gets ready.
The squirrel climbs down . . . then suddenly
The cat chases it up the tree.
To the cat this is victory.

Luke Ashall (13)
The Grange School

THE CAT

By day the cat is an indolent animal,
Wiping his eyes and refusing to travel.
Most of the day, the cat's asleep,
Occasionally rising for bites to eat.

Darkness creates a different creature,
Darting quietly with feline feature.
She makes a move on her innocent prey,
Not knowing it's living its final day.

When the cat is full she returns to the house;
Licking her lips after her final mouse.
Showing to us she's a Jekyll and Hyde,
Through day a friend, yet evil beside.

Phil Clancy (13)
The Grange School

THE YETI

In the eternal world of white,
Camouflaged, quite out of sight,
This fearsome creature stalks alone,
Able to strip men to the bone.

Footprints sighted everywhere,
His colossal roars cry through the air.
This deadly, fearsome ball of white,
Fills explorers full of fright.

If you smell his gruesome breath,
Be sure you know it's certain death.
Is this creature full of sin
Or maybe just protecting kin?

Perhaps there is another one?
Perhaps he's even got a son?
Perhaps he is not alone?
Perhaps some family of his own?

Will we ever know?

Richard Hutchinson (13)
The Grange School

DARK ANGEL

No exordium -
   Diving down from the sky,
     In a stone-like fall,
       Straight plunges down towards me.

So nearby,
   I hear the rush of air,
     As you pass me by,
        Just moving over me.

Close enough
   To note the crack of your wings,
     Who are you headed for?
        See your cool glare pass me,

Look up,
   Your journey's soon complete,
     With one I love in your arms;
Gone . . . until the next time.

Jenny Winter (13)
The Grange School

THE CAT

A beautiful creature that never is seen,
Which hides in the shadows at dusk,
Avoiding the light that would give her away,
She pounces again and again.

She dodges through shadows, chasing her prey;
From one to another she glides -
The picture of elegance, silent and quick,
Enclosed in the blanket of night.

She walks along railings, tightrope thin,
But these cause no problems for her.
She dashes along, sure-footed and swift,
Then somersaults down to the floor.

But now as the day is beginning to dawn,
The cat must return to her home,
And she will be back though she needs not to hunt,
For the darkness is where she belongs.

Lucy Bate (14)
The Grange School

A HERON

I wiped the window with my hand
And looked out to the frosty land.
Hot breath clouded up the pane,
I took my hand and wiped again.
My eyes, accustomed to the glare,
Saw a bird high in the air.
It landed in a nearby tree
And tucked its wings in gracefully.
It looked around from where it perched
And with its eyes the pond it searched.
I knew what it was there to do:
I rapped the window, shouted 'Shoo!'
That heron is a naughty chap,
And likes our Koi carp for a snack.
I rapped again. It flew away.
Our fish will see another day.

Lisa Bramwell (13)
The Grange School

THE MOUSE

The mouse, he does crawl
From his home in a wall.
When he looks for food
He must be very shrewd.
He darts around the home;
Every space he does roam.

Just like Robin Hood,
Courageous he stood.
To steal from the rich to give to the poor,
To feed his family once more.
Although he is almost blind,
More food he will find.

As he runs without a sound,
More food he has found.
Now he must creep through feet,
Where many people are about to eat.
He must go past in a hurry
Not to be seen in his scurry.

Into his hole he will crawl
To finally feed his family in the wall.

Mark Burton (13)
The Grange School

THE DOG

He comes in barking very rude,
Asking his master for some food,
His master comes down the stairs
because he cares

He eats his food making a mess
all over the floor,
His master finds cleaning it up
such a bore,
He goes upstairs to have a bath,
And everyone has a very good laugh.

After his bath he is shiny and clean,
He goes to sleep and he has a dream,
When he wakes up the very next day,
The dog is ready to go and play.

Rajiv Tandon (13)
The Grange School

ANTS

Marching down in single file,
They are standing all in ranks.
Head towards the dirty pile,
Guards upon the flanks.

Underground cadets work hard,
Scurrilous gossip is bad!
The gate to their lair to guard:
Homeless, they'd be sad.

Peter Tipler (13)
The Grange School

Two 'Swallow' Poems

I

The swallow is a delicate creature
Whose chest is its prominent feature.
It's graceful in flight,
Quite powerful in might -
If you're a fly then it's going to eat ya!

II

In winter you start your migration,
Flying from nation to nation.
You come back in spring,
By foot or by wing,
Without needing fuel from a station.

Stephen Willis (13)
The Grange School

The Lion

As he lurks in the darkness,
He waits for his moment.
When he sees his prey,
He then darts into a spring -
Grabs the prey in his jaws:
It's a quick but mean end.

When he's back in his den
With a three-course meal,
He then feeds on the carcass
In a dark pool of blood.
He is hungry for more,
But he rests for the moment.

Guy Campbell (13)
The Grange School

THE MOUSE

A sound from on far,
Catches the attention,
Beckons him forward,
And then a false alarm.

Stealthily and quietly,
Cunning and clever, he waits,
A chance he would take, to get
That piece of cake, balancing
Life and limb.

A life on the edge,
Predators around every corner -
The silence will fall.
The mouse has a meal;
Fastidiously he leaves the moth.

A flash of lightning -
The mouse is gone
Into the distance.
Something must have caught his eyes.
A scrap, a struggle -
The mouse is no more.

Ross McDyre (14)
The Grange School

THE CAT

Prowling through the sable night,
  Strong feeling in her eyes.
Stealing through the backyard, like
  A robber in disguise.

As vicious as a tiger,
  Predacious in her way.
Yet she purrs like a kitten,
  So nothing's left to say.

A queen among her subjects,
  Majestic, proud and grand.
A fierce and savage killer,
  That dominates her land.

She's lying low and waiting,
  She casts an eye around.
She watches like an eagle,
  For movement or a sound.

She creeps across the garden,
  Her victim well in sight.
A struggle breaks; the deed's done;
  She slips into the night.

A shadow by the back fence,
  She knows the time is right.
The patter of her paws, sends
  A whisper through the night.

Debjani Talukder (14)
The Grange School

THE RABBIT

The rabbit,
Small and clever,
Fast as ever,
For more food,
He will endeavour.

He outruns hunters,
And most punters.
A nice smooth coat,
And feet like boats.

No time to get fat,
Or chased by a cat.
Up hill, down hill,
Hoping for a kill.

The cat ends the chase
Exhaustion in its face.
The rabbit is free,
But what's the fee?

None can catch him,
Even with a ferret's whim.
Many try,
But eventually die.

The next week
He hears a shriek!
Off he goes,
Running scared!
No one cared!

Andrew Taylor (13)
The Grange School

DAY AND NIGHT

Day begins with early morn,
Bringing with it, the ascent of dawn.
The sun appears extremely bright,
And opens up the world to light.

The sun stays with us all day long,
But then with mysticism it is gone.
Bats will fly and owls appear,
The darkness sets in and
Night begins.

The following morning the sun will rise,
It runs its course, then once more dies,
Taking with it all the light,
And leaving, yet again, the night.

Gina Percy (13)
The Grange School

UNTITLED

Twigs waltz around like litter,
As icy winds break their hearts,
Snow falls like sparkling glitter,
Shrouding the hedges and carts.

Even with the fire alight,
A chill runs across my spine,
As the darkness of the night,
Takes all the warmth that's mine.

Katie Ferry (13)
The Grange School

The Storm

I saw the lightning flash:
1000, 2000, 3000, 4000, 5000, 6000 . . .
Only six miles away! We must dash.
Into the house we run for shelter:
Last time was 4000 . . .
It looks like a belter.
It's gone dark outside; the daylight is dead.
Thunder and lightning together - it's right overhead!
Then almost as quickly we're back on the grass;
The fright of a lifetime has started to pass.

Natalie Johnson (13)
The Grange School

An Autumn Day

The biting winds of autumn,
Gushing past my face like water.
The golden browns of autumn,
The sways and rants of trees,
Leaves fluttering in the wind.
A dirty ball of wool,
Hopping from branch to branch,
Scratching for a morsel of food.
The tiny ball of wool flew skywards,
To mingle with the desolate sky,
Then the wind turned to a whisper,
Yes, *gone!*

Andrew Hulme (12)
Verdin High School

NIGHT

The sun sets into a golden sky,
The nightingale ushers a sweet lullaby,
The sparrows have all settled down to rest,
The owl starts his hungry quest,
The silent hunters of the night,
Watch until there is no light.

The silence is disturbed once more,
For on the ground a patter of paws,
Out of the mist approaches the fox,
Rummaging around in a worn-out box,
A flick of its tail and it's caught its prey,
And in the darkness carries it away.

The soft miaowing of a cat,
The swiftness of a single bat,
The night gives its last goodbyes
And gives welcome to the new sunrise.

Fiona Ellison-Smith (12)
Verdin High School

THE DEMONS OF DARKNESS

When it falls around, you cannot name it;
This untouchable night is not a game; you cannot play it.
A screech echoes through the foggy vastness.
The deceased lurk beyond the vast, black cover
That calls itself night.
Ghostly ghouls and sour souls dance on their moonlit shadows.
Defeated prey plummet to the cold, dark ground,
Bitter as it is, their life has been taken, their death is true.
Ghosts seize their chance to ambush innocence.
Spineless witches chant their mythical, mystical music.
Music it is to no fair souls' ears, though.
These souls are indecent.
Engulfed in their cowardly consciences.
Despicable.
Children are escorted far from their slumber.
A promise is broken.
Faceless beings wander from a vulnerable heart.
Hopeful demons descend into it.
A million grotesque wonders of the night,
Lie uninhabited until first light.
But then it's far, far, far too late.
In any case, I fear that's fate.

Jenny Maddock (11)
Wilmslow High School

WHISP OF FEAR

Towering walls like a solitary lighthouse
banging doors like a stampede of monsters
dusty shelves like a ferocious sandstorm
howling wind like a hungry wolf
ripped curtains like a piece of torn paper
creaky floor like a piece of old machinery
shattered bricks like a heavy chunk of cement
broken glass like a nail sticking up from the ground
huddling up in a corner like a small mouse hiding from a big cat
chilly air like a winter frost
a whisp of fear on my spine like a tingling shock
a whisp of fear . . . a tingling shock
   whisp of fear   tingling shock
       fear   shock
           fear.

Emma Varney (12)
Wilmslow High School